IMAGES
of America

CEDARBURG

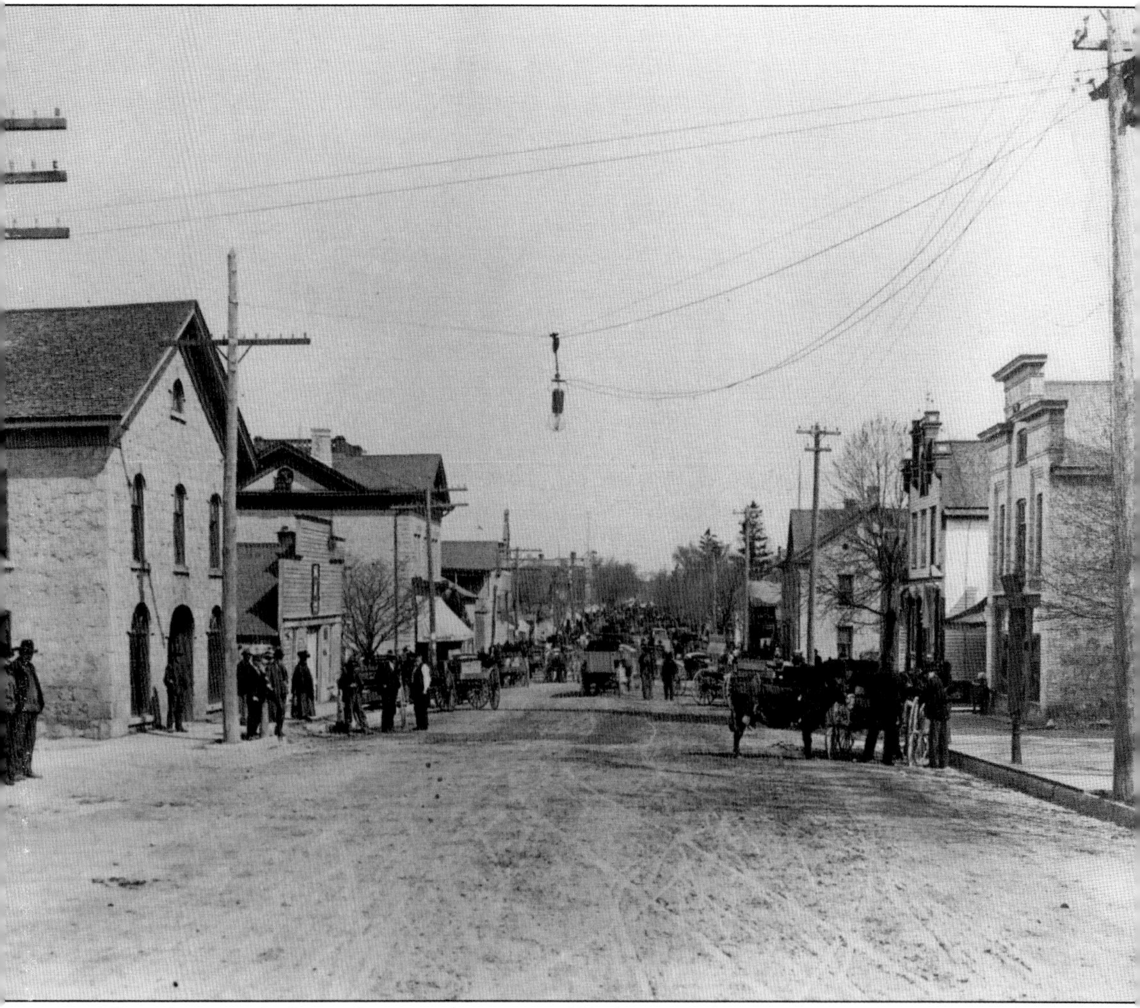

This photograph shows the area that is now Washington Avenue at Western Avenue, looking north. The blacksmith shop is the first building on the left. Two buildings down is Wirth's Store. While Washington Avenue is known today as the main thoroughfare, Hamilton Road saw the most traffic in the pioneering days, as a plank road was built that connected Milwaukee to Green Bay. (Courtesy of the Edward A. Rappold Photograph Collection, Cedarburg Cultural Center.)

On the Cover: Bill Laudon is heralded as the winner of the 50-mile race at the Cedarburg fairgrounds racing track on October 26, 1924. (Courtesy of the Edward A. Rappold Photograph Collection, Cedarburg Cultural Center.)

IMAGES
of America

CEDARBURG

Lisa Curtis

ARCADIA
PUBLISHING

ISBN 978-0-7385-8260-3

Published by Arcadia Publishing
Charleston, South Carolina

Printed in the United States of America

Library of Congress Control Number: 2011925096

For all general information, please contact Arcadia Publishing:
Telephone 843-853-2070
Fax 843-853-0044
E-mail sales@arcadiapublishing.com
For customer service and orders:
Toll-Free 1-888-313-2665

Visit us on the Internet at www.arcadiapublishing.com

For my father, Will Curtis, who showed me that long hours really do pay off, and to Erin Koch, who always pushes me to reach higher.

Contents

ACKNOWLEDGMENTS

Compiling nearly 200 historical pictures and crafting them into the story of a community is no easy project, and I could not have done it without the assistance and support of many people. Deep gratitude goes to Vivian Scherf Laabs, who gave willingly of her postcard collection, her photographs, her memories, and her time. Thanks to Mark Justesen for his unquestioning support and technical expertise. Thanks to Deb Kranitz for sharing her many beautiful images of this city. Thanks to Kay Dahlke for her eyes and ears when I needed them most. Many, many thanks to those at the Ozaukee County Historical Society, especially Ruth Renz, for allowing me liberal access to the photographs, and Jane Butz, whose love for history runs deep. Thank you to Harold Pfhol for sharing the photographs and stories from his unpublished manuscript, *The German-American Farm, A Wisconsin Chronicle*. Much appreciation is extended to Sue Gyarmati at the Cedarburg Cultural Center for taking the time to help me with this project. Finally, special thanks go to Denise Boerner, Robert Armbruster, the Wirth family, Roy Eickstedt, Marge Fay, Pat Ross, Mark Anderson, Jim and Sandy Pape, Brook and Liz Brown, Dave Goggins, Tom Ingrassia, Mark Bertieri, and Jim Culotta at Cedarburg Town Hall for sharing their photographs, their family memories, and their time.

INTRODUCTION

Waterways have long attracted pioneers to unsettled lands because of their vast potential as a power source, and the Cedar Creek 20 miles north of Milwaukee was no exception in the late 1830s and early 1840s. Before the Germans and Irish used the rushing waters to power dams, Indians from the Potawatomi, Chippewa, Menominee, Sauk, and Fox tribes lived off the waters and the nearby lands. Some say the name Cedarburg, said to mean "castle of the cedars," was coined by townsman Frederick Luening. Others speculate it may have come from a combination of the name of the creek, married with the German word *burg*, which means "castle" or "fortress." And the area was indeed a fortress of cedar trees, which required laborious efforts to remove so that plank roads could be made of their lumber.

Those who reached the area during this period include Joseph "Miserly Joe" Gardinier of Ireland and Germans Frederick Hilgen, William Schroeder, Ludwig Groth, and Carl Dobberpuhl. Cedarburg's residents toiled through the harshest of conditions in the second half of the 1800s to build a self-sustainable community that would eventually become home to five dams and mills. Life was not easy in these early days, and the work was especially difficult. Electricity would not be available to Cedarburg's inhabitants until 1901. Clean water and sewers took about 20 more years to develop, so residents relied on the creek, often for both consumption and disposal. Through pure drive and painstaking work, industry was developed in the second half of the 1800s. There were mills to grind farmers' wheat into grain, another to make hats and blankets from sheep's wool, another to make pearl barley, and one to make nails. There were also many sawmills, which took lumber from the trees and made them into wood for buildings. Small business owners of the time ran blacksmith shops, dry goods stores, harness shops, liveries, and saloons. Farming sustained many families and contributed greatly to the Cedarburg economy as a whole. It also required long days and physically taxing work.

Early on, Cedarburg developed a zeal for independence and its residents looked to no one but themselves to contribute to their progress. That philosophy would hold strong in the generations to follow. When other communities joined in with private power companies, Cedarburg established its own utility through friendly negotiations with the operator of the steam generator at the Cedarburg Woolen Mill. It established its volunteer fire department through the contributions of its founders. And more than 150 years later, volunteers still make up the ranks of the fire department. Additionally, they do not rely on city funds to purchase their trucks, as they raise their own money through rental of space at Firemen's Park.

Civility and respect was another hallmark of the city through the generations. The Irish and the Germans and the Catholics and the Protestants worked together to build the community. For instance, when the Catholics needed a larger parcel to build a bigger church for their growing congregation, it was the German Protestants who helped raise money to buy the land. It proved to be a wise decision because the Catholic church with the magnificent steeple provides the gateway into downtown Cedarburg.

Cedarburg was often the center of activity in the county. Market days brought farmers on horseback from miles around to sell their goods and have their grain milled. Even more people flocked to the city every summer for the popular Ozaukee County Fair, which to this day is still held in Cedarburg. One of the biggest attractions around in the late 1800s was Hilgen's Spring Resort, a 72-acre resort that contained two hotels, a bandstand, spring, bathhouse, gardens, and trails. It drew visitors from as far away as Chicago and St. Louis.

Despite its lure, Cedarburg was overlooked as the county seat of Ozaukee County in what is one of the more colorful stories in Cedarburg's past. Prior to 1853, Ozaukee County was actually part of Washington County, and elected officials moved around from community to community for their meetings. Citizens who needed county services also went to different cities, depending on their needs. A vote was taken in April 1846 to see where residents thought the county seat should be located. Port Washington received the most votes, with 164. Cedarburg received 100 and Grafton 74. But a clear majority was needed and none emerged. So in 1847, the territorial legislature declared that Port Washington would be the county seat for five years.

When Wisconsin became a state in 1848, the new legislature asked citizens to vote again. This time, Cedarburg and West Bend received the most votes. Another vote was needed to narrow the choice, only this time there was clear evidence of ballot stuffing, presumably from Port Washington–area residents and their allies, who loaded the ballot boxes with votes cast for "neither place." The state eventually tried to solve the struggle by dividing the county into two counties: Tuskola to the south and Washington to the north. But many still pressured the legislature for another change—dividing the county along an east-west line. That met with approval from the legislature, which was growing tired of the dispute, and they created Washington County to the west and Ozaukee County to the east. They also appointed Port Washington as the county seat of Ozaukee County.

Of course, Cedarburg wasn't contained to the street blocks around the creek and the mills. The town of Cedarburg extends miles west and north of the city, and offers the best of the community in a wide-open, rural setting. The earliest residents of the town include the Kaehlers, Uhligs, Mintzlaffs, Ernsts, Niemans, Lueders, Malones, and Rintelmans. Within the town were small hamlets with their own stores, churches, schools, and livelihoods.

That so much of the city's past is visible today can be credited largely to former mayor E. Stephan Fischer. In 1966, he lobbied St. Francis Borgia to retain the iconic church and steeple at the south end of the city, even though they wanted to build a new, larger church for their growing membership. He also fought to keep one of the former mills from being demolished to make room for a gas station. That mill is now the Cedar Creek Settlement, which has become a must-see for thousands of visitors annually. Those preservation coups were not easily won, and there were some losses. Turner Hall, for example, could not be saved as "the Modernists" argued it was cost prohibitive to save and maintain the old buildings or construct new ones of similar materials. But many others were saved through the perseverance and political determination of Fischer and those who worked with him. It was during this time that preservationist groups like the Cedarburg Landmarks Commission, the Cedarburg Landmark Preservation Society, and the Historic Restoration and Preservation Corporation of Ozaukee County were formed. The first two would last until the present time; the third did not. Cedarburg now has three districts listed in the National Register of Historic Places: the Washington Avenue Historic District, the Hamilton Historic District, and the Columbia Historic District.

Today, Cedarburg is known throughout the Midwest for its quaint, turn-of-the century character. The old stone buildings, the rushing waters of the creek, and the twin steeples acting as a gateway to downtown are the envy of cities throughout the country. It is also a community that is home to one of the most vibrant arts communities in the state. There are museums, two performing arts centers, countless artist studios and more than half-a-dozen major arts events each year. And Cedarburg is located in one of the wealthiest counties in the state, known for its staunch conservative political policies. Its resident pride themselves on taking care of those who need help. It is home to a community foundation, two women's clubs, two education foundations, a Rotary Club, a Lions Club, and many more organizations that give hundreds of thousands of dollars each year to those in need.

One

The Settlement Years

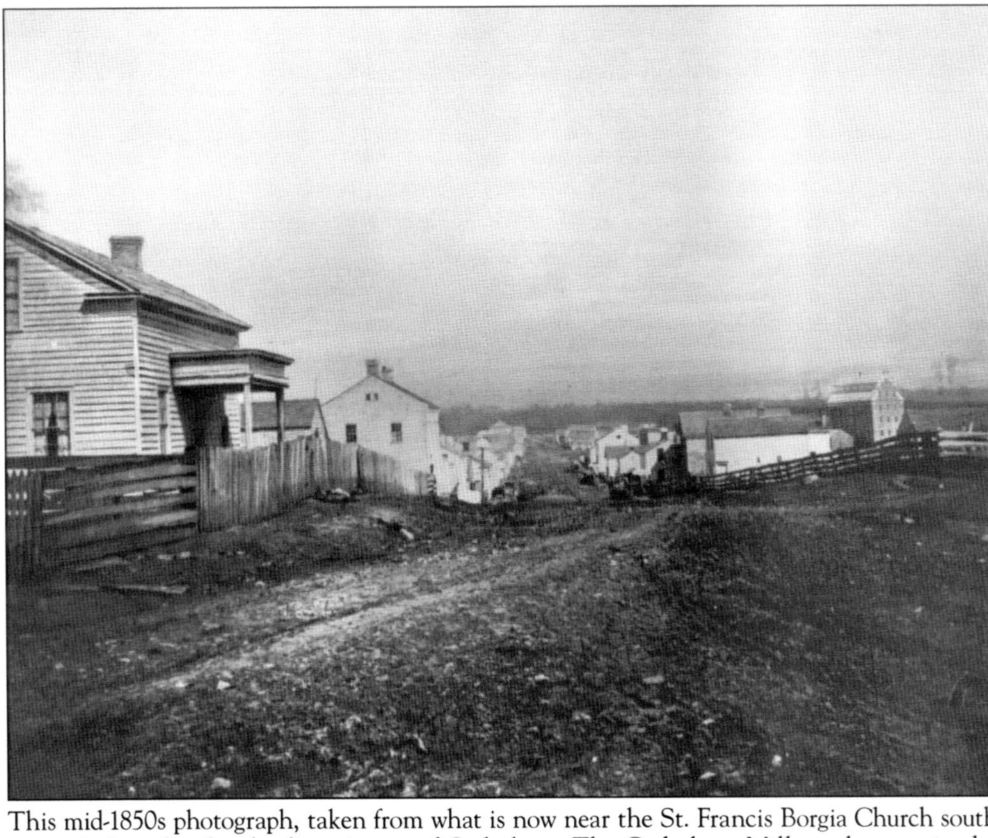

This mid-1850s photograph, taken from what is now near the St. Francis Borgia Church south site, is believed to be the first picture of Cedarburg. The Cedarburg Mill can be seen in the background to the right. Records show that it cost $22,000 to construct the mill, which translates to roughly half-a-million dollars in today's market. (Courtesy of the Edward A. Rappold Photograph Collection, Cedarburg Cultural Center.)

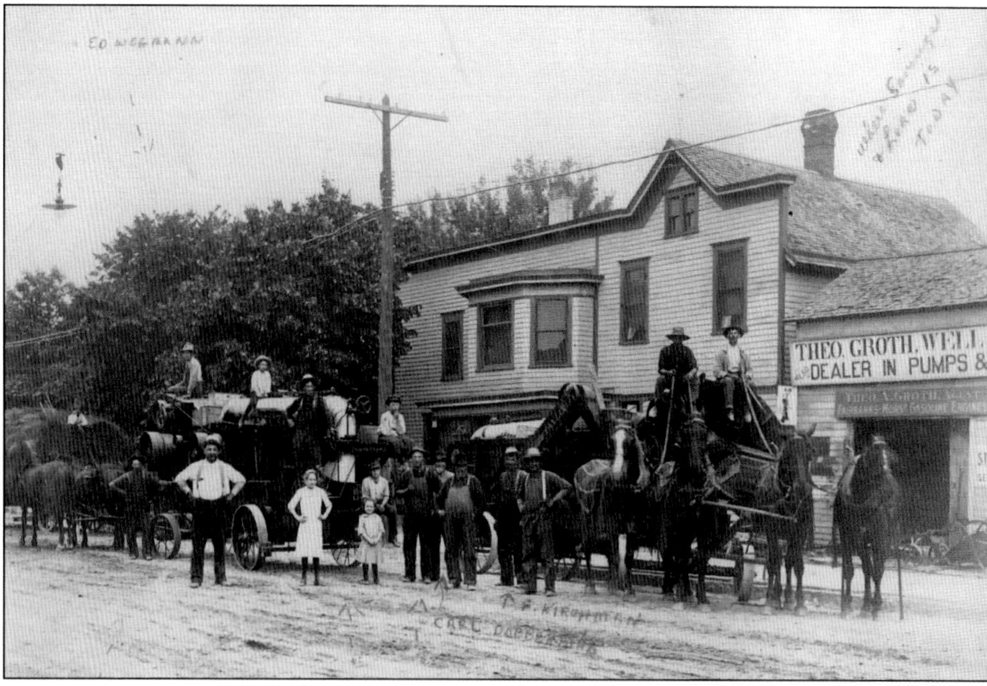

Two of the more influential families in early Cedarburg were the Groths and the Dobberpuhls. Ludwig Groth came to America from Treptow, Germany, in 1842. He was an early land speculator, and along with his brothers, he initially bought 120 acres around Cedarburg, including much of the land along Cedar Creek. Carl Dobberpuhl arrived in Cedarburg in 1842. He was a deacon at Trinity Lutheran Church and, along with Groth, donated the land on which the original church was built. Here, members of the Groth and Dobberpuhl families take a break from threshing. (Courtesy of Mark Anderson.)

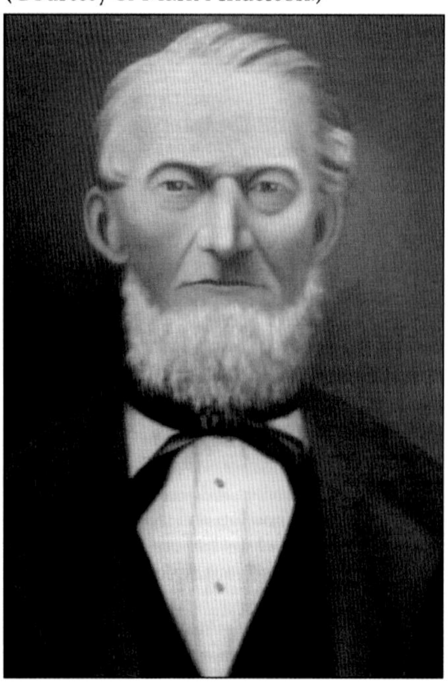

Frederick Hilgen left Germany in 1832, making his way first to Baltimore, then Charleston, South Carolina. He came to Cedarburg with friend and business partner William Schroeder in 1844, when they began buying land for development. He was often referred to as "Father Hilgen" because of his leadership in developing Cedarburg into a thriving community. Schroeder served as postmaster of Cedarburg for many years. (Courtesy of the Ozaukee County Historical Society.)

Christoph Friedrich Boerner was born in Hatten, Germany, in 1812, and he came to Cedarburg in 1849. Prior to that, he ran a store in Charleston, South Carolina. He was the financier for many of Hilgen's and Schroeder's ventures, loaning them thousands of dollars at a modest six-percent interest. (Courtesy of Denise Boerner.)

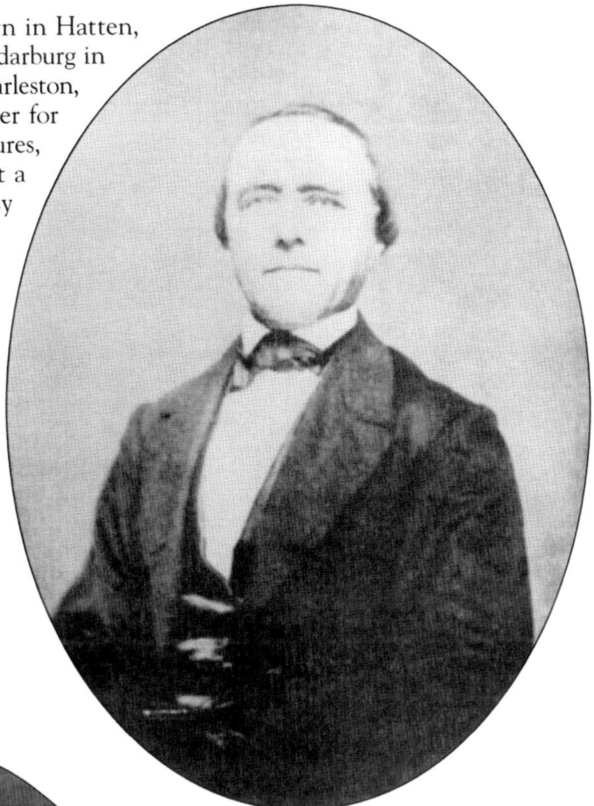

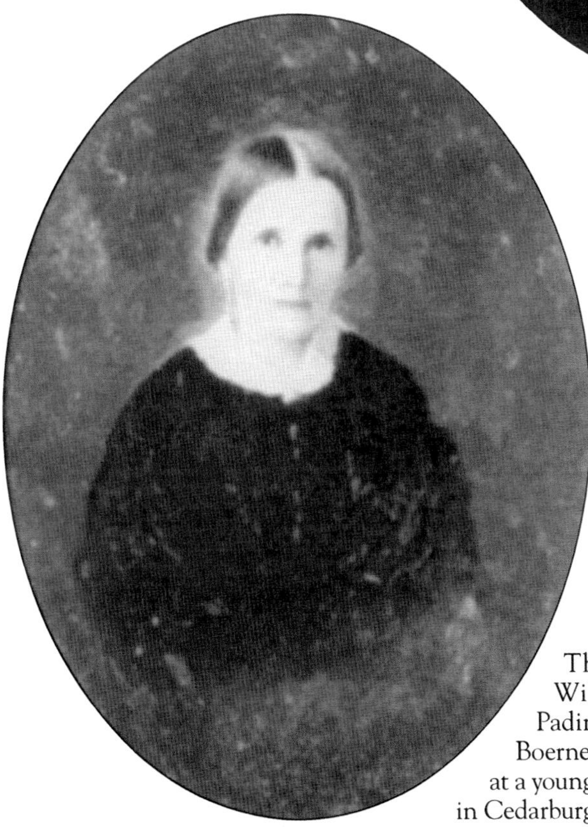

The first wife of C.F. Boerner, Helena Wilhelmina Hussmann, was born in Padingbuettel, Germany, in 1824. She and Boerner had six children, many of whom died at a young age from diphtheria. She died at age 34 in Cedarburg. (Courtesy of Denise Boerner.)

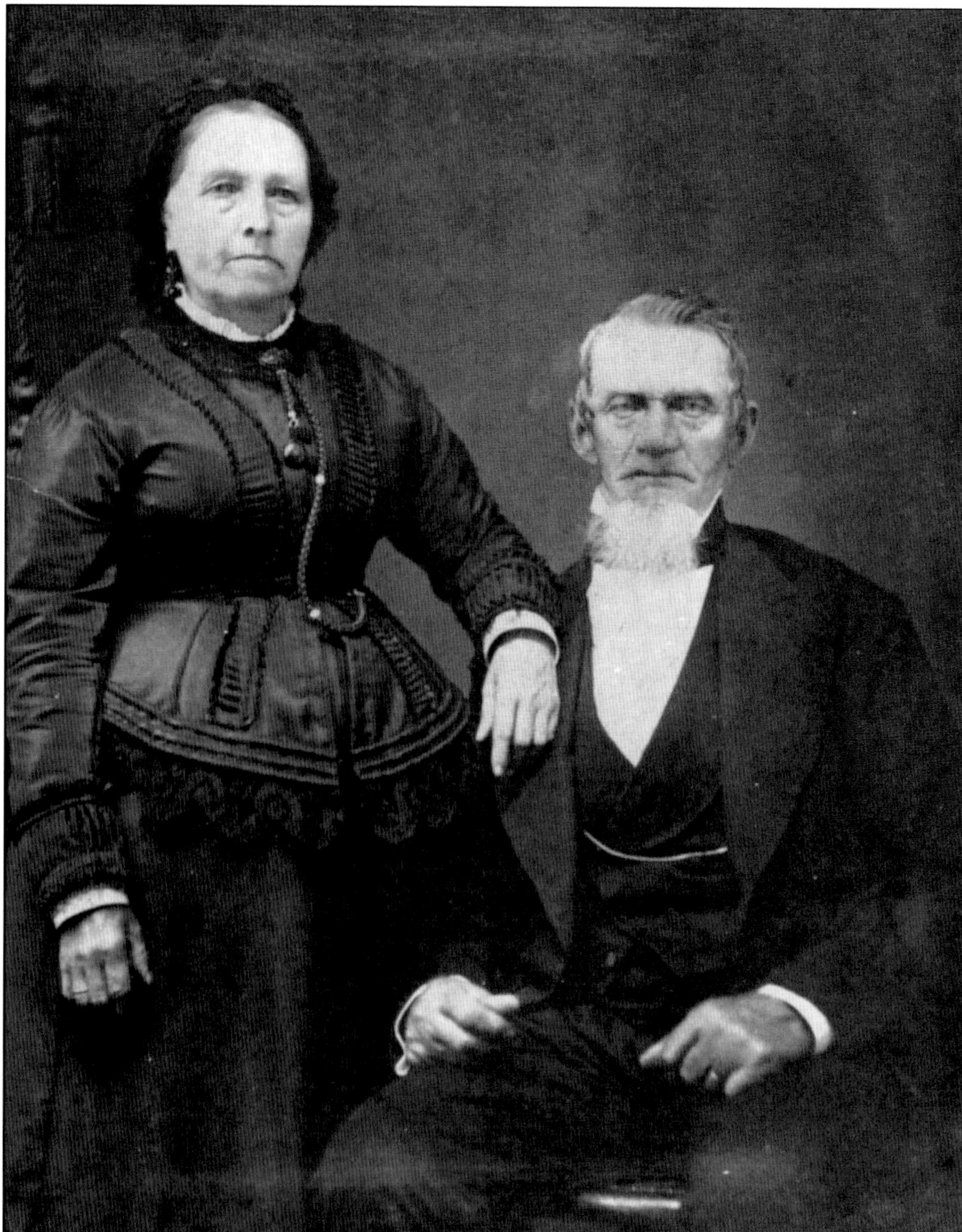

The Hilgen and the Boerner families were very close friends and remained so in Germany, South Carolina, and eventually Cedarburg. So close were they that Frederick married Christoph Boerner's sister Louise in Germany. The couple had 13 children, nine of whom lived to maturity. When Frederick died in 1877, special railway cars were added from Milwaukee to bring his many friends and business associates to his funeral. (Courtesy of the Ozaukee County Historical Society.)

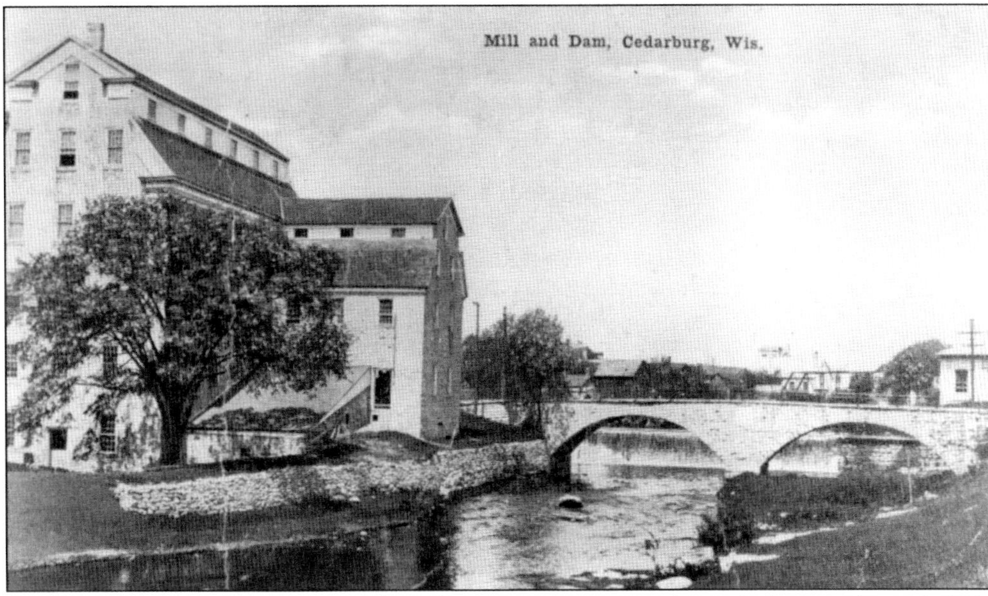

The five-story Cedarburg Mill must have been quite a structure for Cedarburg in the mid-1800s. Hilgen and Schroeder bought the land for the mill as part of a 35-acre purchase from Ludwig Groth. The present mill was constructed in 1855 of limestone quarried from the site. During the quarrying process, the stream was diverted to the east so stone could be gathered from the creek bed. Powered by a dam, the mill produced 120 barrels of flour a day at its peak. (Courtesy of the Edward A. Rappold Photograph Collection, Cedarburg Cultural Center.)

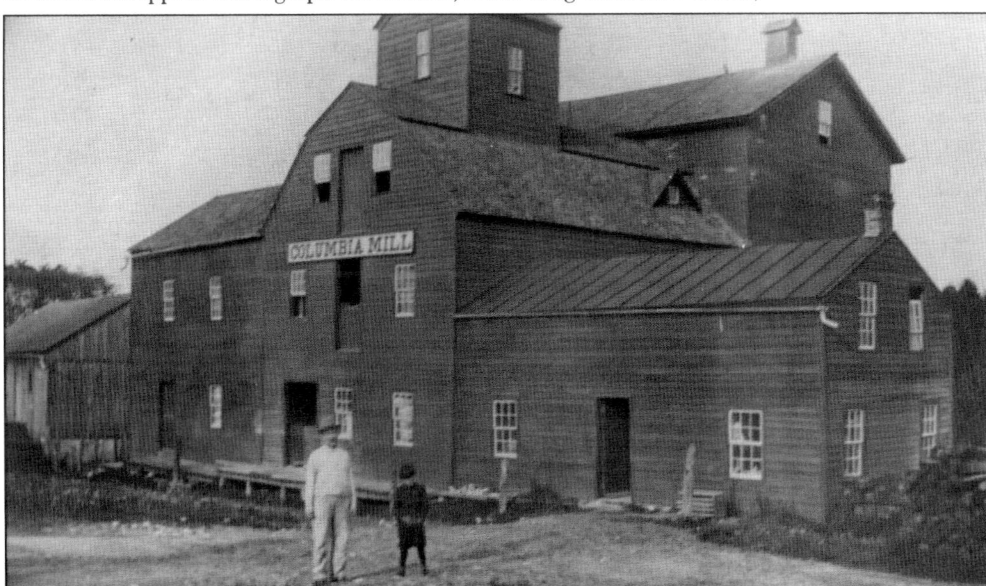

The land on which the Columbia Mill was built in 1846 was obtained in 1839 by an Englishman named Jonathan Spencer. Dr. Frederick Luening later bought the land and had the Columbia Mill built to serve the east side of the city. Cedarburg historian Ed Rappold said Ludwig Groth tried to make the streets on a grid system, but the creek always made that a challenge. City leaders solved the problem by removing a mass of trees and building Columbia Road. Today, a bank sits on the site of the former mill. (Courtesy of the Edward A. Rappold Photograph Collection, Cedarburg Cultural Center.)

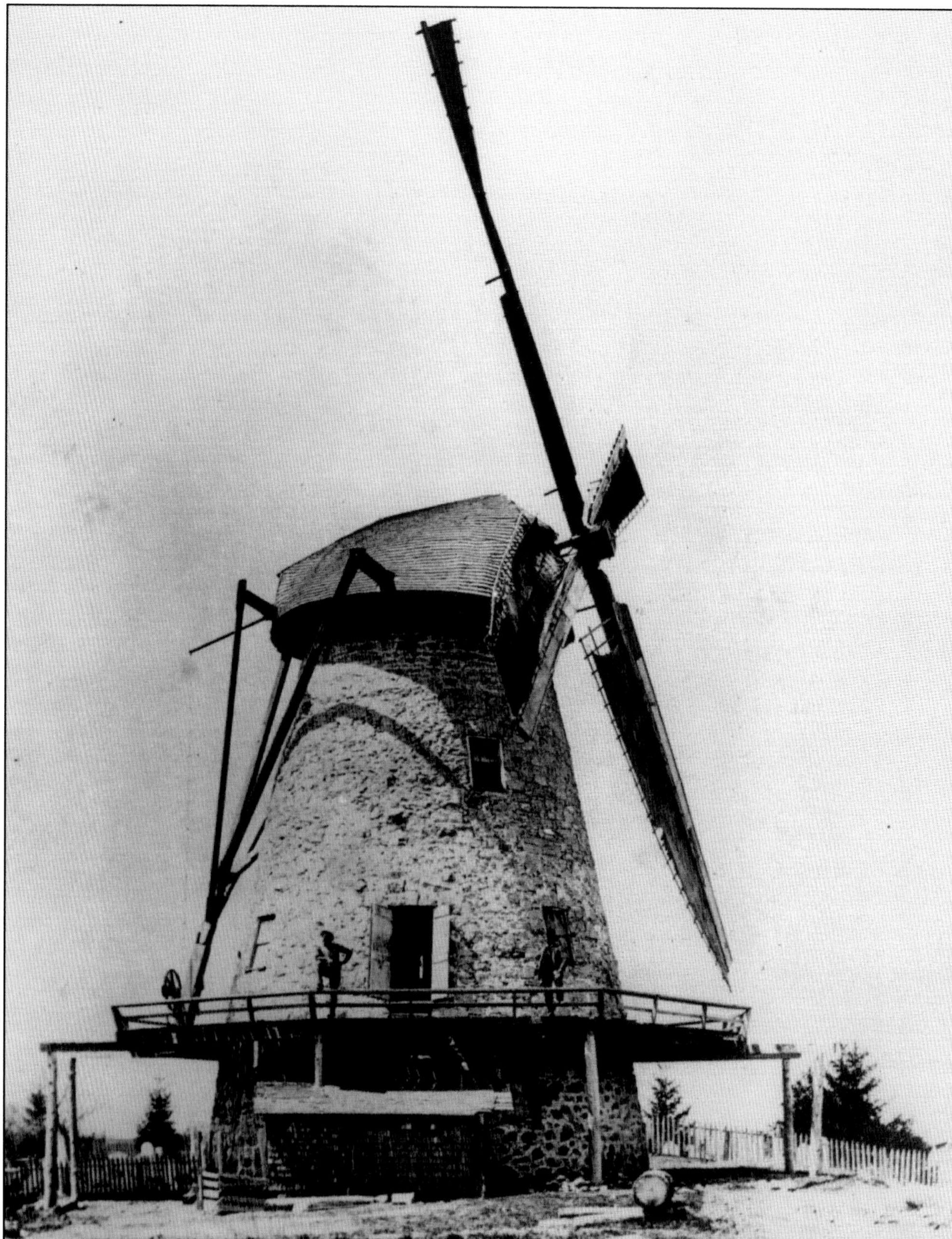

Another gristmill was built in Cedarburg in 1872 on what is now Bridge Street. And while the five-story gristmill further south was powered by water, this one ran on wind, which was much less predictable. The main product was barley, which the owners of the mill hoped they could create a market for in America. Barley was used for soups and sausage filler, but public demand was not enough to keep the mill going. It suffered a great fire in 1894, and stone from the structure was later used to build several homes in Cedarburg. (Courtesy of the Edward A. Rappold Photograph Collection, Cedarburg Cultural Center.)

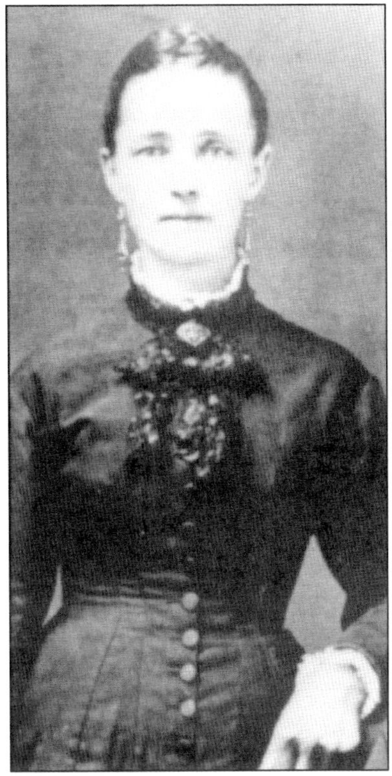

Anna Gesina Vosteen was the second wife of C.F. Boerner. Together, they had nine children. Their sons would later run Boerner Bros. Store. The Boerner family remains a vital part of the Cedarburg community and generations of Boerners have served in the Cedarburg Volunteer Fire Department. (Courtesy of Denise Boerner.)

Theodore Hartwig is said to have been Cedarburg's first doctor, arriving there in 1846. He left twice and returned both times, prompting the *Cedarburg Weekly News* in October 1884 to welcome him back, stating, "In the course of this week, we may look for the old runaway." The Hartwig home still stands just north of the corner of Washington Avenue and Sheboygan Road. (Courtesy of the Edward A. Rappold Photograph Collection, Cedarburg Cultural Center.)

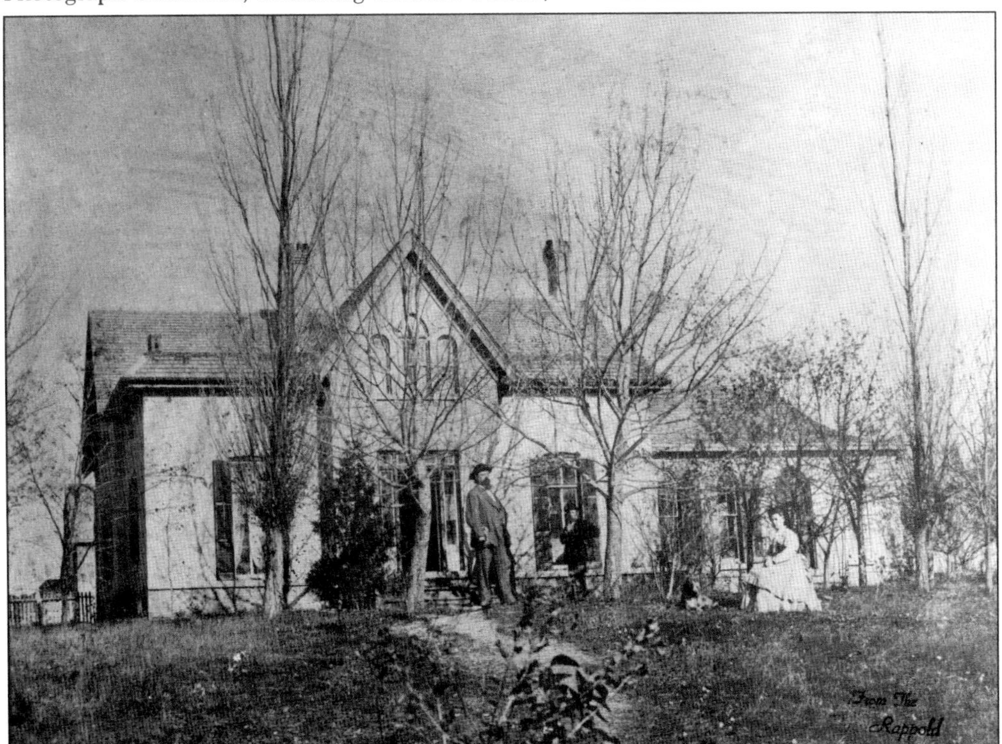

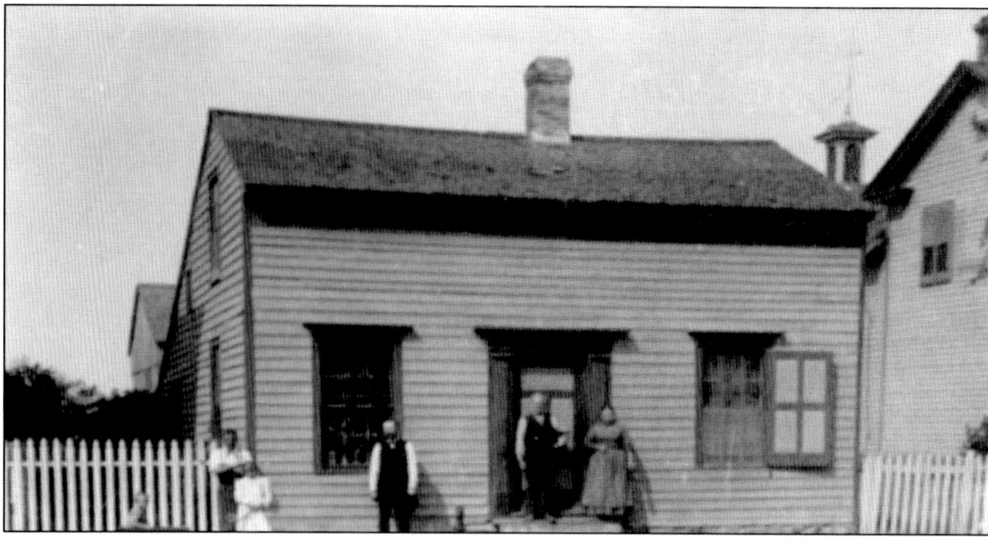

Another early settler in Cedarburg was J.P. Wirth, a native of Bavaria, Germany. Wirth immigrated to America in 1843, settling first in Dayton, Ohio. The next year he moved to Milwaukee, then Cedarburg, where he opened Wirth's Store, which began by selling shoes but expanded to other merchandise in later years. Several members of the Wirth family are pictured in this undated photograph. (Courtesy of the Wirth family.)

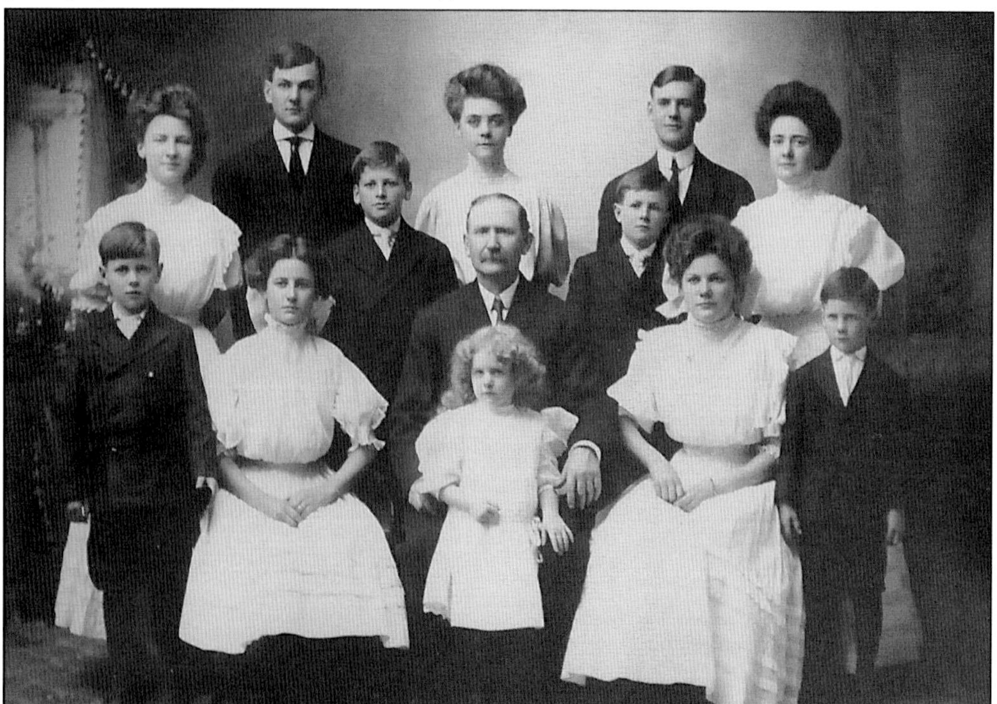

Gustav Wirth Sr., son of J.P. Wirth, was a widower raising 12 children when this photograph was taken. Pictured standing, from left to right, are (first row) Delwin, Wincic, Glady, Roma, and Gus Jr.; (second row) Palmer, Gus Sr., and Joy; (third row) Livia, Etz, Teekla, Utz, and Hertha. (Courtesy of the Wirth family.)

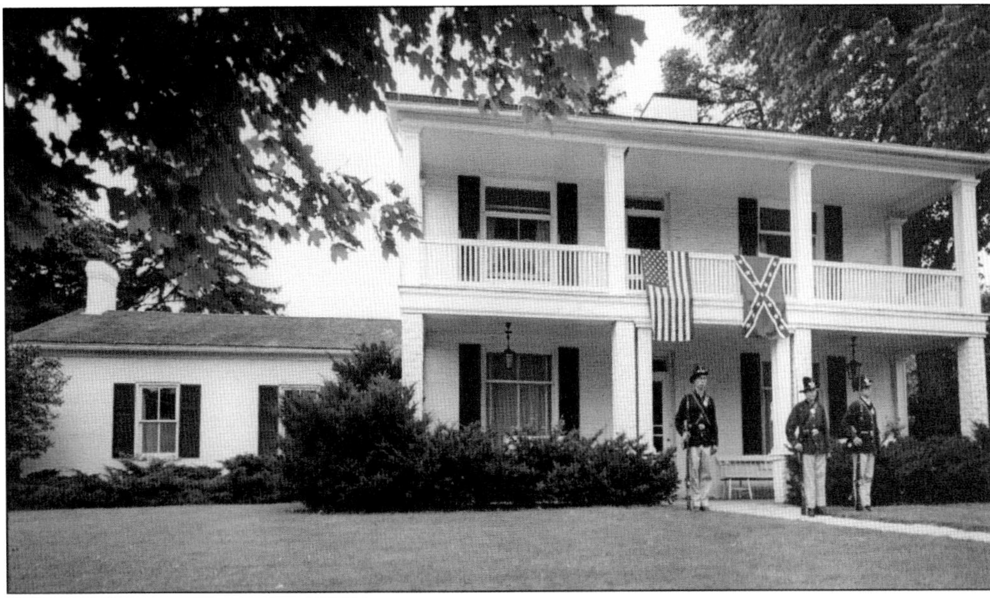

Frederick Hilgen built his family homestead in 1846 on a hill overlooking the creek. The architectural style of the home is in tribute to the time he spent in Charleston, South Carolina, as is the Confederate flag, pictured at an open house during a Civil War centennial celebration. It is said that he built the house on a hill so he could see the homes of his children from his second story. (Courtesy of Kathy Lanser.)

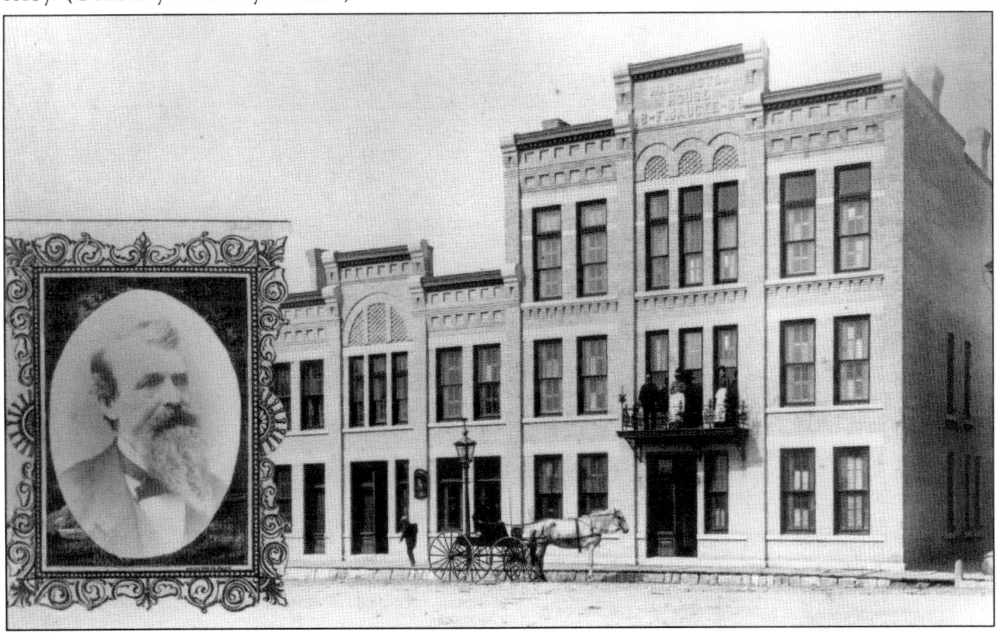

The Washington House Inn was Cedarburg's first inn. It was founded in 1846 by German immigrant Conrad Horneffer. In the early days, hotels functioned mostly to house travelers and pioneers making what were then long, difficult journeys, such as from Chicago to Green Bay. The original structure was wooden, replaced in 1886 with the cream city brick building that still functions as the Washington House Inn today. Builder F. Jaucke is pictured in the inset photograph. (Courtesy of Jim and Sandy Pape.)

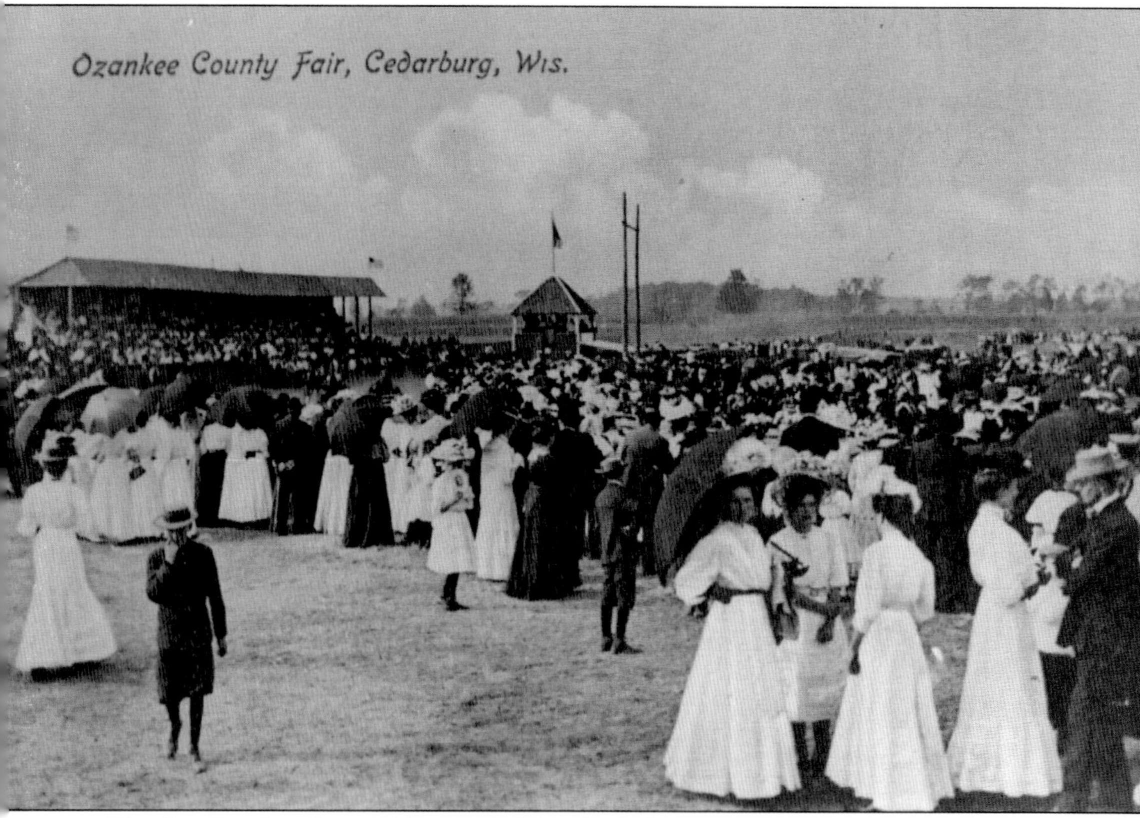

The first Ozaukee County Fair was held in Cedarburg in 1859. The early fairs were held in October to coincide with harvest time. The midway rides were steam-driven from pails of water, filled and carried by hand from a pump 500 feet away. They were then fired by coal from a large boiler. Other events included balloon rides, spelling bees, contests to make homemade butter and cheese, and dog and horse races. (Courtesy of the Edward A. Rappold Photograph Collection, Cedarburg Cultural Center.)

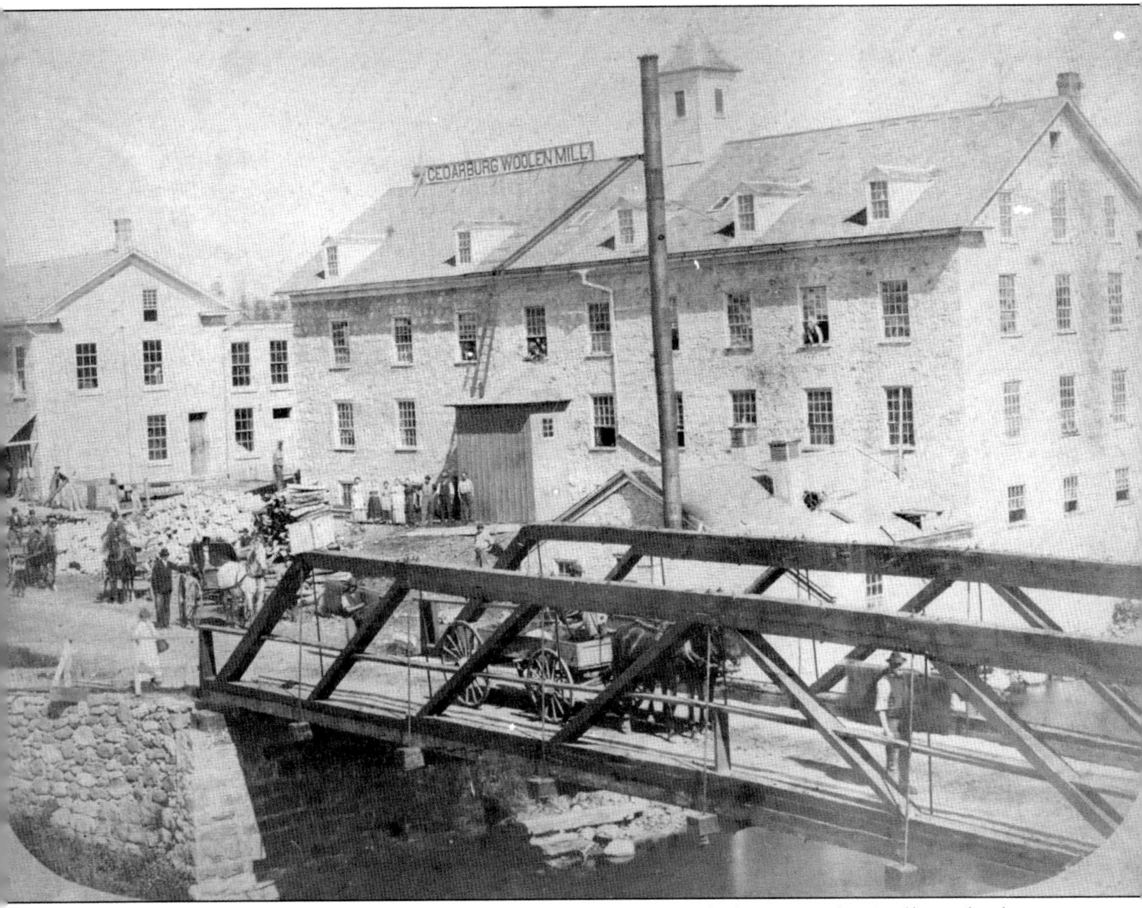

The north side of Cedarburg bustled with activity after the Cedarburg Woolen Mill was built in 1864 to make hats for Civil War soldiers. The bridge over the creek survived many severe winters. A sudden thaw after the long winter of 1881 sent huge ice blocks crashing against the structure. While the weather brought down other bridges in the city over the years, the woolen mill bridge lasted until structural improvements were made in the 1970s. (Courtesy of the Ozaukee County Historical Society.)

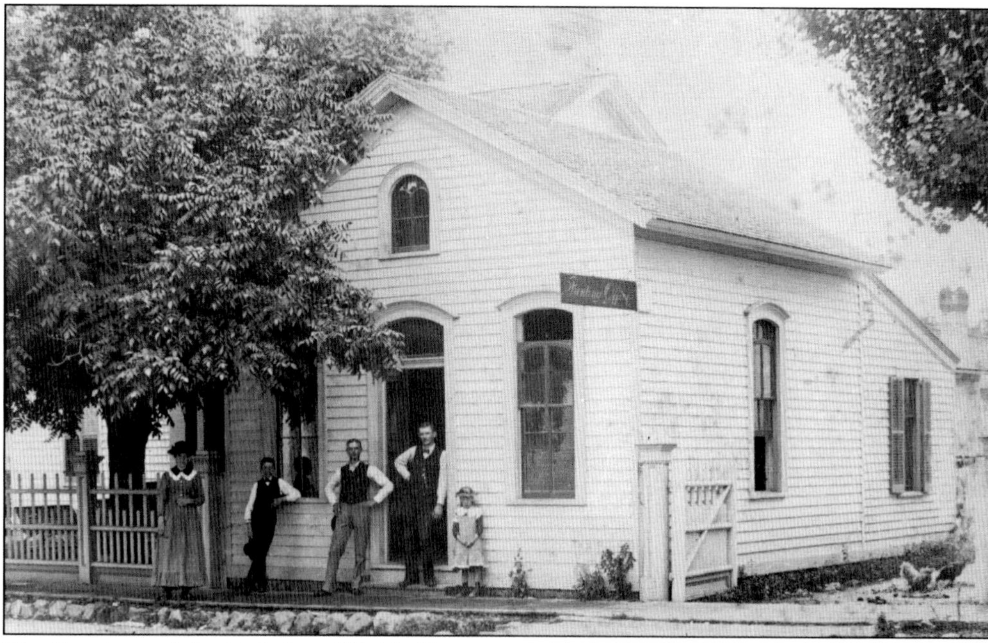

The first issue of the *Cedarburg Weekly News* was published on Jan. 17, 1883. Its first publisher, Frederick Horn, was also a state legislator and left much of the newspaper business to his son Alexander Horn. The early papers were all of four pages and subscriptions cost $1.50 per year. The paper stayed in the Horn family for 105 years. It became the *News Graphic Pilot* in 1979. (Courtesy of the Edward A. Rappold Photograph Collection, Cedarburg Cultural Center.)

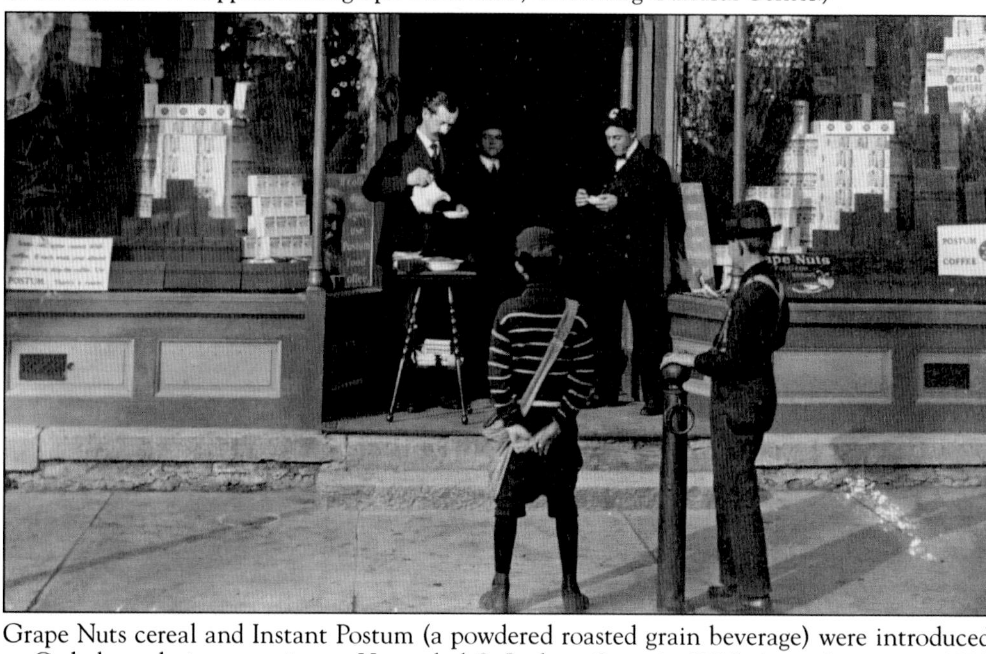

Grape Nuts cereal and Instant Postum (a powdered roasted grain beverage) were introduced to Cedarburg during a tasting at Hentschel & Jochem Store in 1905. According to an 1883 advertisement in the *Cedarburg Weekly News*, the store sold dry goods, groceries, clothing, hats, and a "choice line of wines and liquors for medicinal purposes." The location is now home to Amy's Candy Kitchen. (Courtesy of Jim and Sandy Pape.)

The Cedarburg Volunteer Fire Department was formed in the fall of 1866 by a group of 31 residents following a series of meetings in the homes of Conrad Horneffer and William Boxhorn. The first firehouse, pictured here, was built on what is now Washington Avenue and Cleveland Street. The land cost $600, and members were required to donate work and $2 toward the construction costs, though many contributed much more. (Courtesy of the Cedarburg Fire Department.)

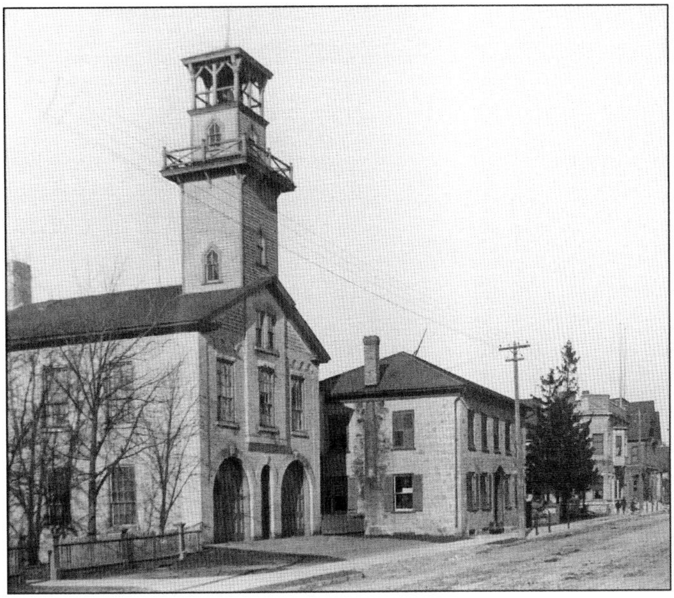

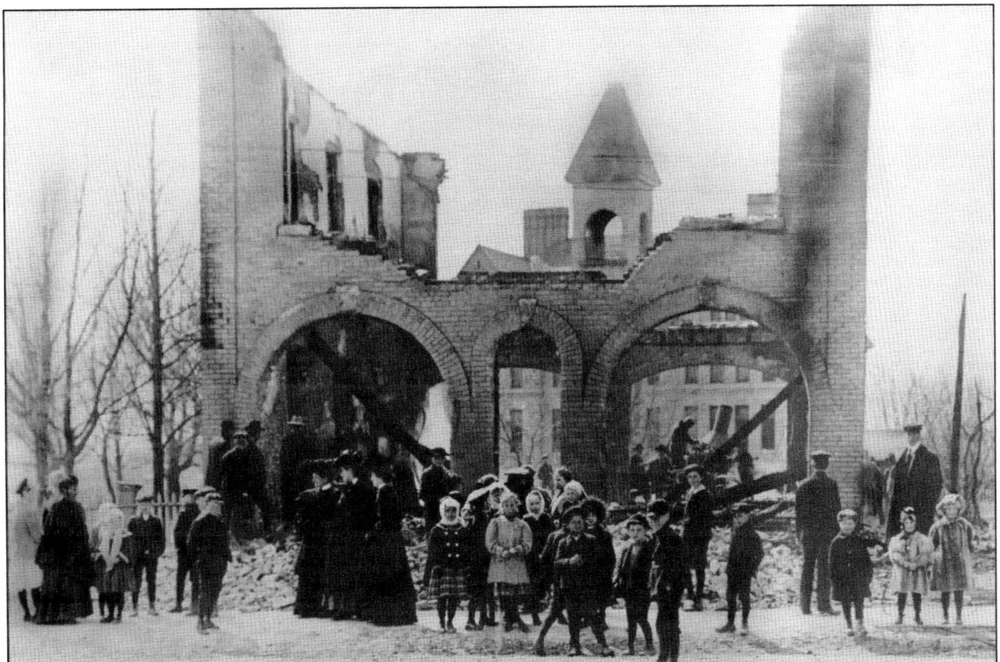

The worst fire to occur in Cedarburg's young history occurred on April 1, 1907, at the fire department itself. A Grafton man named Charles Riulling noticed the fire at 2:00 a.m. The fire started in the basement of the building, which housed the firehouse on the lower level and a school for sixth- and seventh-graders on the second level. According to the *Cedarburg Weekly News* account at the time, "In the building at the time of the fire were the steamer, the old hand engine, hook and ladder wagon, several hose wagons, and everything belonging to a first class fire apparatus outfit, such as this city really possessed." (Courtesy of the Cedarburg Fire Department.)

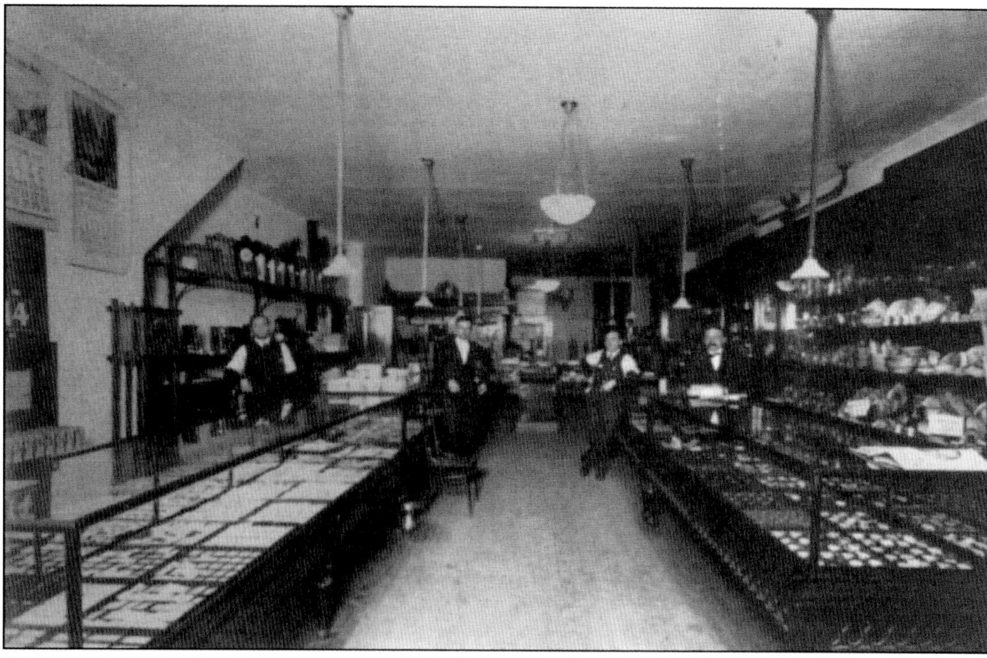

Watchmaker John Armbruster came to Cedarburg in 1884 and opened what is still known today as Armbruster Jewelers on the east side of Washington Avenue. In the store's early years, sheet music, clocks, and clock repairs were a large part of its sales. Armbruster also served as mayor of Cedarburg from 1910 to 1925. Today, the store is run by Armbruster's great-grandson John and his family. (Courtesy of Robert Armbruster.)

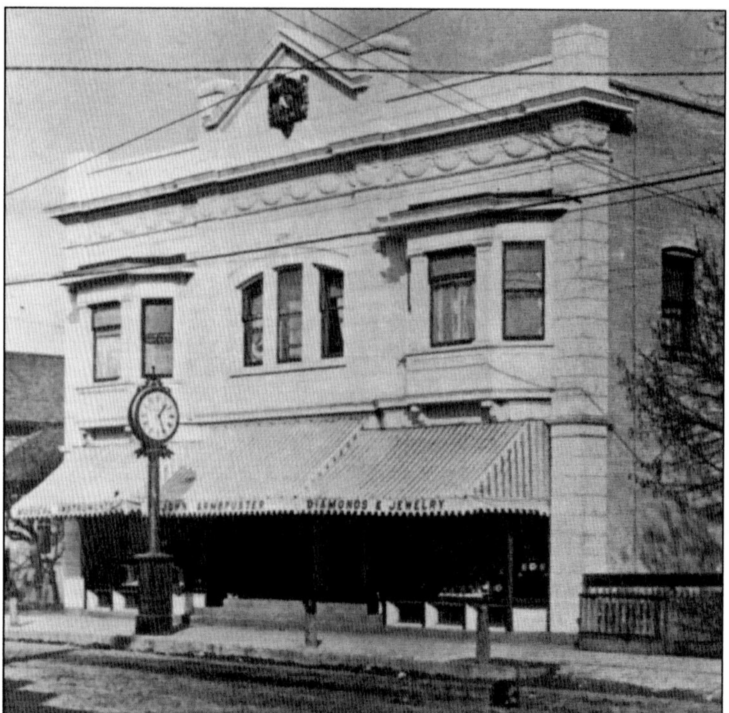

The clock outside Armbruster Jewelers has been a fixture of downtown Cedarburg since the store's beginning. Early on, the clock had to be wound every eight hours to keep it operating. It was also replaced once when a team of horses knocked it down. (Courtesy of Robert Armbruster.)

Two

A City Takes Shape

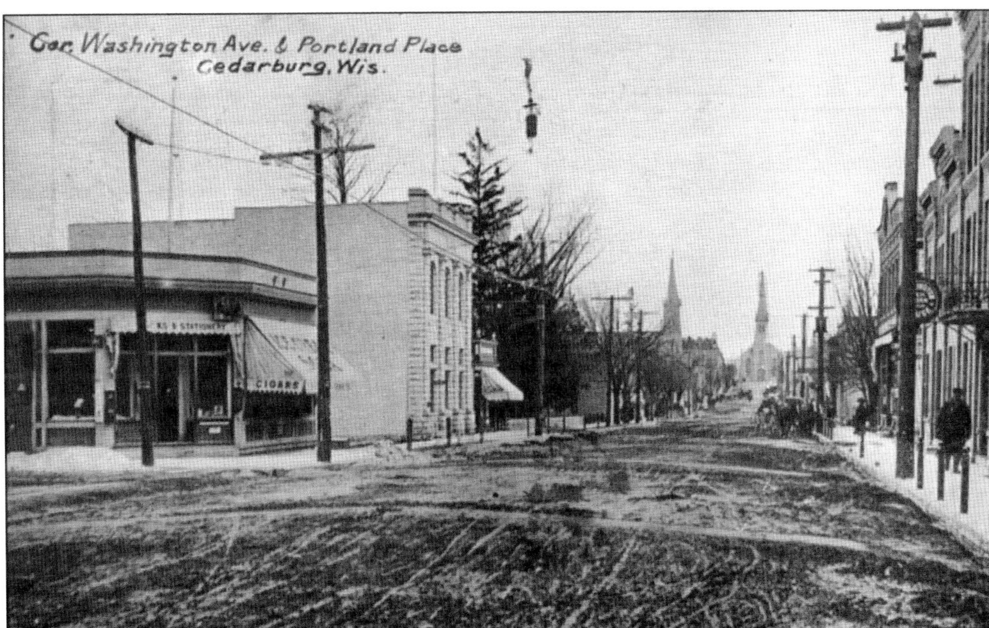

Electric lights made their debut in a Cedarburg home in 1897, when a wire from a direct current generator at the woolen mill was connected to the nearby Wittenberg house. Four years later, an electric arc was hung over the main street, as shown here, looking south on Washington Avenue. Also, in 1901, the city formed its electric utility. While the city was seeing much advancement by the early 1900s, paved roads were still a few years away, as evidenced by the muddy dirt road in this photograph. (Courtesy of Vivian Scherf Laabs and Arnold Laabs.)

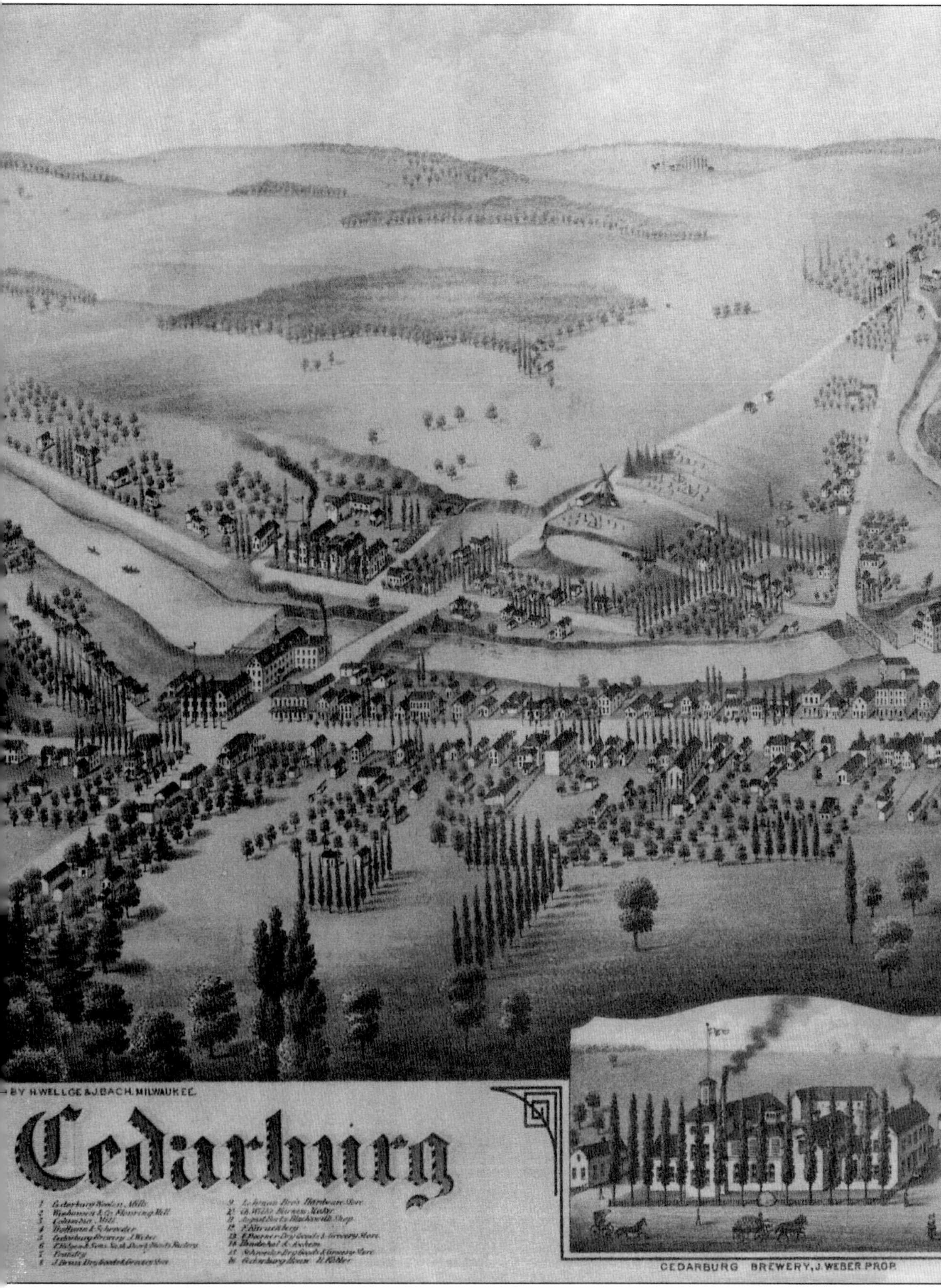
BY H. WELLGE & J. BACH, MILWAUKEE.
Cedarburg
CEDARBURG BREWERY, J. WEBER PROP.

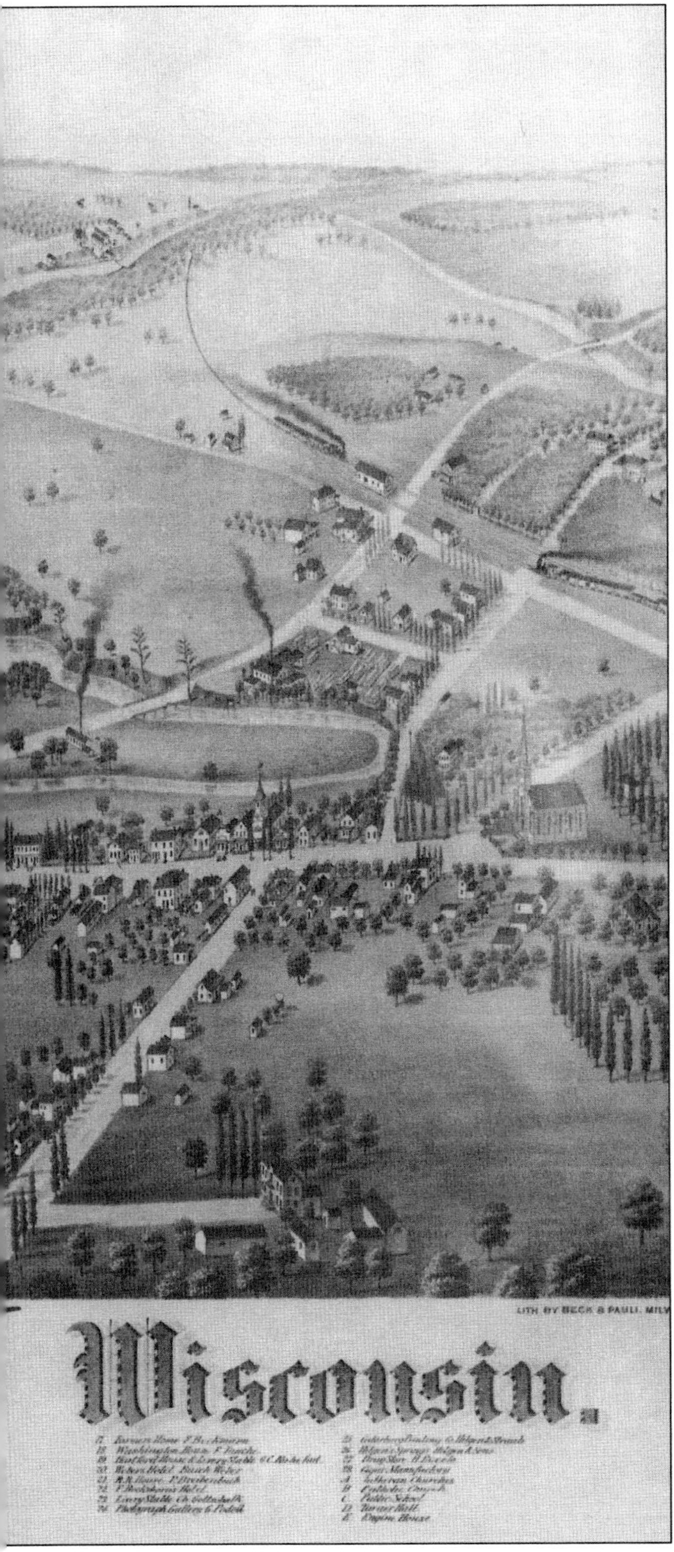

This artist's rendering of a growing Cedarburg in the late 1800s shows a city dotted with mills, stores, and homes. The first stagecoach came through Cedarburg in 1847, along what is now Green Bay Road. It is said that up to 12 people, along with their luggage and trunks, were squeezed into one stagecoach. In 1859, Cedarburg had a population of about 1,175, and the stagecoach was rerouted through the downtown area of the village. Cedarburg became a city in 1885, with Frederick W. Horn its first mayor. Horn was a politically ambitious man who also served as an independent in the state senate. By 1896, Cedarburg's population was around 1,400. Though the city lost out to Port Washington as the county seat of Ozaukee County, Cedarburg was a hub of commercial and agricultural activity. (Courtesy of the Ozaukee County Historical Society.)

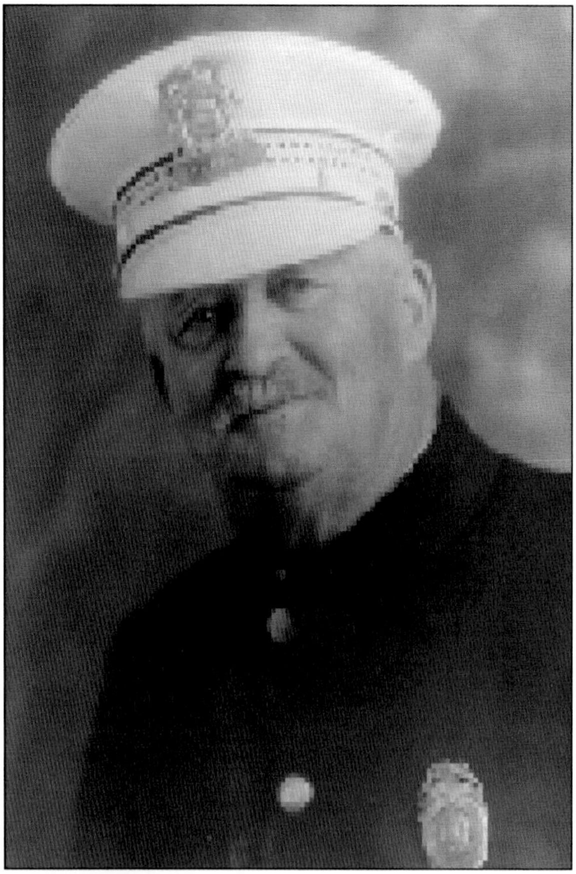

The city's police department was formed in 1885. Otto Beckmann was the city's only constable in the early 1900s, serving from 1904 to 1934. He used a stopwatch and whistle to clock speeders between two posts. If he whistled and the driver stopped, he would arrest him. He had no car to pursue those who did not stop. The city's first jail was located in the basement of the former Turner Hall. (Courtesy of the Cedarburg Police Department.)

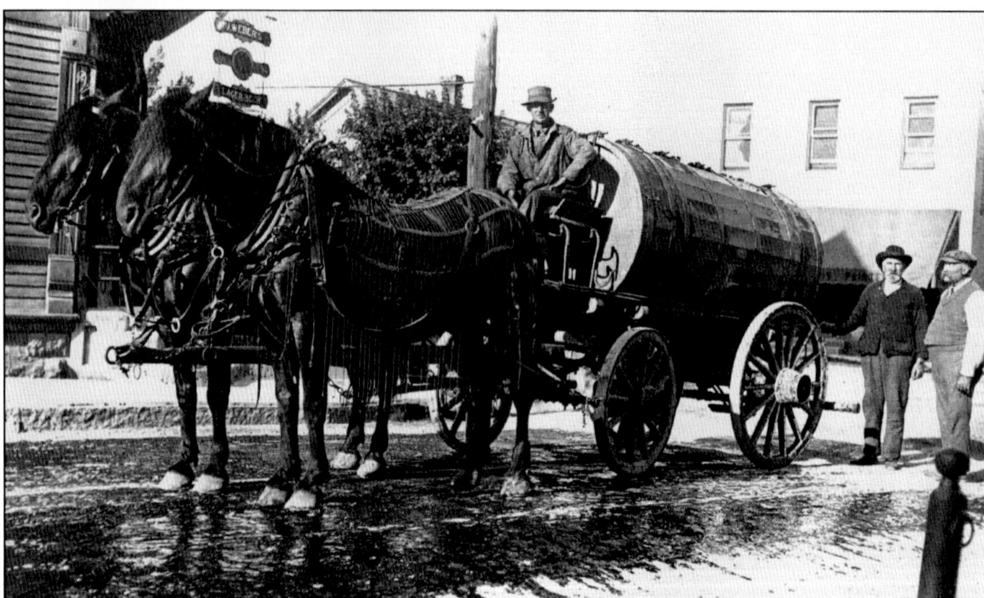

Water wagons pulled by horses were often used to sprinkle the street in an effort to contain dust from the dirt roads. (From the Edward A. Rappold Collection, courtesy of Cedarburg Light & Water.)

Postcards were an extremely common form of communication in the late 1800s and throughout the 1900s. They also allowed for a unique form of artistry. This postcard, from around 1907, allowed Cedarburg's German heritage to show through. (Courtesy of Vivian Scherf Laabs and Arnold Laabs.)

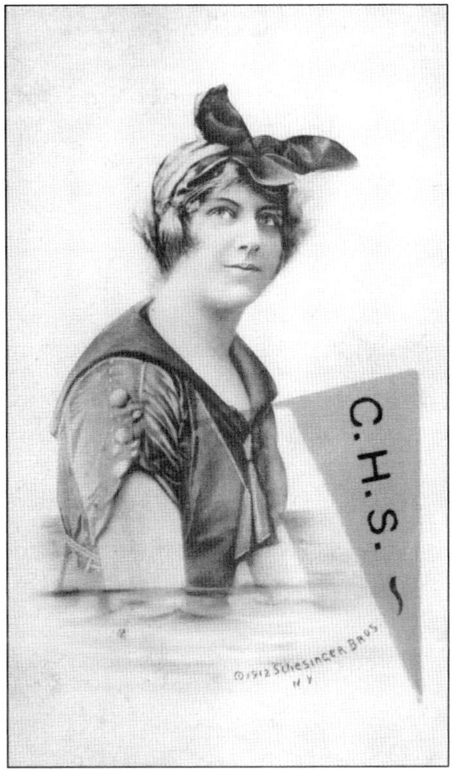

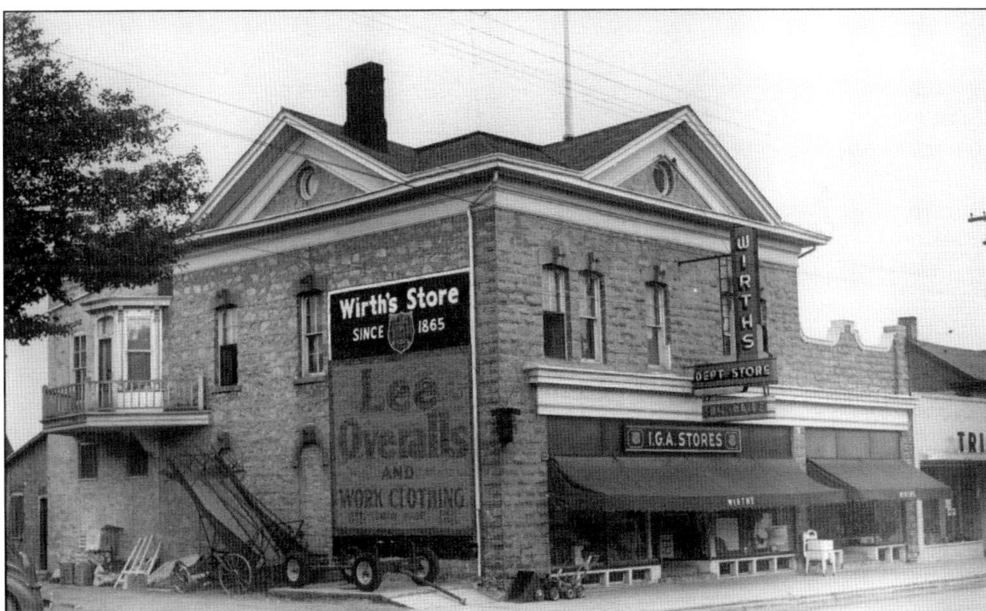

Wirth's Store was a fixture of downtown Cedarburg for generations. It was known for its quality shoes and boots, although it added more merchandise through the years. G.H. Wirth, Inc., which was established in 1865, still exists, though not as a grocery store. J.P. Wirth's great-grandson Gustav W. Wirth Jr. runs a commercial and residential real estate business under the name. (Courtesy of the Wirth family.)

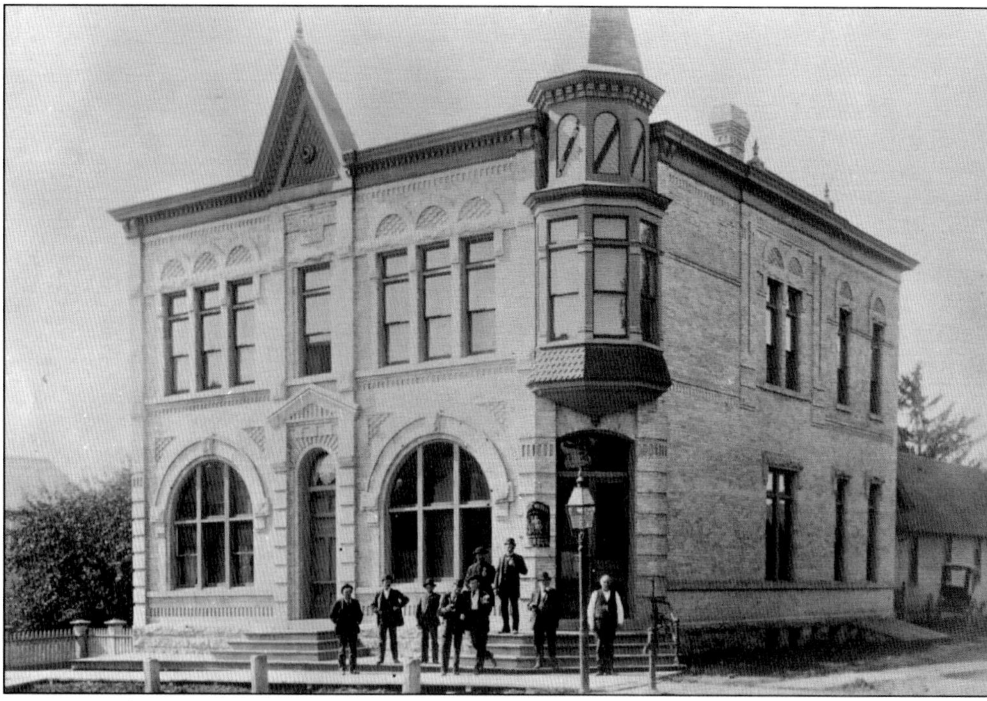

Constructed in 1888, the building at Washington Avenue and Bridge Street was home to Roth Saloon. Henry Roth was known as much for his days as a Civil War bugler as he was for his tavern. Today the building is still a bar—and restaurant—called Maxwell's. (Courtesy of the Ozaukee County Historical Society.)

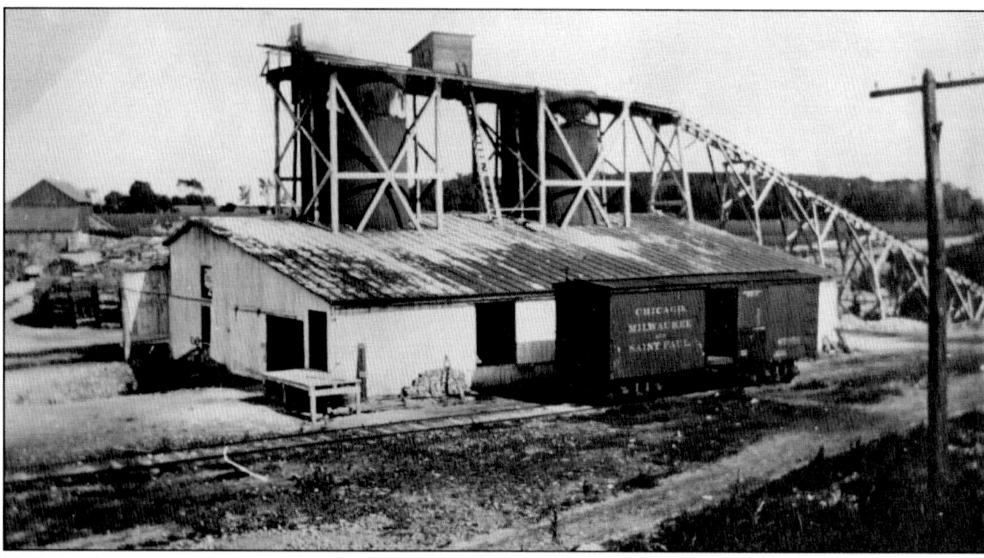

If Cedarburg was a fortress of cedar trees above ground, it was rich with stone below. While the hard bedrock made building a challenge at times, it provided unlimited amounts of limestone and fieldstone for many of the city's buildings. In this photograph, the Groth Lime Kiln is one such quarry in operation in Cedarburg in the early years. The former quarry has since been filled with water and is a lake at Zeurnert Park. (Courtesy of the Edward A. Rappold Photograph Collection, Cedarburg Cultural Center.

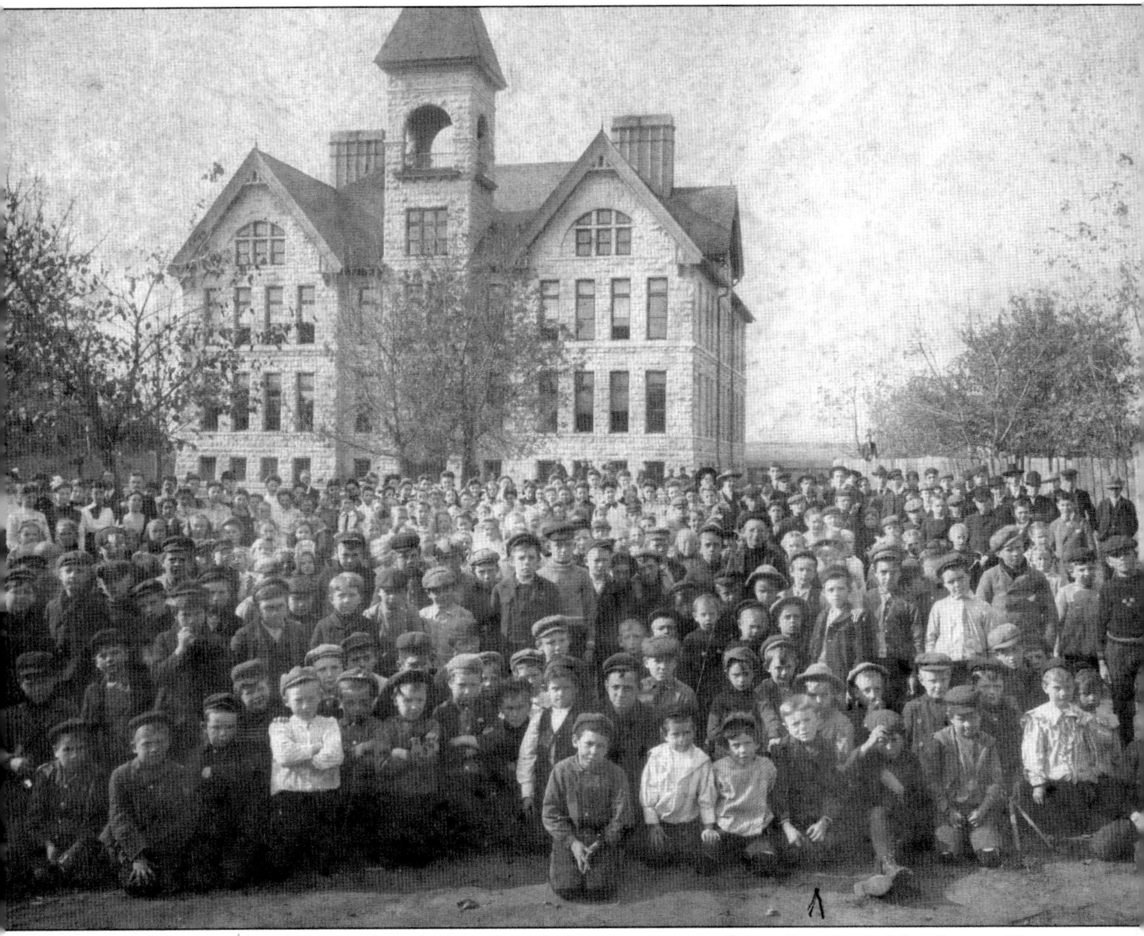

Early Cedarburg schools were church-based, and classes were taught in German. The first public school in Cedarburg was located in a small frame building on Washington Avenue, where Advent Lutheran Church now stands. The Lincoln School was built across the street in 1894 to serve the city's grade school students, but it also housed high school students for several years. Charles Lau was the first principal, and he was paid an annual salary of $1,000 in 1901. (Courtesy of the Ozaukee County Historical Society.)

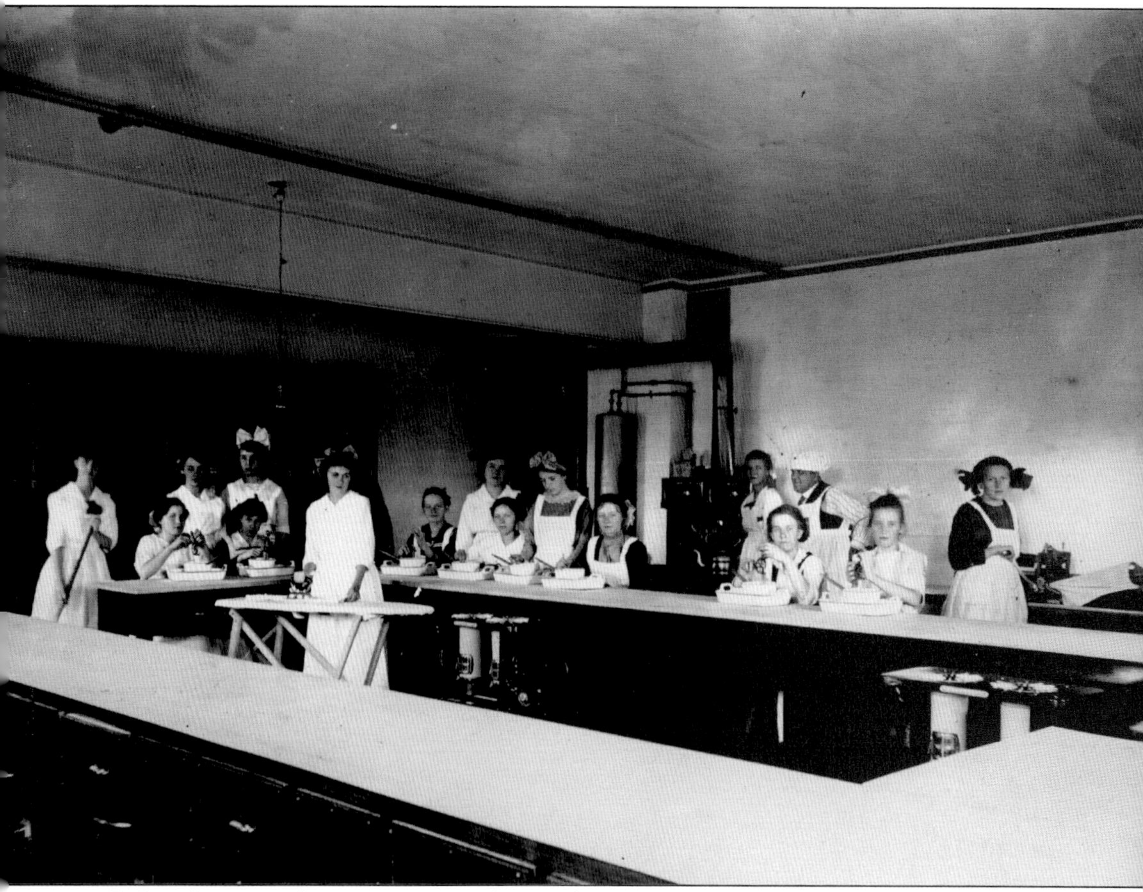

Before there were home economics classes, there were domestic science classes to teach young women how to cook and sew. This undated photograph shows a class of women learning how to iron, cook, and clean. While women were graduating from high school in the early 1900s, they still were not allowed to vote and were largely expected to marry and raise children. (Courtesy of the Ozaukee County Historical Society.)

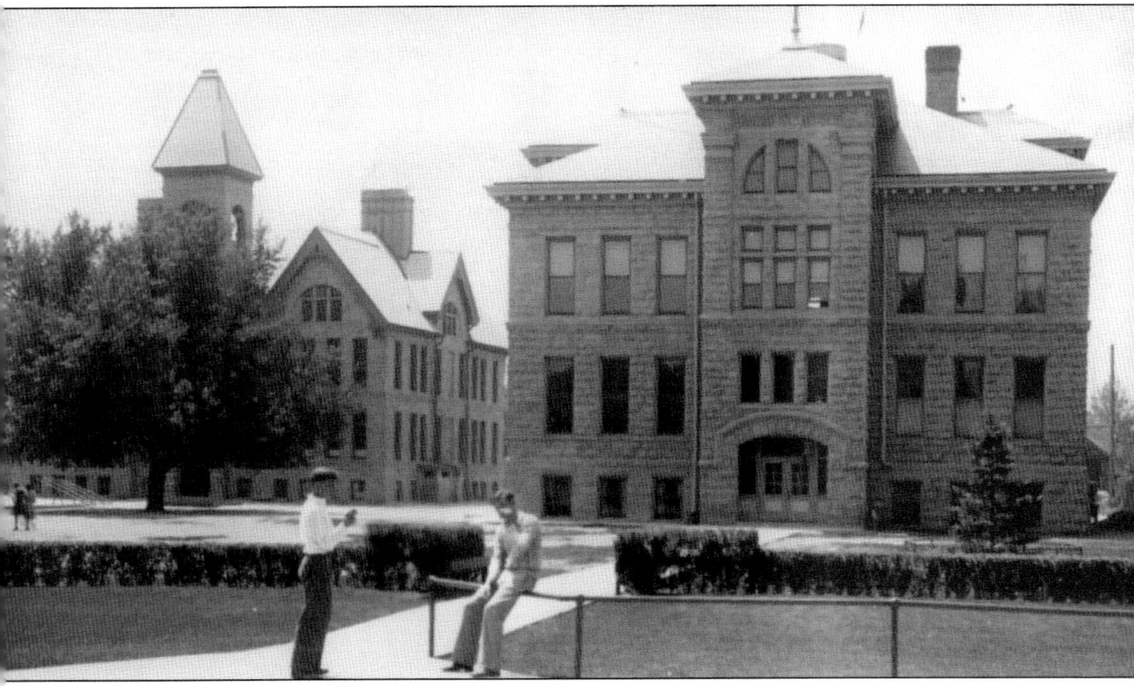

The first high school graduation in Cedarburg occurred in 1899. According to newspaper accounts, the ceremony took place with a backdrop of orange and black, which are still the school colors today. According to the book *Cedarburg History: Legend and Lore*, there were no graduates in 1900 and just 10 in 1901. In 1908, the first high school was built behind where the firehouse was located before it burned. The old high school, pictured here, is now Cedarburg City Hall. (Courtesy of Vivian Scherf Laabs and Arnold Laabs.)

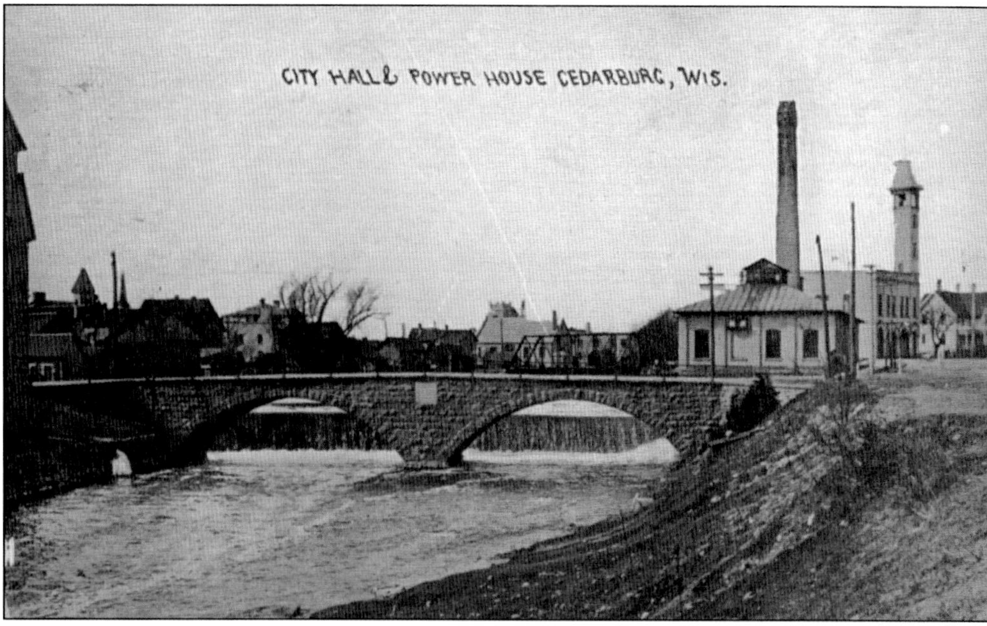

In late 1901, Cedarburg formed its electric utility after it purchased an electric light plant that was built by J.E. Bruss, the steam generator operator at the woolen mill. The plant was located on Mequon Avenue, at right. The first utility superintendent was Ernst Schneider, who served in the role until 1950. (Courtesy of Vivian Scherf Laabs and Arnold Laabs.)

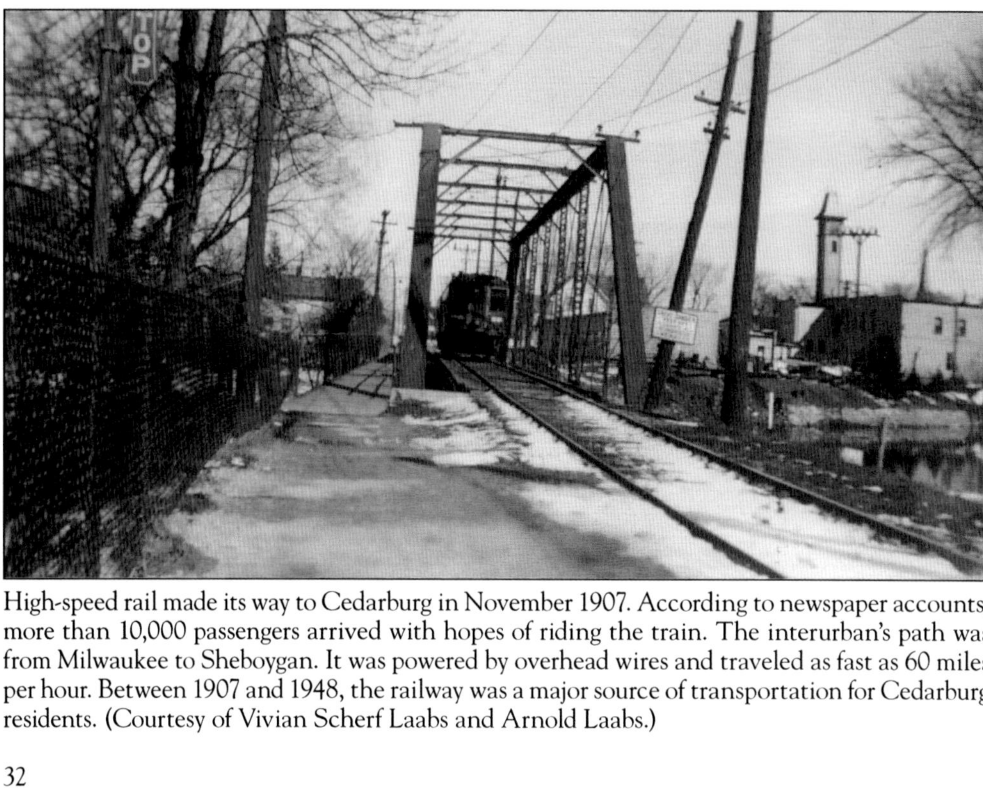

High-speed rail made its way to Cedarburg in November 1907. According to newspaper accounts, more than 10,000 passengers arrived with hopes of riding the train. The interurban's path was from Milwaukee to Sheboygan. It was powered by overhead wires and traveled as fast as 60 miles per hour. Between 1907 and 1948, the railway was a major source of transportation for Cedarburg residents. (Courtesy of Vivian Scherf Laabs and Arnold Laabs.)

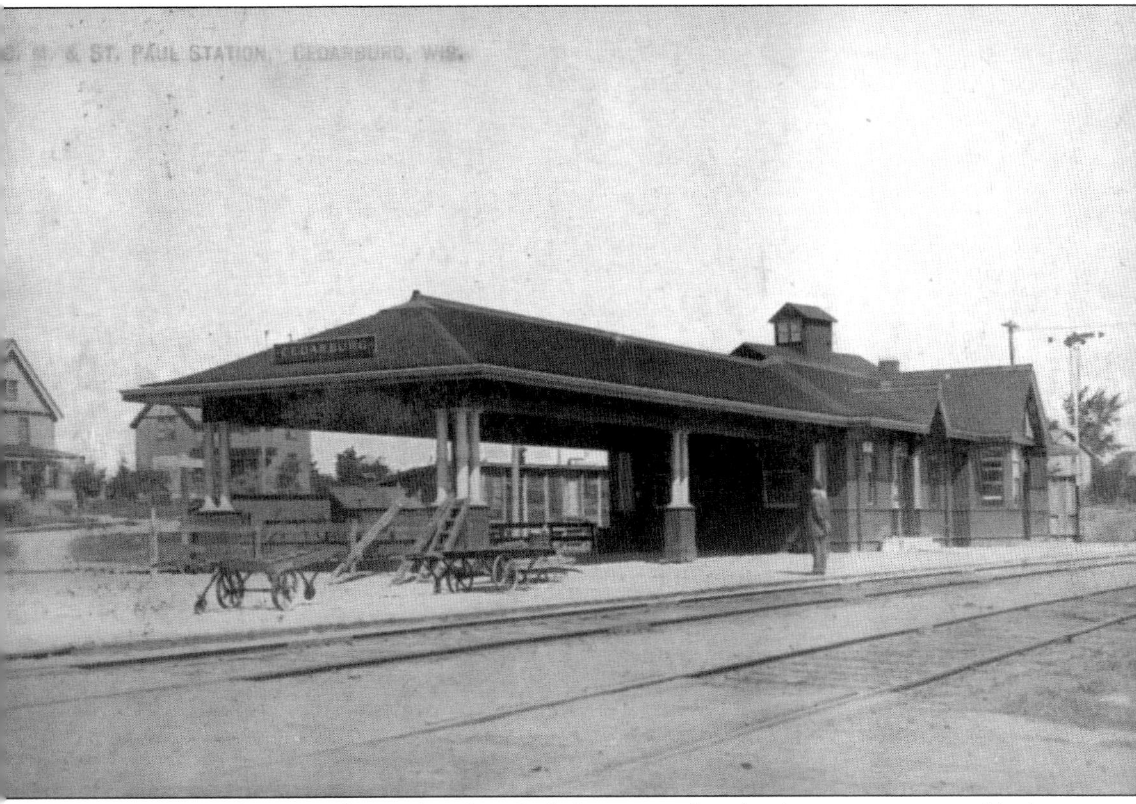

Passengers using the interurban railroad in Cedarburg waited at the depot station just a block west of downtown. The train is said to have been so dependable that locals set their watches to it. After World War II, the number of passengers fell, and people began to rely more and more on automobiles. The last interurban cars ran on March 28, 1948. The next day, the Greyhound bus station moved into the depot. Today, the restored depot is home to the Ozaukee County Historical Society's archives and research center. (Courtesy of Vivian Scherf Laabs and Arnold Laabs.)

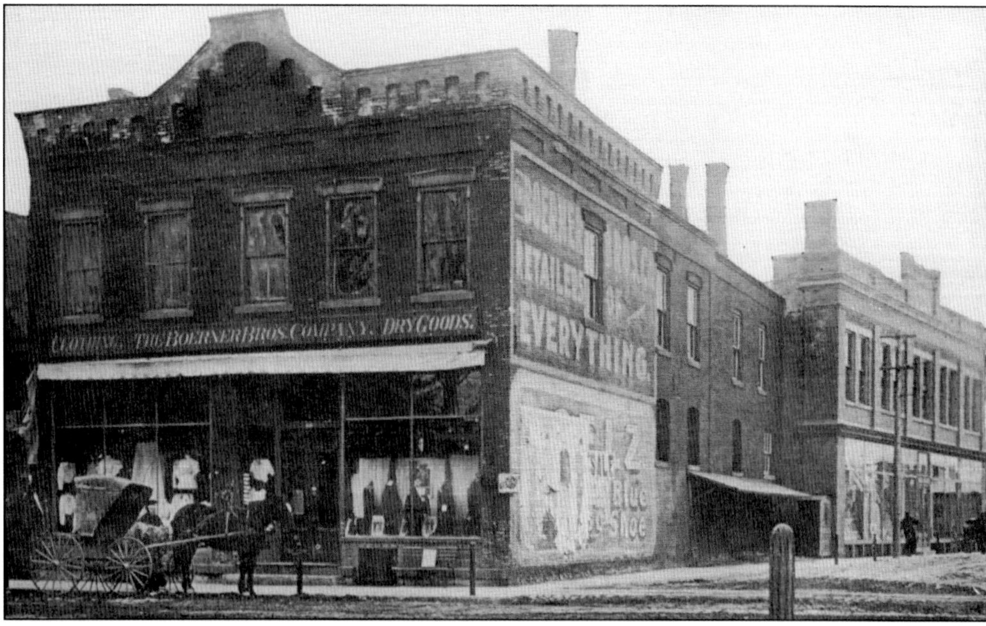

Boerner Bros. Store was one of several stores located in Cedarburg in the late 1800s. The store carried items like sugar for 8¢ a pound, Turkish prunes, and New Holland herring. It is said that C.F. Boerner preferred to run the family farm, Cedar Hedge Farms on Sheboygan Road, and left the store business to his sons. A catalog from Cedar Hedge Farms shows the business carried some 800 varieties of seeds, trees, and shrubs. (Courtesy of Deb Kranitz.)

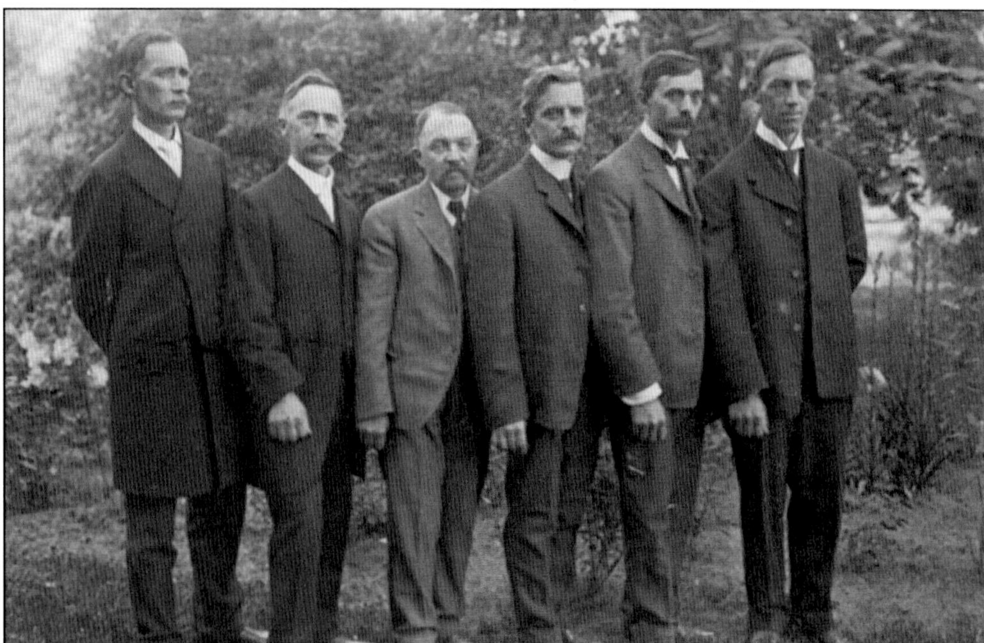

This undated photograph shows the six brothers involved with the Boerner Bros. Store. From left to right are Arthur Richard, Gustave Adolph, Henry Christian, Theodore Andrew, Oscar Franklin, and Albert Frederick. (Courtesy of Denise Boerner.)

When Cedarburg officials told the owners of Nick Schuh's saloon that he couldn't build a second story, Schuh got creative and raised the entire building. The structure is still standing, though it now has a first story. It is located next to the former Interurban Railroad Bridge. (Courtesy of the Ozaukee County Historical Society.)

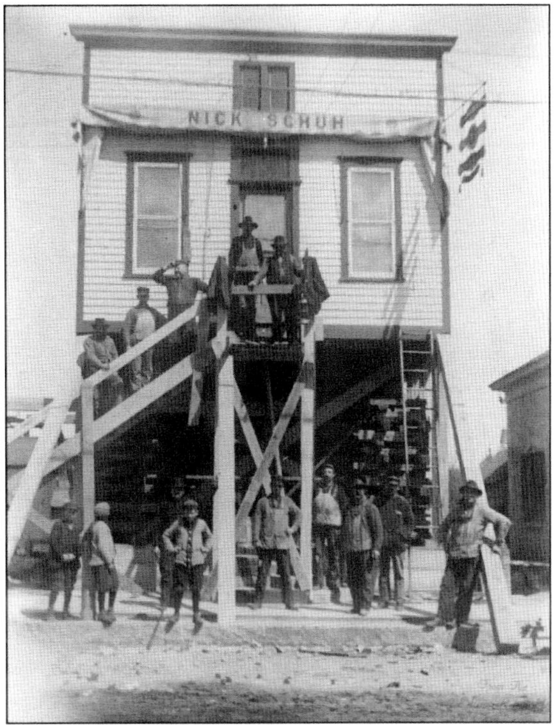

Hoffmann's Meat Market was a staple of Cedarburg for nearly a century. The market was founded in 1917 and was operated by four generations of Hoffmanns through 2008. The Hoffmanns were known for their fresh summer sausage and mock chicken legs. Pictured from left to right are Charles, Walter, and Ernst Hoffmann. (Courtesy of the Ozaukee County Historical Society.)

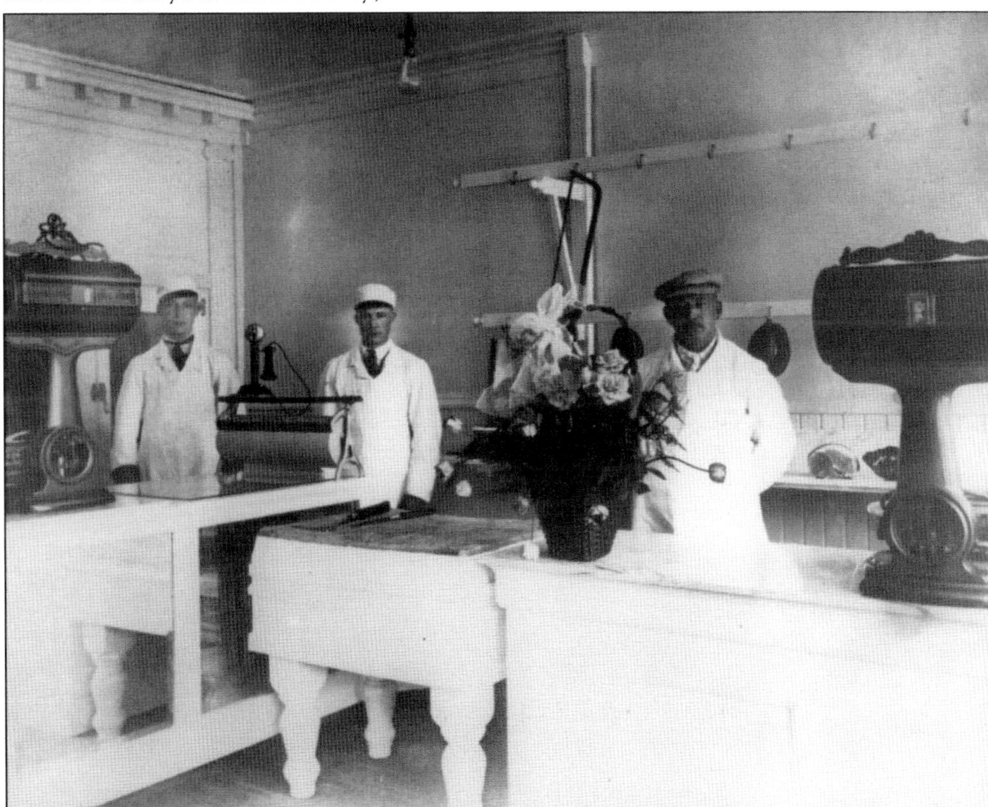

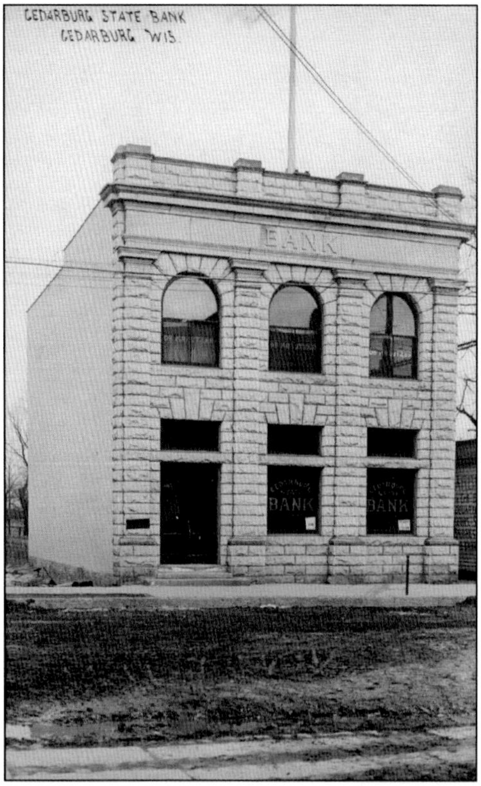

Like any good community of the 1900s, Cedarburg saw the creation of its local financial institution when the Cedarburg State Bank was built in 1908. J.P. Wirth's son Charles was the longtime president of the bank. The building also housed the early telephone switchboard on the second floor. (Courtesy of the Edward A. Rappold Photograph Collection, Cedarburg Cultural Center.)

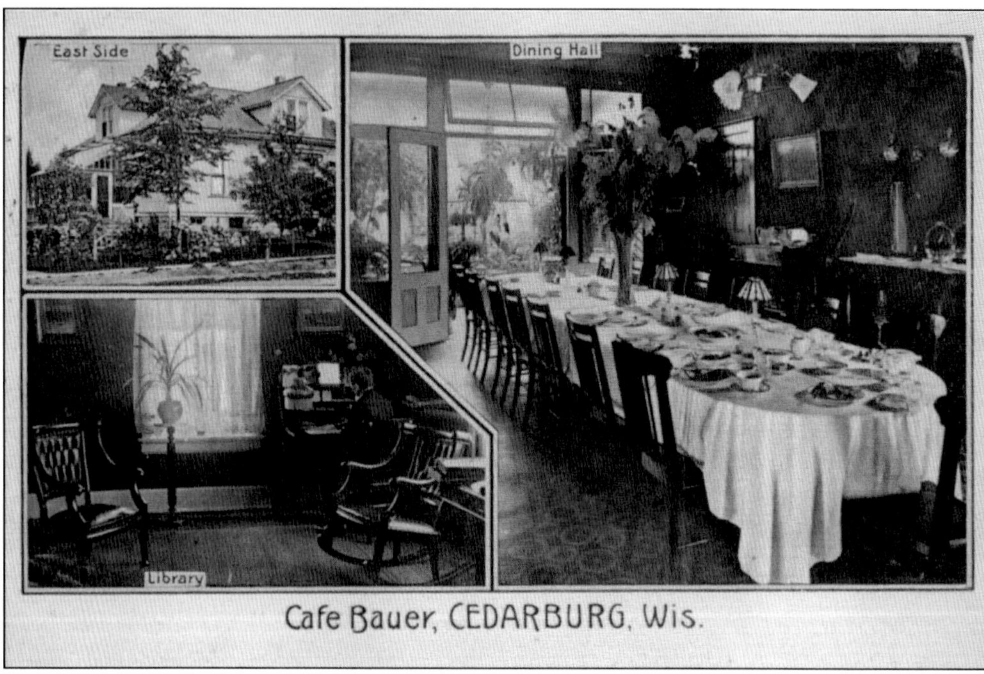

Located on Hilbert Street near Spring Street, Café Bauer served as a meeting place for many of Cedarburg's leaders. It was known for its open-air atmosphere and gardens. It also provided several hotel rooms. (Courtesy of Vivian Scherf Laabs and Arnold Laabs.)

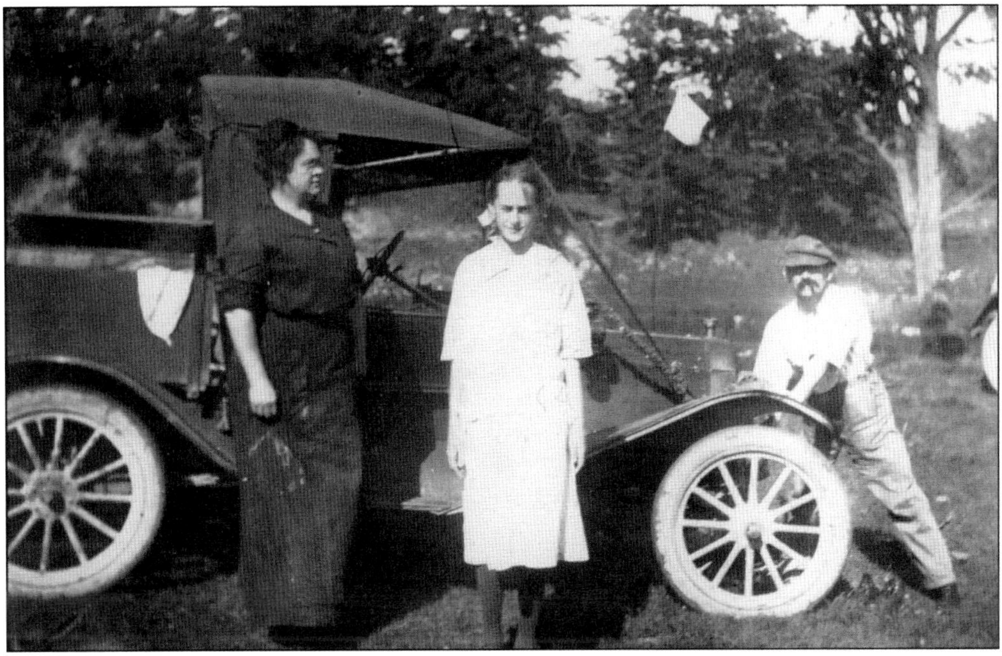

Automobiles reached the streets of Cedarburg in the early 1900s. By then, gasoline cars had begun to outsell all other types of motor vehicles. In Cedarburg, the availability of automobiles decreased the need for the interurban railway. Pictured from left to right with their car in this undated photograph are Emma Bauer, Evelyn Straub, and Alfred Bauer. (Courtesy of the Ozaukee County Historical Society.)

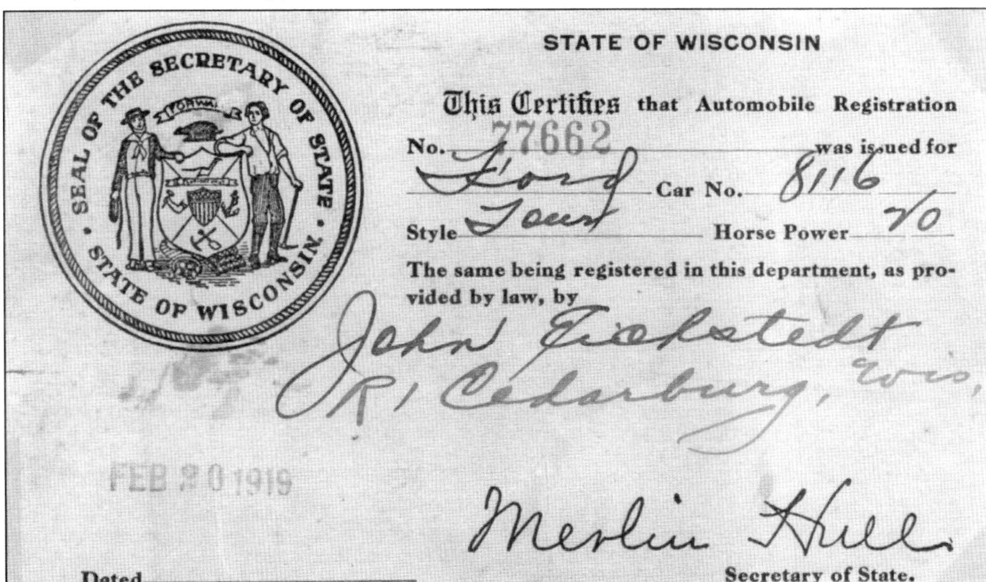

SEAL OF THE SECRETARY OF STATE • STATE OF WISCONSIN •

FORWARD

STATE OF WISCONSIN

This Certifies that Automobile Registration No. 77662 was issued for Ford Car No. 8116 Style Tour Horse Power 20

The same being registered in this department, as provided by law, by

John Eickstedt
R1 Cedarburg, Wis.

FEB 20 1919

Merlin Hull
Secretary of State.

Dated

John Eickstedt purchased a Ford touring car in 1919 and registered it with the state of Wisconsin. He may have bought the car in downtown Cedarburg, where Lauterbach Ford Sales & Services was located. It is unclear whether the car required a hand crank or had an electric starter, which became available in most cars sold after 1919. The car had a 20-horsepower engine, compared to the average 150-horespower engines in cars today. (Courtesy of Roy Eickstedt.)

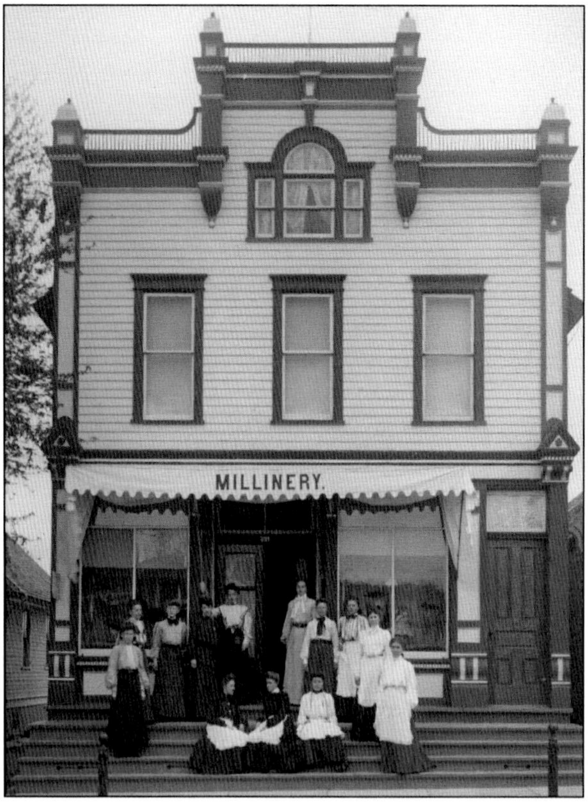

The Ziemer sisters owned a millinery shop in downtown Cedarburg for many years. Early millinery shops were almost always owned by women, who made items such as aprons, ruffles, trim for gowns, neckerchiefs, and dresses. The 1880 census for Cedarburg showed there were seven members of the Ziemer family living in Cedarburg at the time. (Courtesy of the Ozaukee County Historical Society.)

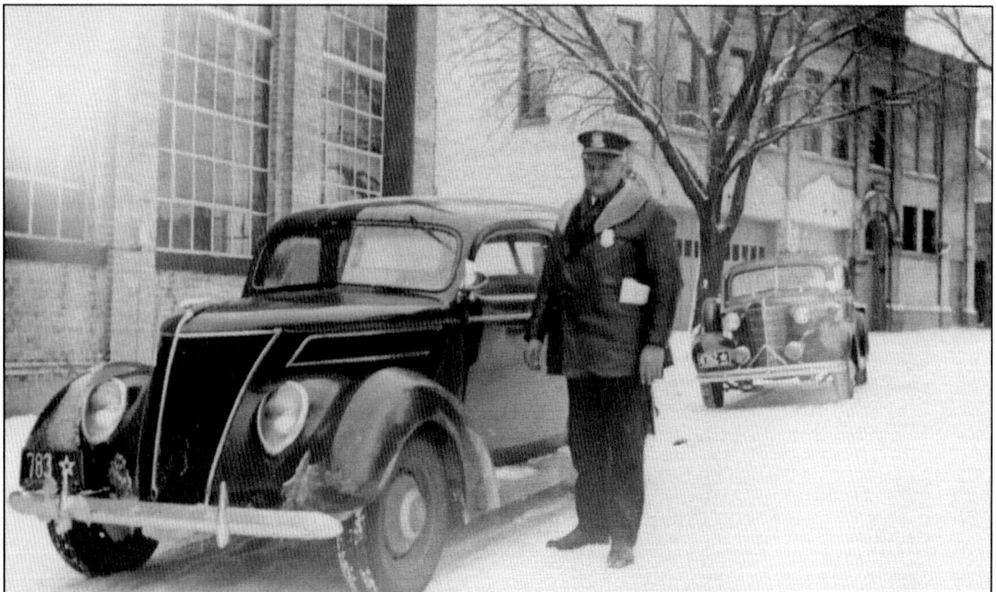

Police Chief August Frank is pictured in front of Cedarburg's power plant, where calls for police service came through. If the chief was reached, the employees at the power plant would dim all the street lights in the city. Frank served from 1932 to 1944. His grandson Tom Frank is now the chief of police for Cedarburg. (Courtesy of the Cedarburg Police Department.)

Three

Town of Cedarburg

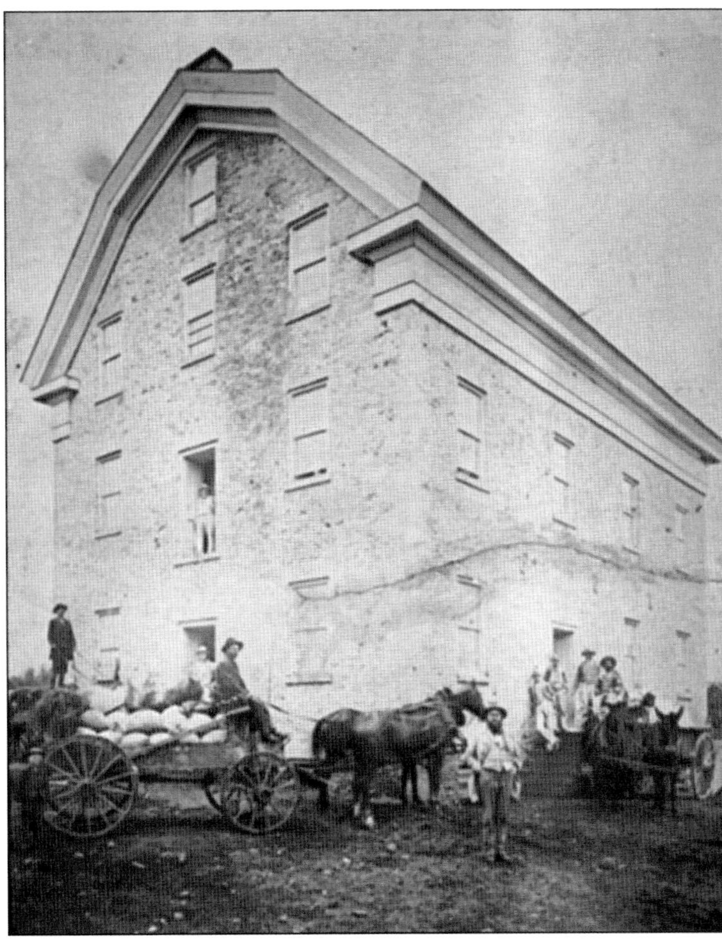

One of the first buildings to be erected in the town of Cedarburg's Hamilton district was the Concordia Mill, constructed in 1853 by Edward Janssen, his brother Theodore, and William Gaitsch. It replaced a sawmill that had been built on Cedar Creek in New Dublin several years earlier. Around the same time, Hamilton also had a post office, general store, and shoemaker. (Courtesy of the Ozaukee County Historical Society.)

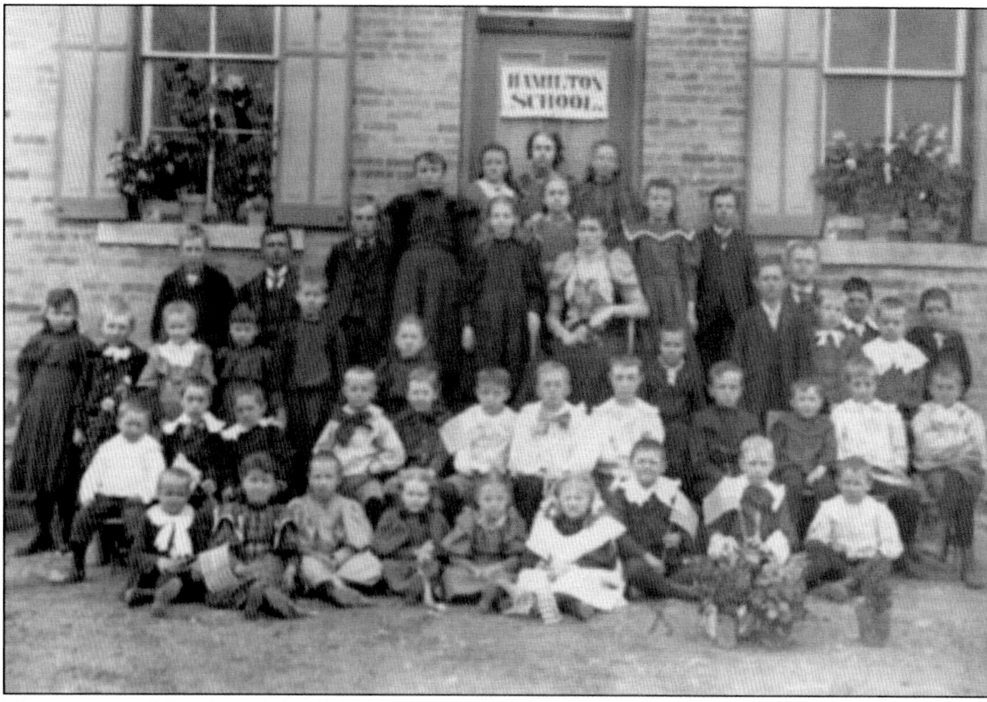

The one-room Hamilton School, built in 1887, was one of several schoolhouses located in the town of Cedarburg before the advent of public school systems. Children in first through eighth grades attended classes there until 1958, when the school closed and town children began attending the Cedarburg School District schools. Today, the restored school is home to a quilt shop known as Ye Olde Schoolhouse. (Courtesy of the Town of Cedarburg.)

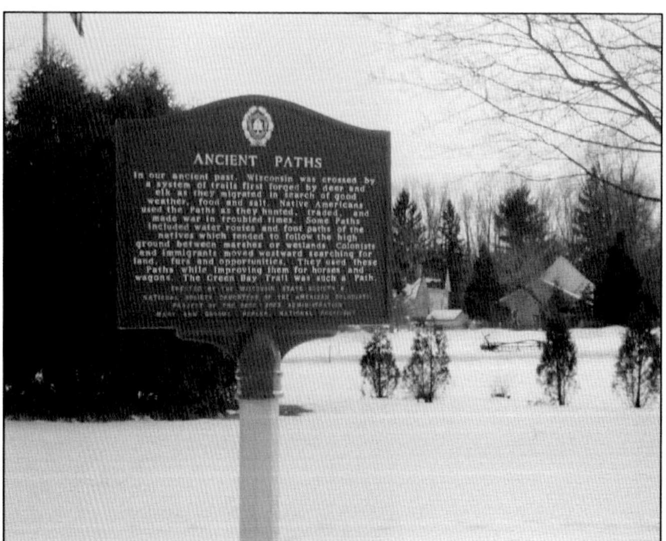

This "Ancient Paths" sign gives a brief history of the activity that took place in the historic Hamilton area before woodcutter Joseph Gardinier came through in 1839. This area of Cedarburg was originally called New Dublin by its Irish settlers. It was renamed Hamilton in 1847 after Alexander Hamilton's son William Stephen stopped at a New Dublin tavern on his way from Green Bay to Illinois and bought drinks for the house. (Courtesy of the *News Graphic*.)

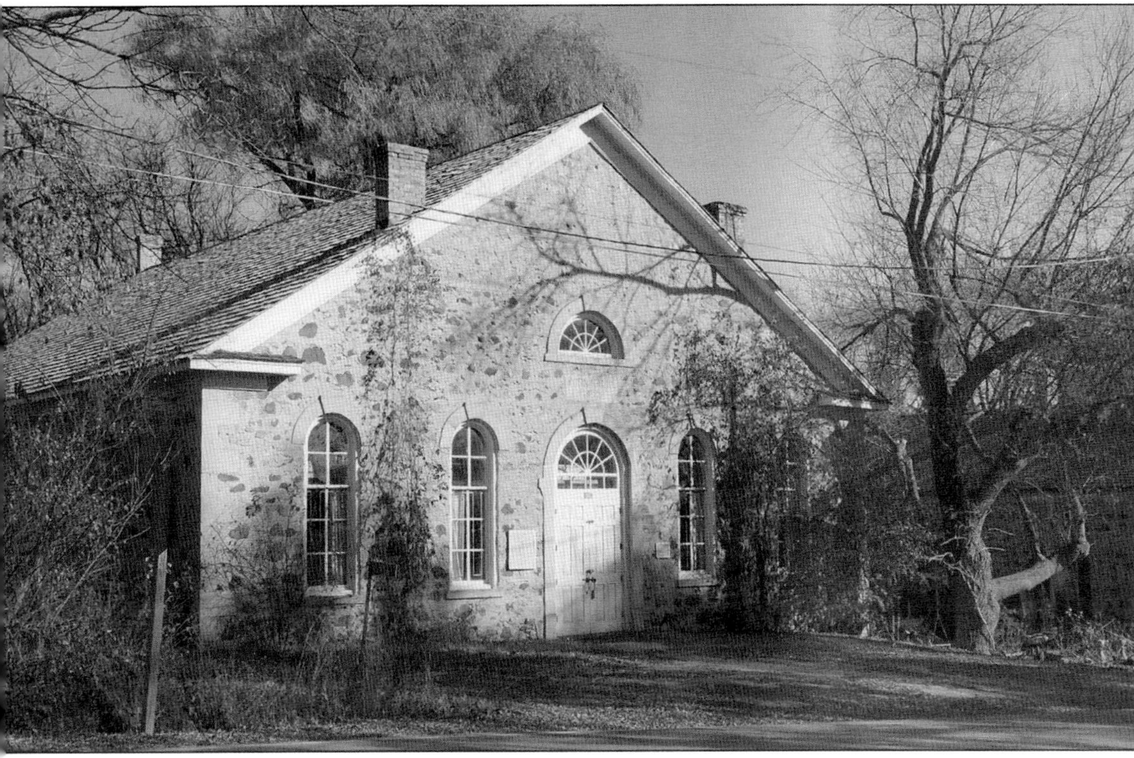

Considered the treasure of Hamilton, Turn Halle was built of fieldstone in 1867 by William Janssen as home to the new chapter of the Turnverein Society, which split off from the Cedarburg chapter. For several years, the hall was home to gymnastics and other recreational activities on the first floor, and dining, dancing, and concerts upstairs. But the popularity of the turnverein faded in Hamilton, and by the late 1870s, Andrew Bodendorfer used the building to store grain for the Columbia Mill. Over the years it has housed a cider mill and an antique racing car museum. It was listed in the National Register of Historic Places on July 1, 1976. It was donated to the Town of Cedarburg and the Cedarburg Landmark Preservation Society by Adelaide B. Mille. In 2010, the marketing firm of Henke and Associates purchased Turn Halle. It made significant upgrades without compromising the integrity of the original building. (Courtesy of the *News Graphic*.)

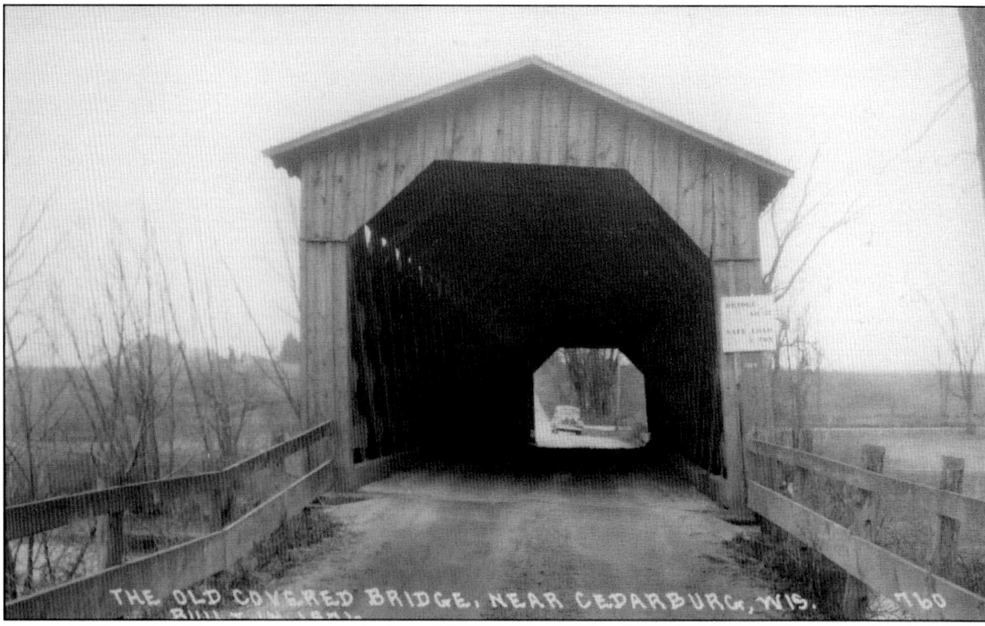

Cedarburg's iconic covered bridge was built in 1876 after neighboring farmers petitioned for a bridge that didn't wash away in heavy rains. Many theories have been given as to why the bridge was covered. One is that it protected travelers from the elements. Some have speculated it gave refuge from the Indians. Long closed to automobile traffic, Cedarburg's covered bridge is now the last remaining original covered bridge in Wisconsin. (Courtesy of the Ozaukee County Historical Society.)

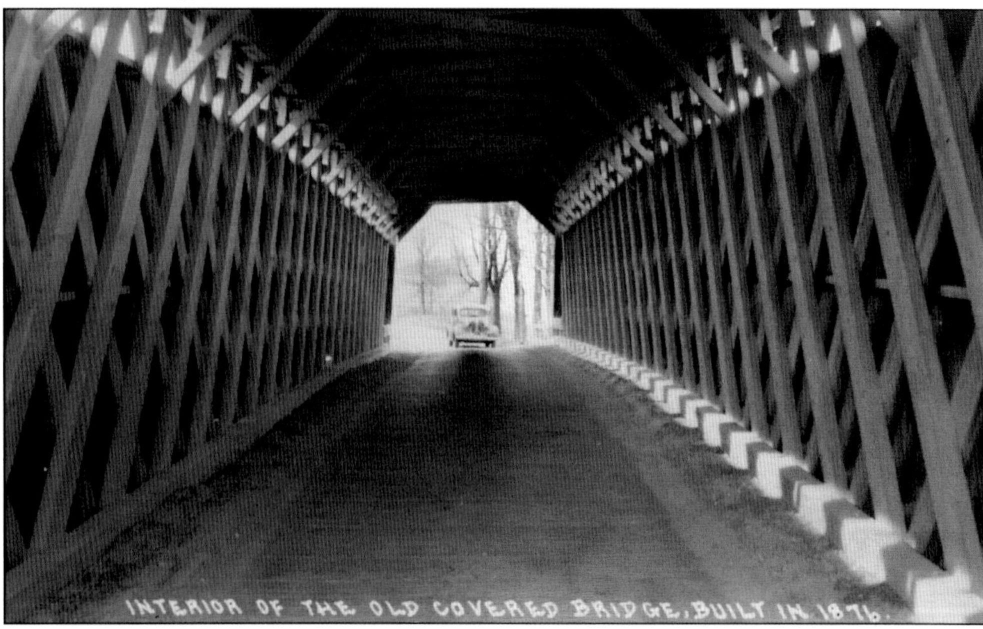

The original span of the covered bridge measured 12 feet wide and 120 feet long. The pine lumber was cut and prepared in Baraboo, Wisconsin, then hauled to Cedarburg, where the bridge was constructed. A center abutment was added in 1927 to carry the heavier traffic. It was originally known as "the red bridge." (Courtesy of the Ozaukee County Historical Society.)

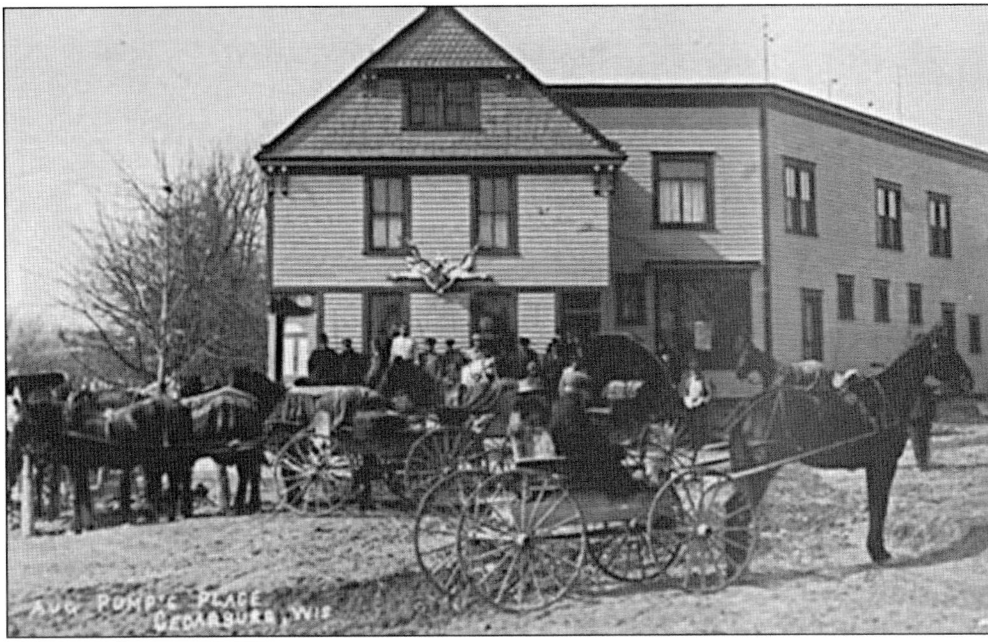

August Pump's Place, a saloon at Five Corners, was a popular destination for town and city residents in the early 1900s. Pump was the third owner of the business, which he bought around 1910. Over the years, the saloon and restaurant was a place for dances, weddings, banquets, and receptions. The original structure still stands and is home to Roadhouse Bar and Grill. (Courtesy of the Town of Cedarburg.)

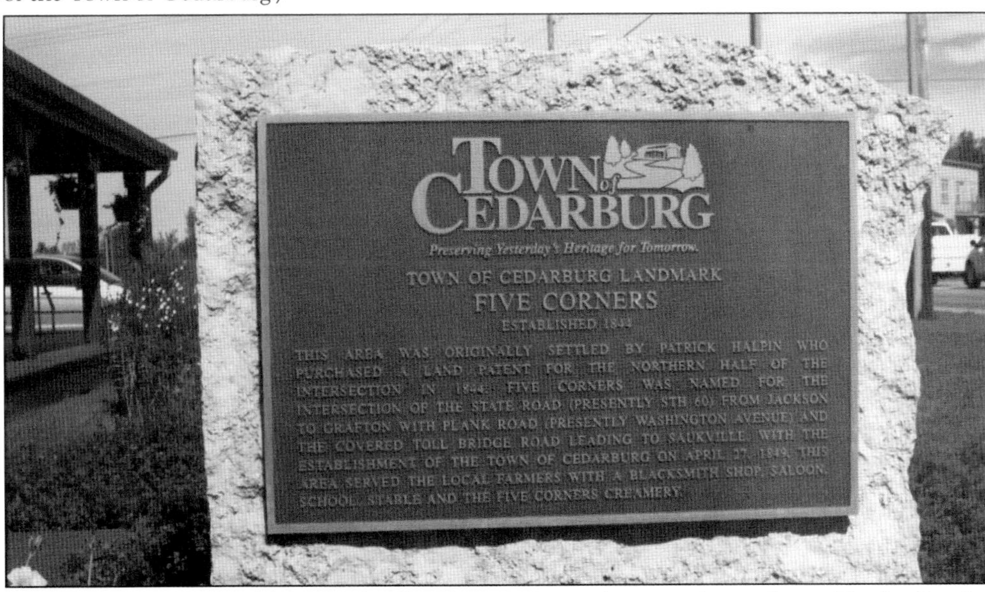

The Five Corners area of the town has long been a nexus of activity for residents. Charles Goeden operated a blacksmith shop there for some 30 years. Across from there was the Five Corners Creamery, organized in 1893 by 20 farmers. Today, town hall, a gas station, a car dealership, and a bar and grill occupy the area. Town leaders plan to build a 95-acre outdoor athletic complex and a commercial town center near Five Corners in the coming years. (Courtesy of the Town of Cedarburg.)

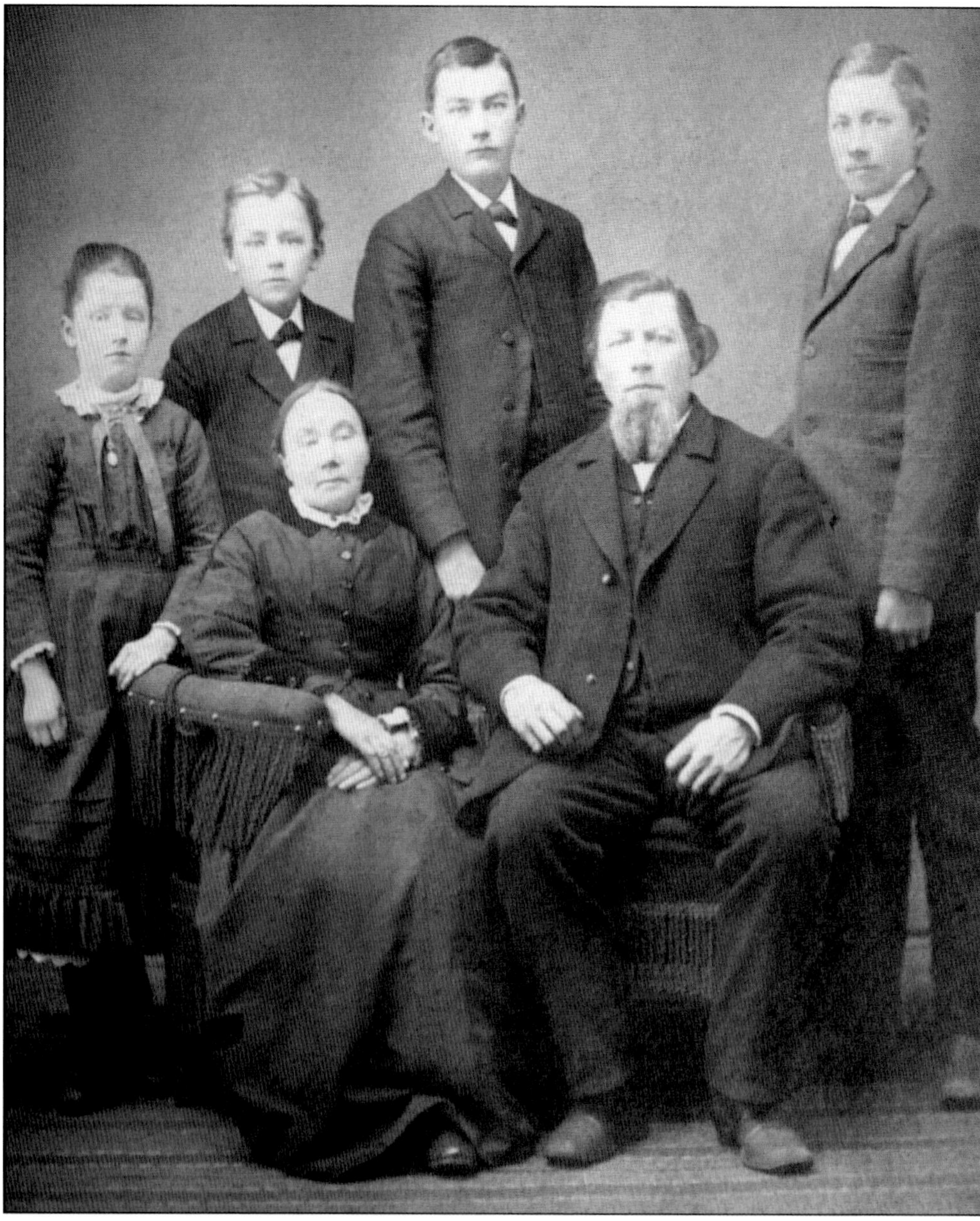

One of the earlier settlers in Cedarburg was the Lüders family (now Lueder and Lueders) of Spornitz, Mecklenburg-Schwerin, Germany. They left Spornitz early in 1854 and reached what would be their farm near Western Road and Granville Road in November of that year. In 1860, the family bought another farm on Bridge Road. By 1863, the family's combined holdings equalled 260 acres. One of those in the traveling party was Joachim, who came with his wife, Henrietta. They had three young children when Henrietta died of tuberculosis in 1863 at age 33. Joachim married Albertina Bruss two months later, and together they had five children. Joachim was a pillar of his church, Immanuel Lutheran, and was chairman of the committee assigned to raise money to build the new Immanuel Lutheran Church. Albertina and Joachim are pictured in this c. 1879 photograph with their children, from left to right, Martha, William, Albert, and Otto. (Courtesy of Harold Pfohl.)

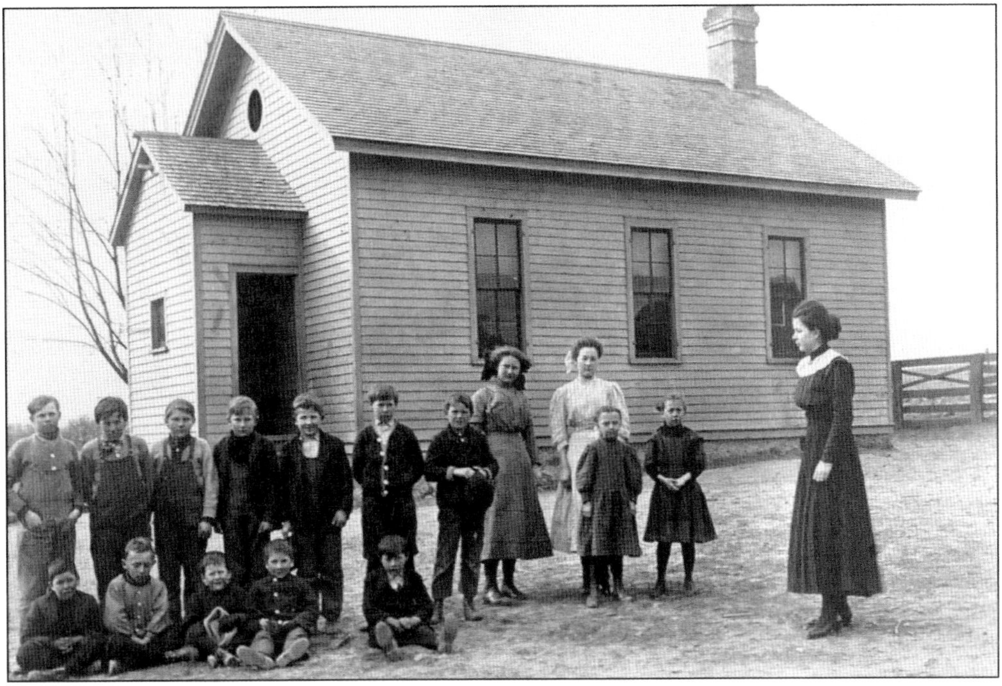

Sherman School was another one-room schoolhouse in the town. It was located on Western Avenue. Other schools in the town included Pleasant Valley, Deckers Corner, Horns Corners, and Five Corners. Children in this era were often required to clean the blackboard, sweep the floors, carry in drinking water from the pump, rake leaves in autumn, and clean the schoolyard in the spring. (Courtesy of Harold Pfohl.)

One of the rather unique schools in the town was the octagonal schoolhouse on Pleasant Valley Road. It was built in 1860 of stone. At one time, as many as 48 students attended the school. When the number of students was greater than the available seats, children sat in the windowsills. The former school is a home today, one of the dwindling number of octagonal buildings left in Wisconsin. (Courtesy of the *News Graphic*.)

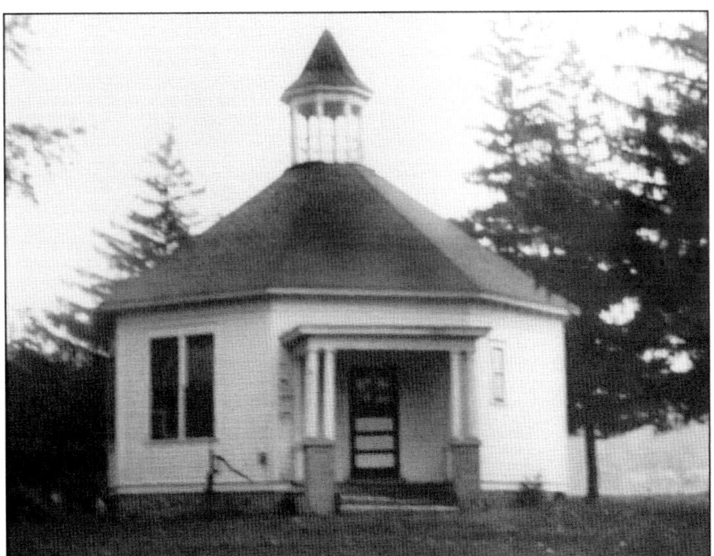

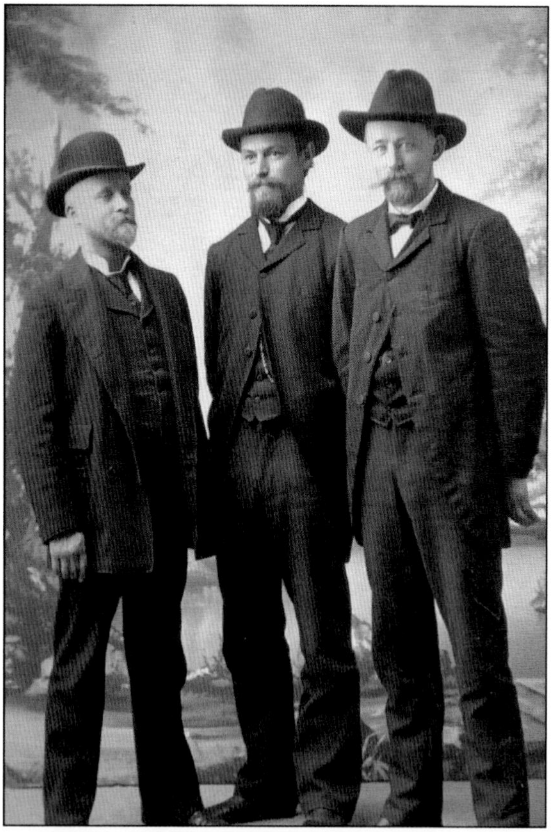

This trio may look like tough cowboys, but historical accounts indicate they were fun-loving and mischievous. From left to right, they are Otto Beckmann, Charlie Nieman, and William Lueder. Beckmann was the Cedarburg constable. Nieman loved photography, and many of the old family photographs were taken by him. Lueder married Nieman's sister, Augusta. (Courtesy of Harold Pfohl.)

For many years, the Lueders family used a pasture that required herding cows along Bridge Street each morning and evening. Bridge Street was still a country lane and traffic was light. Pictured in this photograph from the 1940s is Ronald Pfohl. (Courtesy of Harold Pfohl.)

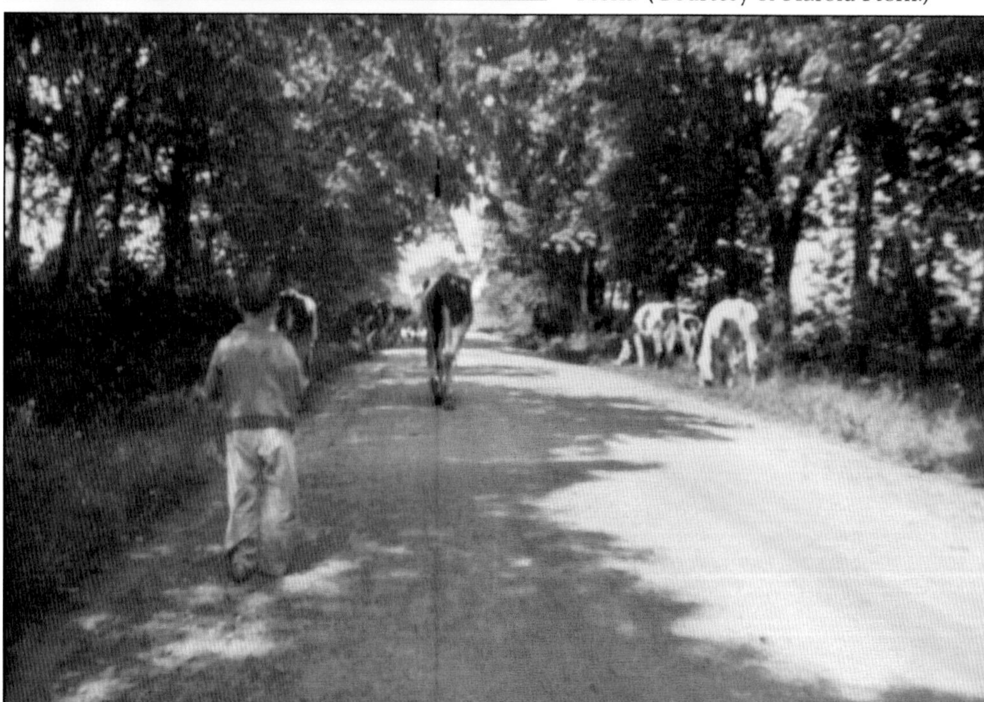

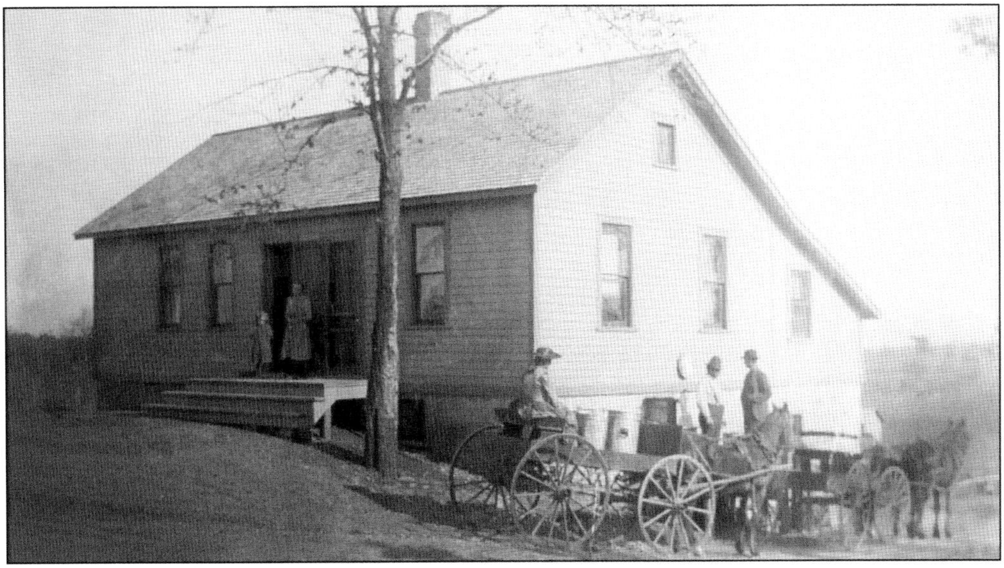

Before butter was mass-produced in factories, area creameries were the norm. Farmers would regularly—sometimes every day—deliver whole milk supplies to the creamery, where the cream was separated and churned to make butter. One creamery was located in the Five Corners area of the town and operated until the 1950s. Another was located on Bridge Street and Granville Road, pictured above in what may have been the 1890s. (Courtesy of Harold Pfohl.)

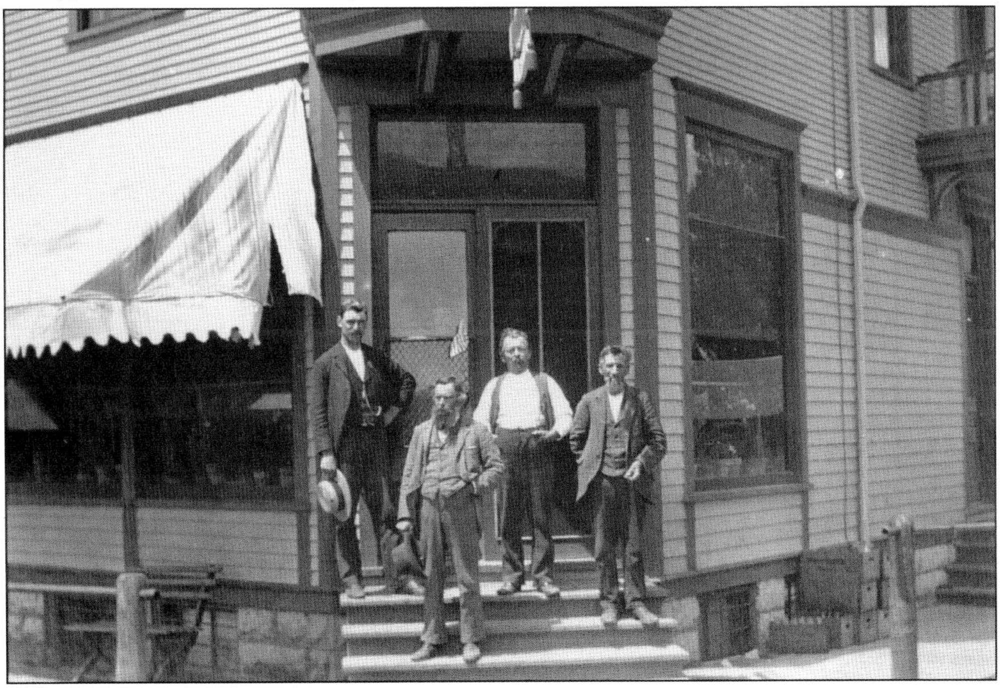

The Cedarburg Town Board is pictured in front of Schullenberg Hall at Horns Corners in this photograph from 1900. The hamlet of Horns Corners was named in tribute to Frederick W. Horn, who bought 140 acres surrounding the intersection of what is now County Highway NN and Horns Corners Road. The area included a general store, post office, church, mill, and school. (Courtesy of Harold Pfohl.)

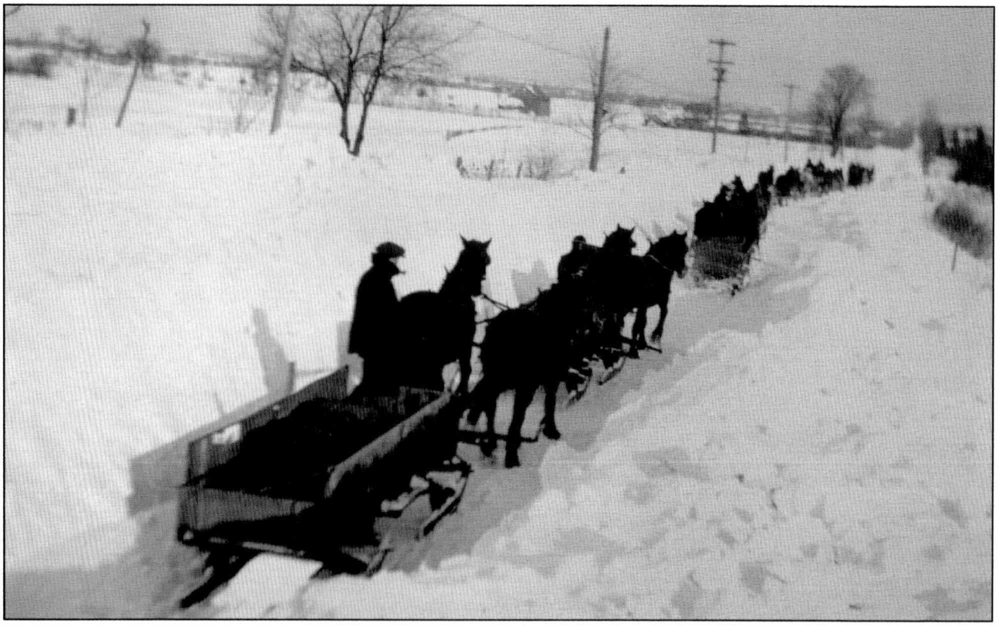

While automobiles were the norm when this photograph was taken in 1936, they were no match for the heavy snowfall that year. Streets remained unplowed for days, and farmers were required to deliver milk using horses and trailers. This photograph is believed to have been taken on either Bridge Street or Western Avenue. (Courtesy of Harold Pfohl.)

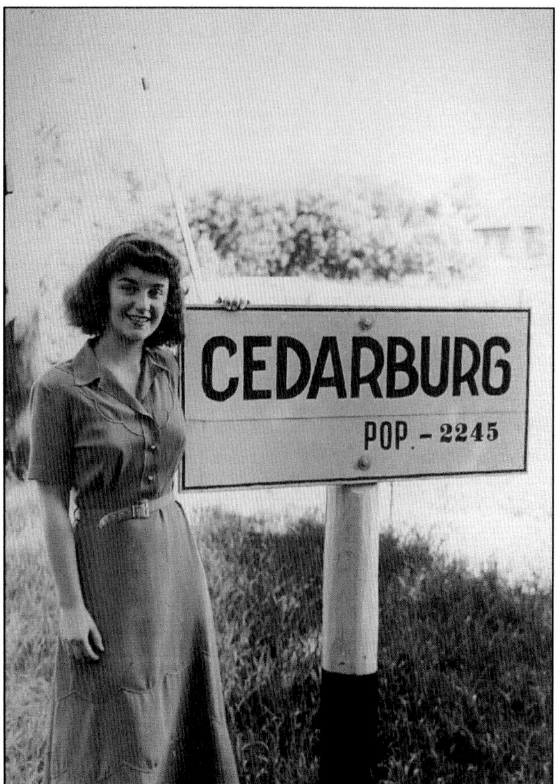

The Town of Cedarburg was officially incorporated in early 1849, and the first meeting of town supervisors was held on April 3 of that year. The first town board was comprised of William Vogenitz, Henry Krohn, and Edward Nolan. Charles E. Chamberlin was the town clerk, and Valentine Hahn Jr. was the superintendent of schools. In 2008, the town's population was 5,789. (Courtesy of the Town of Cedarburg.)

Four

AGRICULTURE AND INDUSTRY

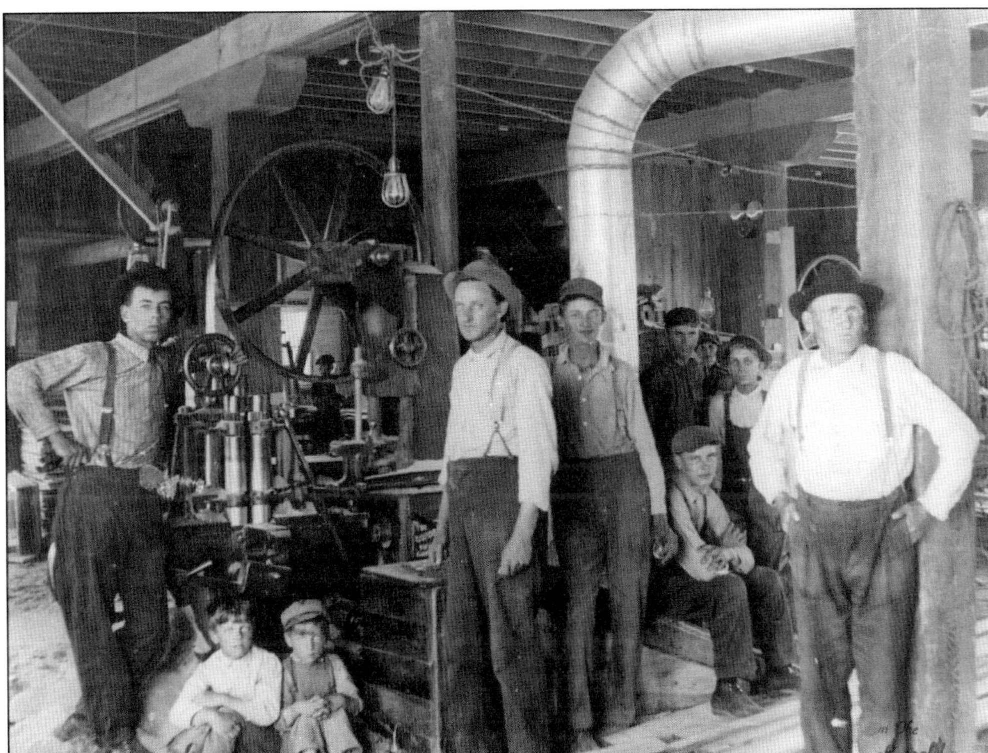

The conditions in the woolen mill may look antiquated and even unsafe, but at the time this photograph was taken in the late 1800s, the world had undergone an industrial revolution. Machines and other technology provided vast improvements in agriculture, textiles, and metal manufacturing, though workers were still considered "hands." The Wisconsin Historical Society recognized the mill as helping the regional economy transform from one of frontier agrarian into one capable of producing manufactured goods for market. (Courtesy of the Ozaukee County Historical Society.)

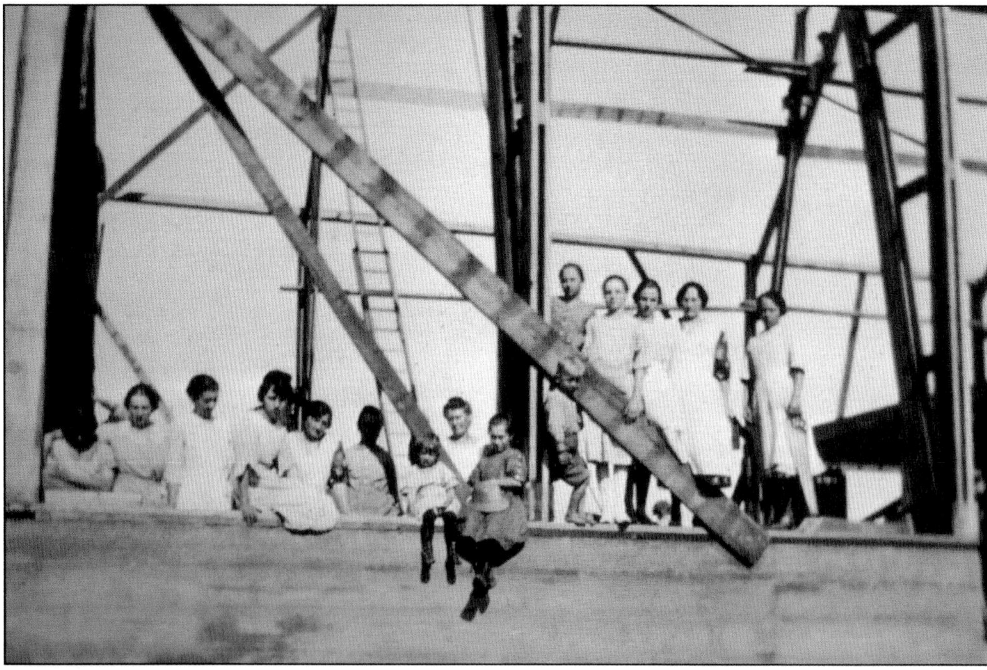

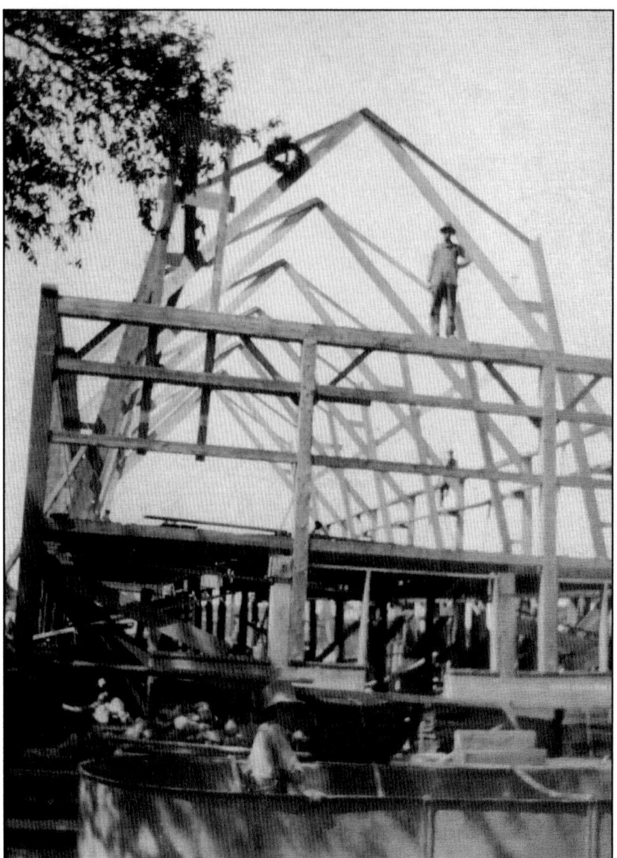

A barn raising in the 1800s and early 1900s was a community event in which families came together to help construct what was probably the most important structure on a farm. The women typically prepared the food, while the men did the heavy lifting. A 1996 survey of barns in the Town of Cedarburg found 154, many of them original. Thirty-one were still in agricultural use, many by "gentleman farmers who have settled for a few acres and a few horses," according to the survey's authors. (Courtesy of Harold Pfohl.)

The construction of the Lueders barn following a fire in 1923 may have brought the community out to observe, but Lueders hired a contractor to rebuild his barn. A young man named Robert Krause was the construction superintendent on the project. (Courtesy of Harold Pfohl.)

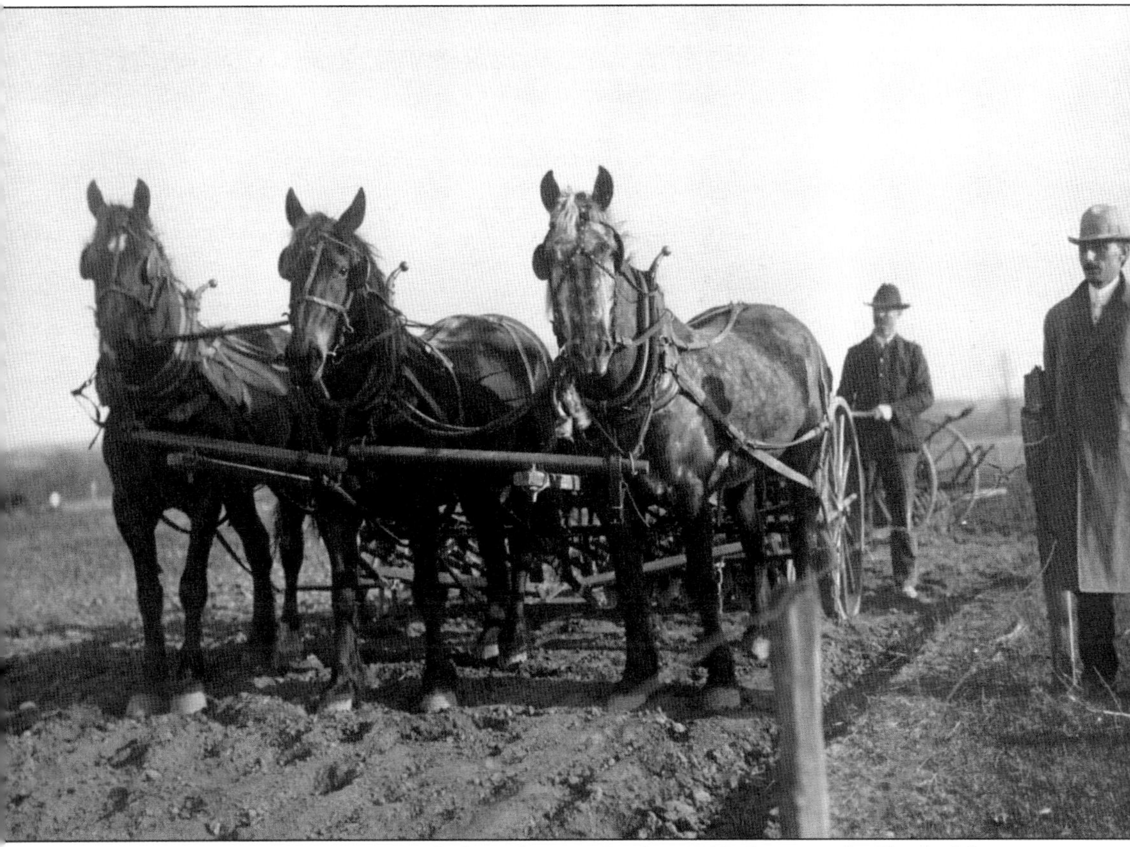

Peas were a common crop among Cedarburg farmers. In this 1909 photograph, Charlie Nieman is seen walking behind horses to guide the seeding process. Nieman was an early practitioner of diversifying one's assets. He had a dairy farm, a sawmill, and a fox farm, among other business ventures. (Courtesy of Harold Pfohl.)

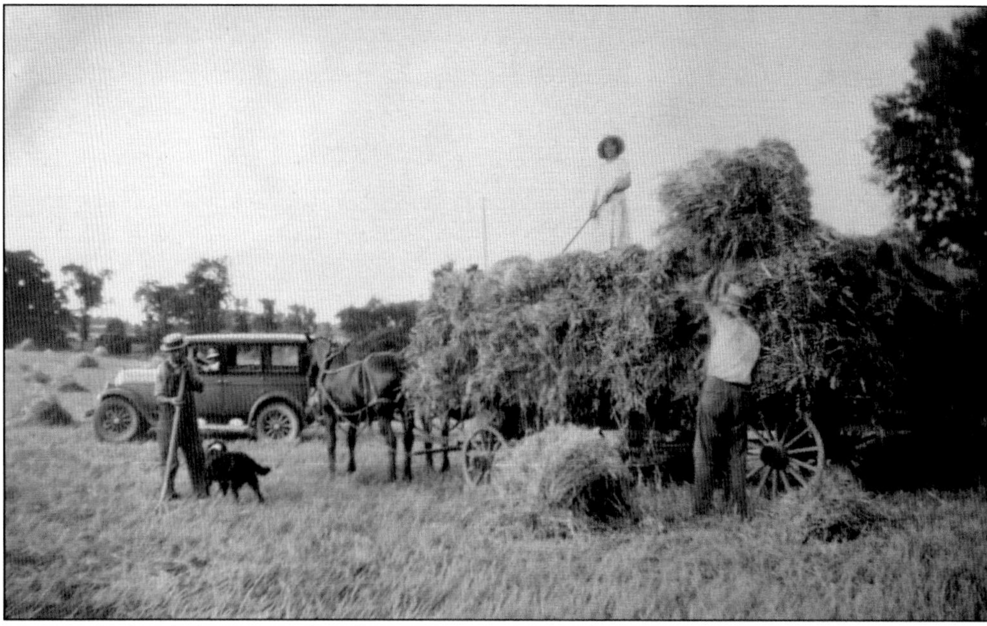

The Lueder family loads grain bundles onto a wagon on July 30, 1931. Elda Lueder is on the wagon. Her brother Edgar is on the ground at left. (Courtesy of Harold Pfohl.)

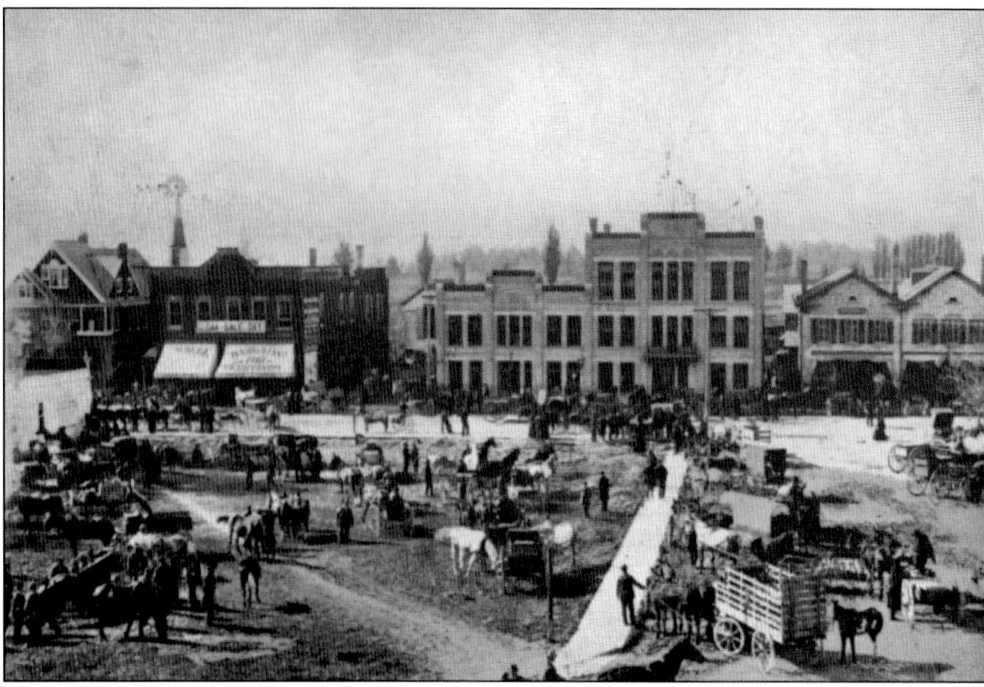

When it came to agricultural activity in Ozaukee County, Cedarburg became the center of activity on cattle fair day, also known as market day. Held the last Monday of the month, farmers throughout the county came to exchange goods or bring grain to the mill for processing. Sometimes the men stayed on into the evening and took in the city's saloons. Legend has it that fights would sometimes break out among the drunks, who broke pickets off the fences and used them as weapons. (Courtesy of Vivian Scherf Laabs and Arnold Laabs.)

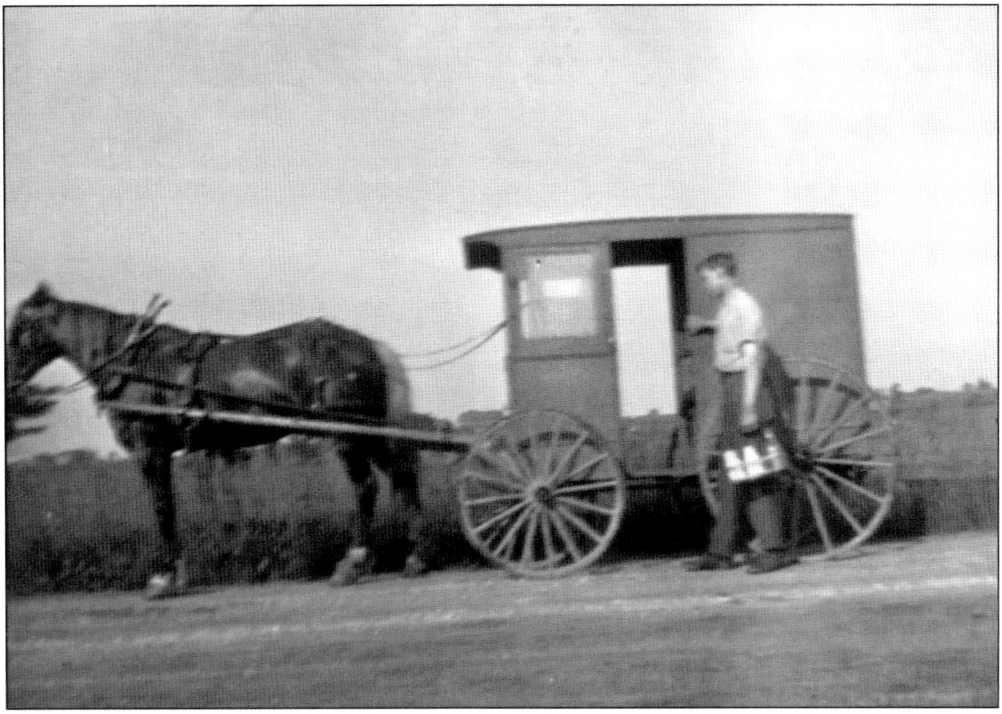

Before accepting a job as a motorman with the old interurban railroad line in 1923, Arnold Scherf delivered milk for Tews Dairy with a horse and wagon. Scherf told his daughter that the horse knew the route, and when it was coming to an end, he would head to the barn. Tews Dairy received recognition for 72 years of continuous service in Cedarburg in 1974. (Courtesy of Vivian Scherf Laabs.)

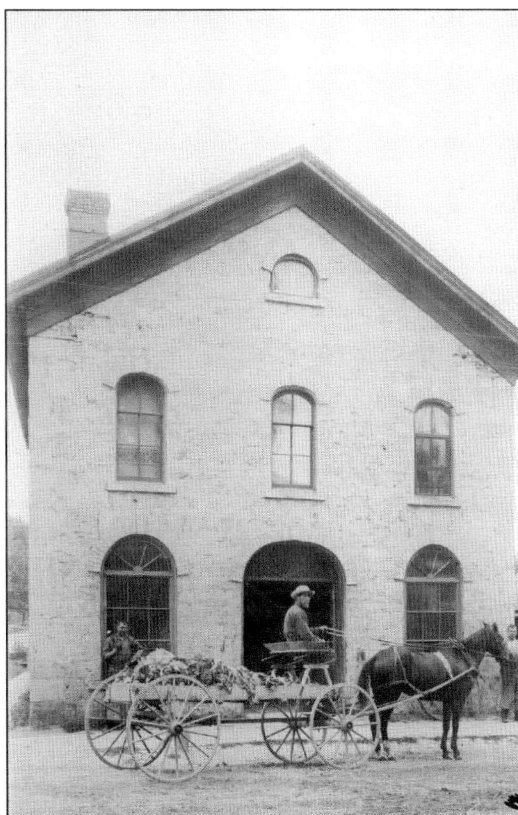

The Krueger Cedarburg Blacksmith shop, located on the corner of what is now Washington Avenue and Western Road, was one of several blacksmith shops that operated in Cedarburg in the late 1800s and early 1900s. Blacksmiths made farm implements, horseshoes, and tools for carpenters. There were many such shops in Cedarburg in its early years. Until 2007, Cedarburg still had a blacksmith, Dan Nauman, although his work was more of an art. (Courtesy of the Ozaukee County Historical Society.)

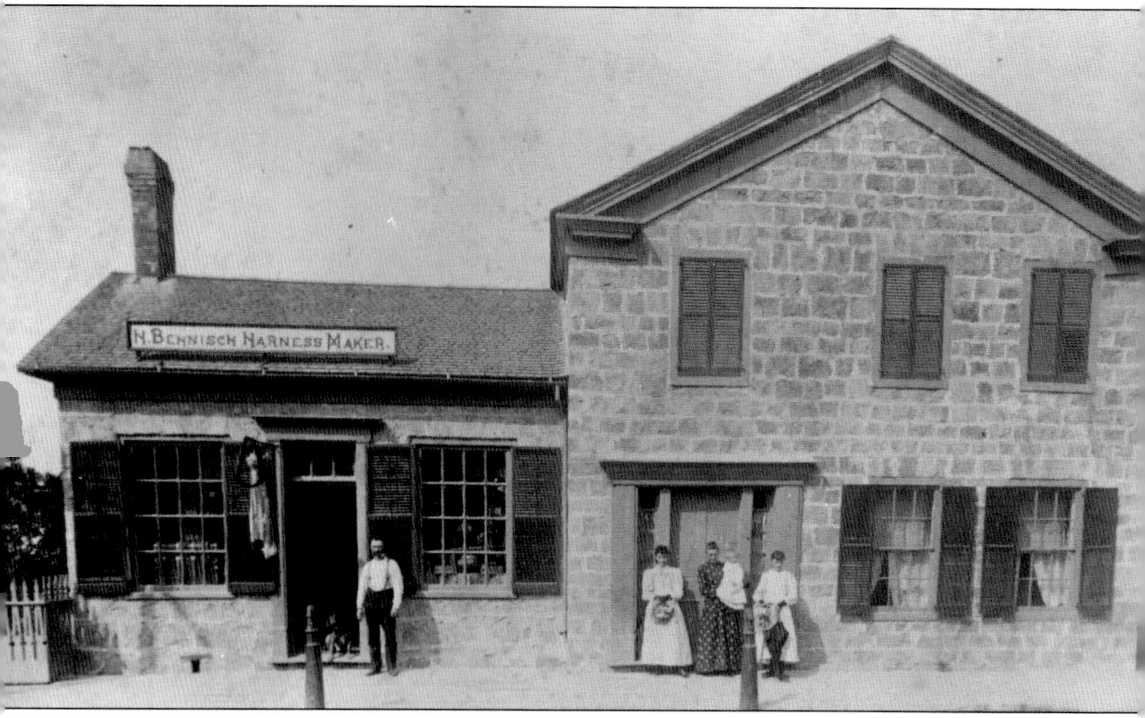

The first harness shop was opened in Cedarburg in 1846 by Conrad Horneffer. It became the Behnisch Harness Shop in 1868, when Heinrich Behnisch bought and ran it with his wife and four sons. The shop, located at the corner of Washington Avenue and Mill Street, remained until 1927, when it was razed and a garage was built. (Courtesy of the Edward A. Rappold Photograph Collection, Cedarburg Cultural Center.)

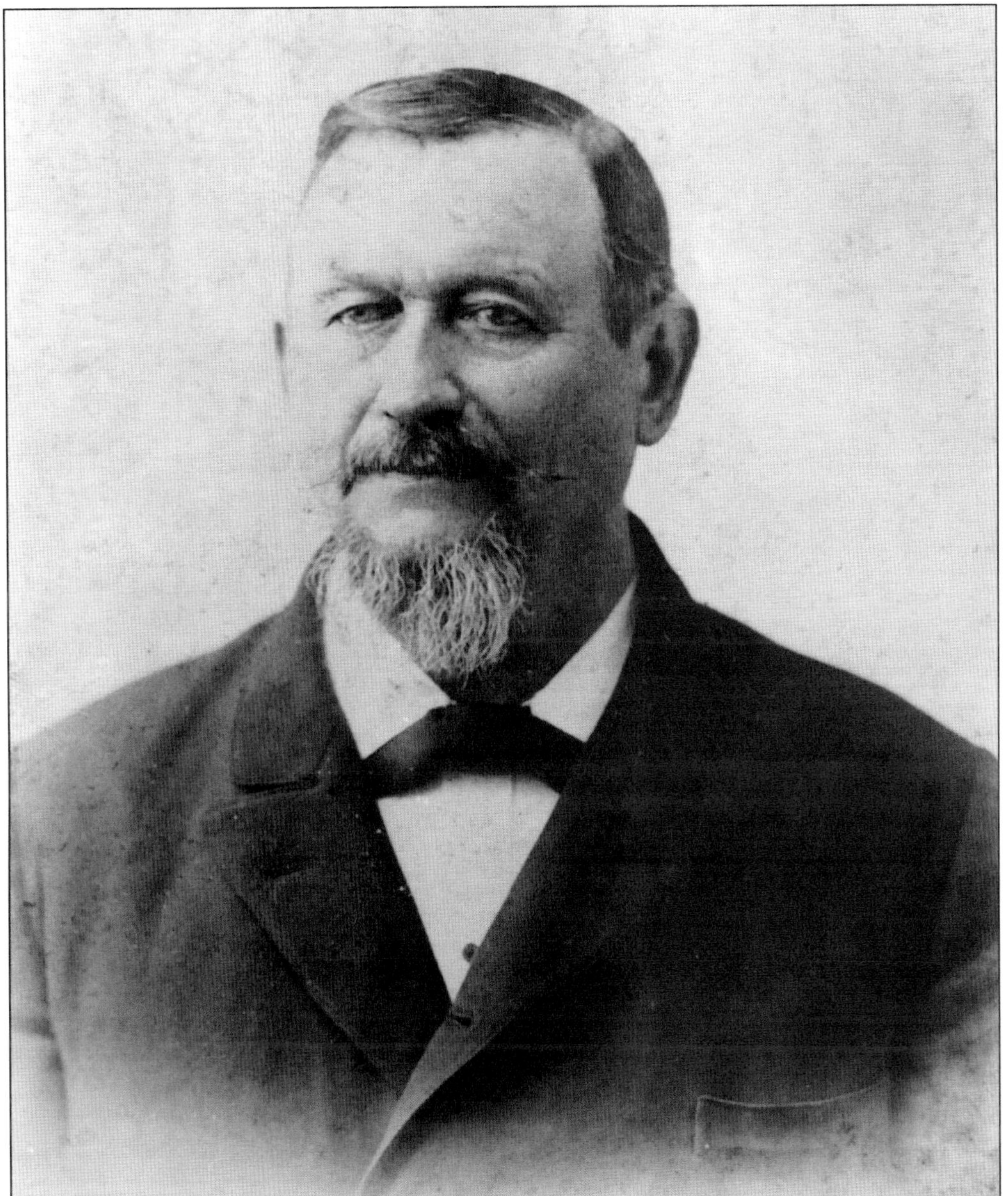

Diedrich Wittenberg Sr. was working for Hilgen and Schroeder hauling flour from the gristmill in Cedarburg to Milwaukee, when he met and later married Hilgen's daughter Margaret. He later went into business with his father-in-law, forming the Hilgen-Wittenberg Woolen Mill. According to the *Cedarburg Weekly News* obituary for Wittenberg in December 1907, it was through his "nurturing efforts and rare business ability" that the mill grew from a small operation to one of "the largest establishments of its kind in the Northwest." Wittenberg was also active in helping to incorporate Cedarburg as a city and was one of the founding members of the turnverein. (Courtesy of the Ozaukee County Historical Society.)

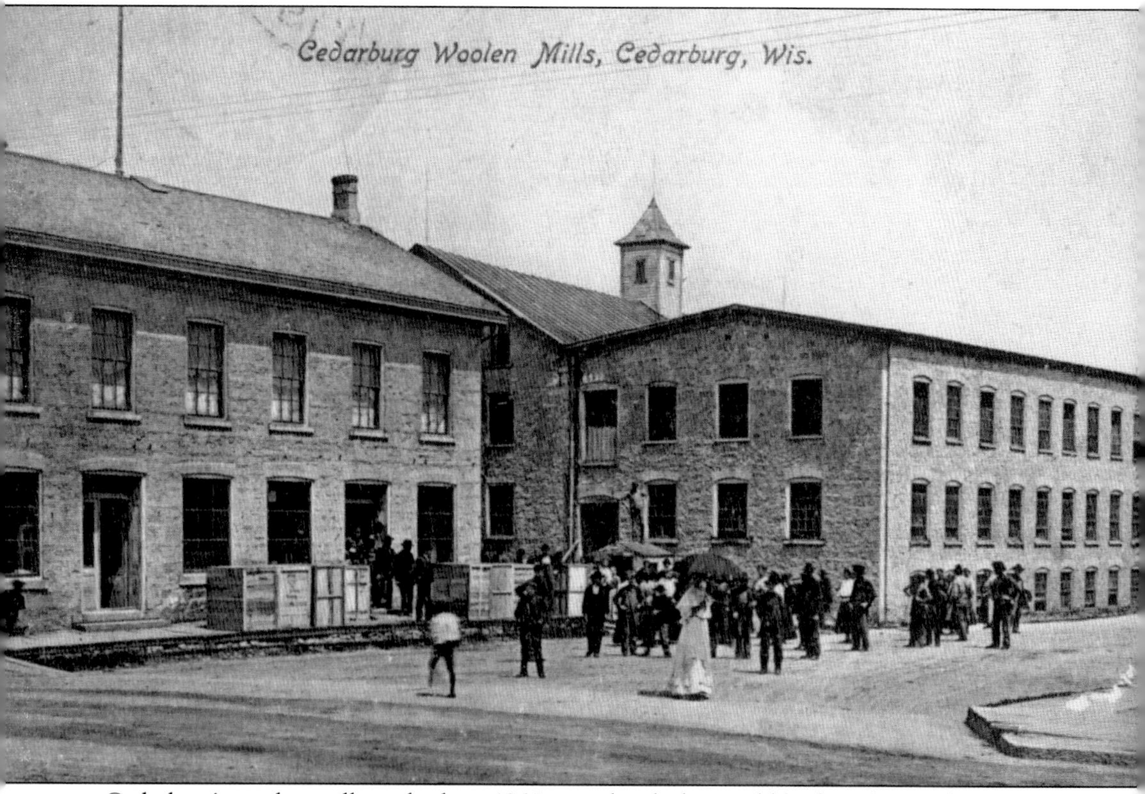

Cedarburg's woolen mill was built in 1864 to make clothes and blankets for Civil War soldiers. After the war, it made cardigans, flannels, scarves, and other wool- and fiber-based items. Its operations were powered by a giant waterwheel, which produced as much as 50 horsepower. The basement housed washing and dying activities, carding machines occupied the first floor, and weaving and spinning took place on the second floor. (Courtesy of Mark Anderson.)

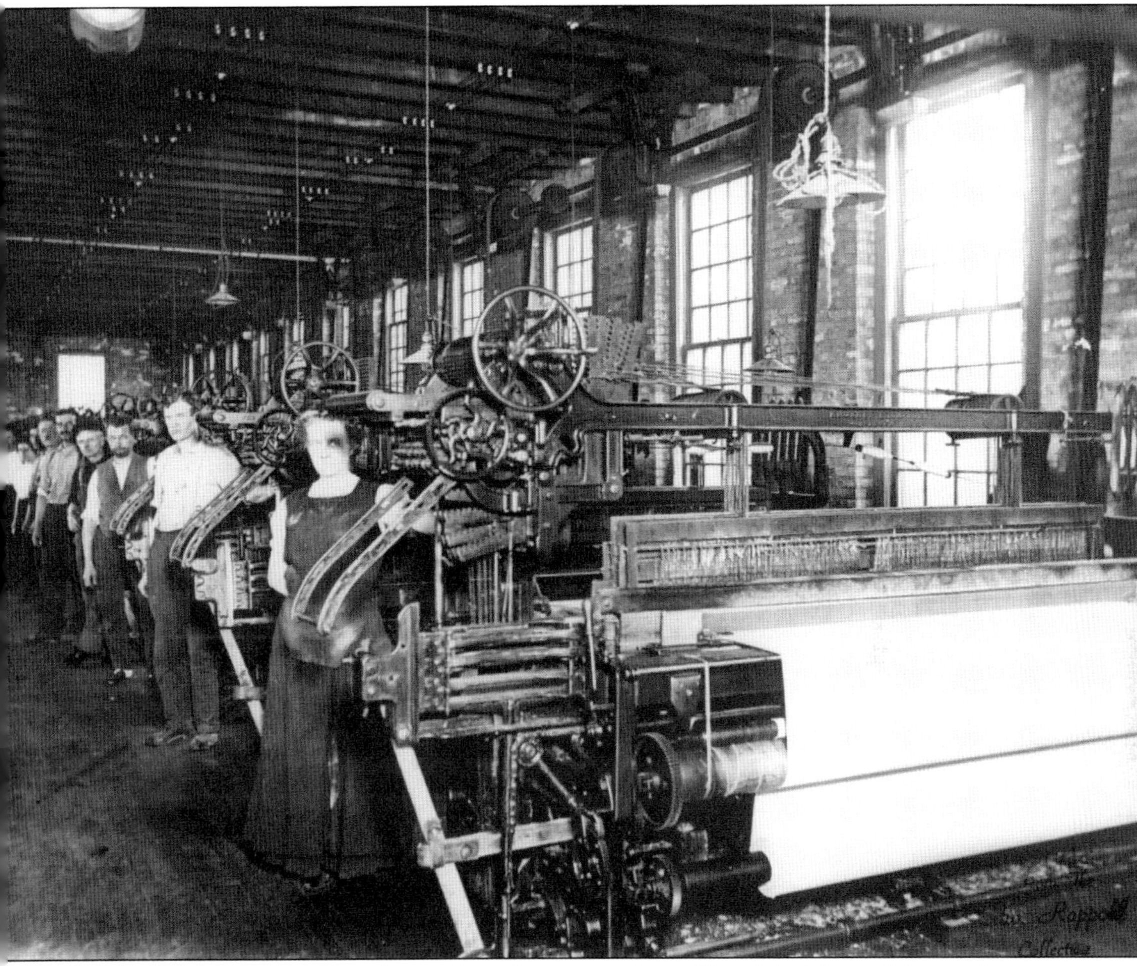

Accounts of the number of woolen mill employees vary from 50 to 200. Many of the employees were women who may have worked on looms or knitting machines. According to an essay by Rita Edquist, the mill executives were paid $3 a day for 12 hours of work. Hilgen and Wittenberg built a second woolen mill in Grafton on the Milwaukee River. (Courtesy of the Ozaukee County Historical Society.)

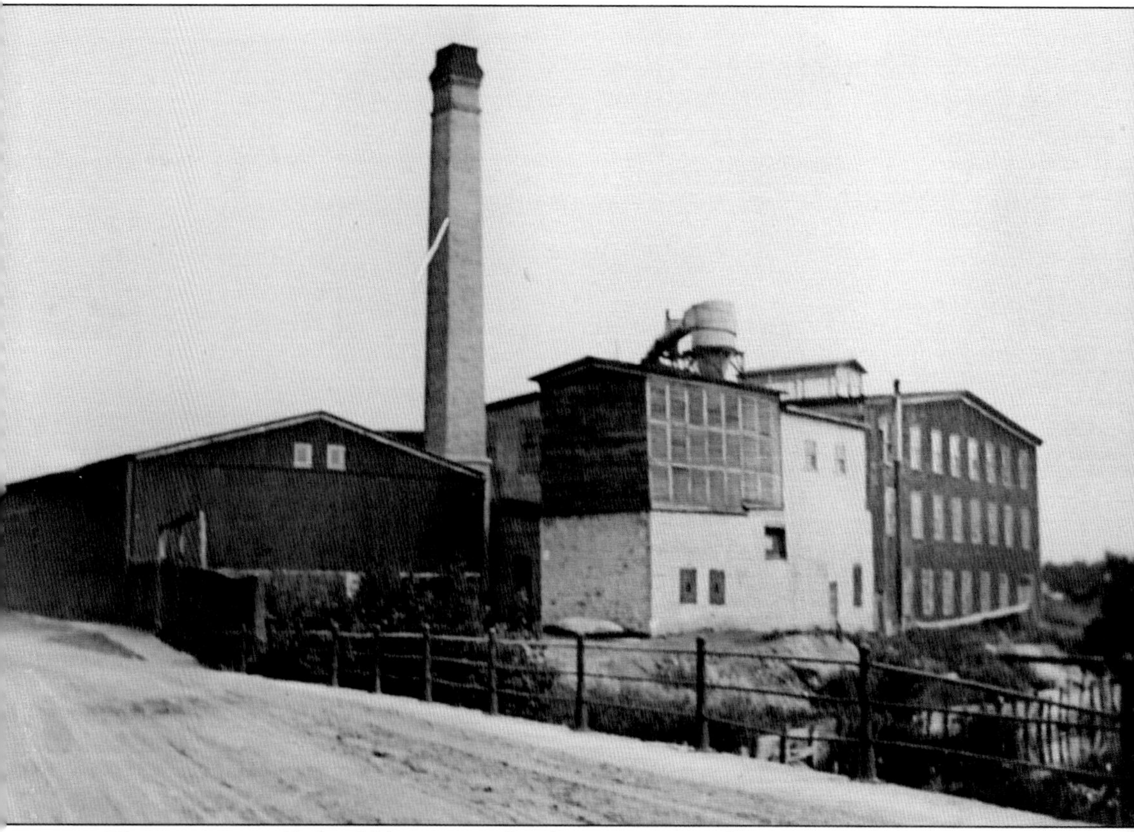

The enterprising Father Hilgen opened a planing company known as Hilgen Manufacturing in 1872. The company made doors, railings, newel posts, and stairs. It was located on what is now Behling Field on Portland Road. The planing company was one of many business ventures for Hilgen. His holdings included grocery stores, the Cedarburg Mill, a mill store, and real estate. (Courtesy of the Ozaukee County Historical Society.)

Sack Suits

The sack suit is the staple thing in clothes; habitually worn by ninety-nine men in a hundred; you are probably one of them. The styles vary somewhat from one season to another, but the only variation in the making so far as we are concerned is that we try to make ours a little better each season.

There are some changes in our popular Varsity style. The 1902 Varsity has "army" shoulders and padded front, and almost no flare to the skirts; the back is form-fitting, in the military style. It will be very popular again this season.

Fabrics and Prices

There's a big list of fancy fabrics to choose from; the prices go from about $12 to, say, $25.

From $12 to $18 there are fancy cassimeres, grays, greens, olives, in stripes, overplaids and checks. At $15 you will find cheviots, gray, brown, olive, blue; fancy outing stripes, and broken plaids, greens, blues, browns, black; also gray, brown and fancy mixed homespuns; worsteds in olive, blue, gray, stripes and checks; unfinished worsteds in outing stripes, black, blue, olive, green and gray. The prices on some of these lines will go as high as $25; on others, to $20 and $22.

We have also a very attractive line of black and white cheviots, a very soft gray effect, at $15 to $25; some of these with overplaids. At $18 and upward, fine worsted cheviots, nut brown, blue, olive, fancy stripes and mixtures; and at $25, a superior imported Scotch tweed, black and white.

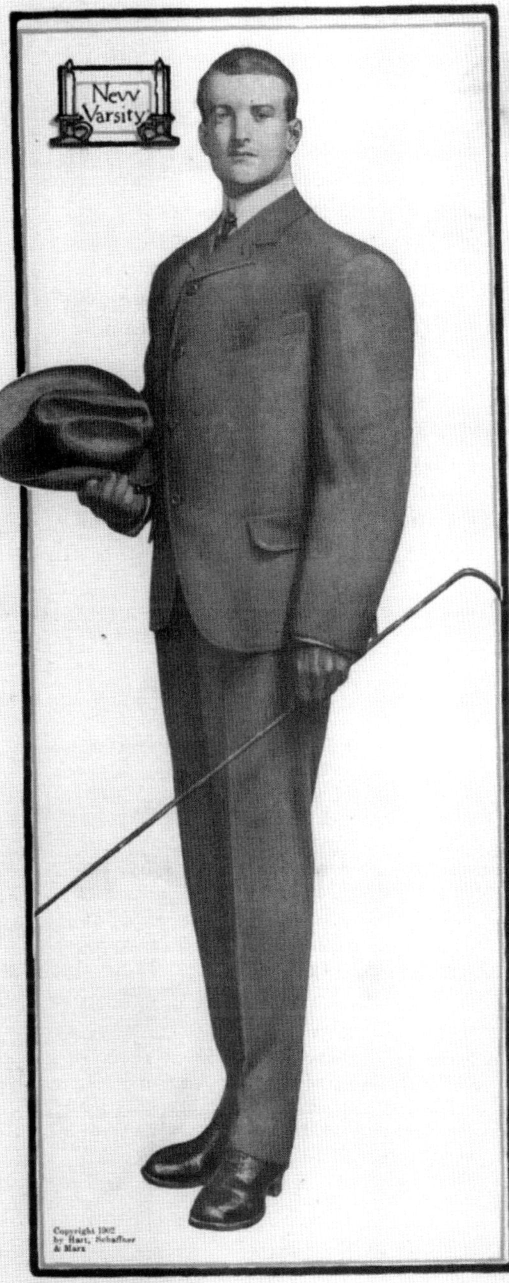

The Boerner Bros. Store sold, among many items, a variety of men's suits. When needed, the store provided a *Handbook of Styles*, which was produced by Hart, Schaffner & Marx tailors. The handbook guided men through the maze of different suit styles available, such as the sack suit, pictured here, which was a staple of men's wardrobes and sold for between $12 and $18 in 1902. (Courtesy of Vivian Scherf Laabs.)

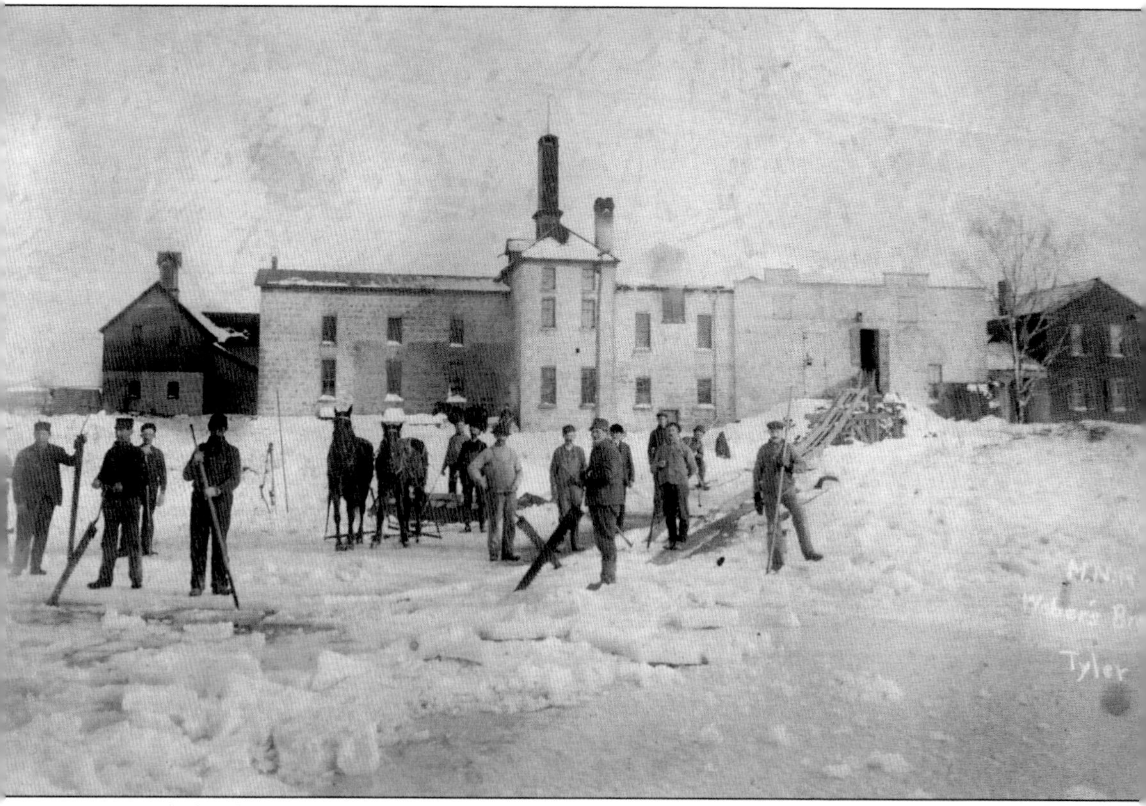

Long before brewpubs sprang up, John Weber Sr. and Dr. D.T. Fricke partnered to purchase the old Cedarburg Brewery, located across the creek from the woolen mill. It operated under the name D.T. Fricke & Co. until 1864 when Weber bought out Fricke's interest and renamed it. The brewery employed about five people and produced as many as 2,200 barrels per year. Ice blocks from the creek were gathered to keep the beer cold. Today, the building is home to Ozaukee Arts Center and Brewery Works. (Courtesy of the Ozaukee County Historical Society.)

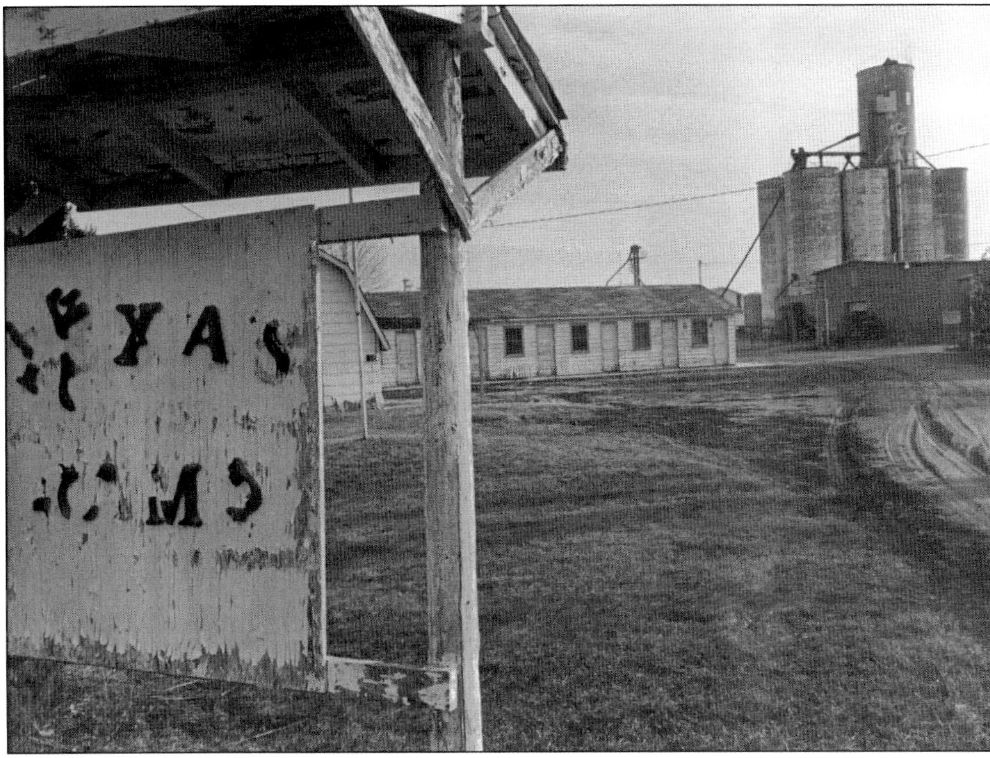

The Nieman Cannery was one of several businesses operated by the Nieman family. The cannery operated in 1908 and processed peas, corn, carrots, beets, squash, and tomatoes brought in by area farmers. Children looked forward to "pea raids" as they picked up the freshly picked pea pods that fell from trucks on their way to the factory. The factory has since been converted to offices and artist studios. (Courtesy of the Ozaukee County Historical Society.)

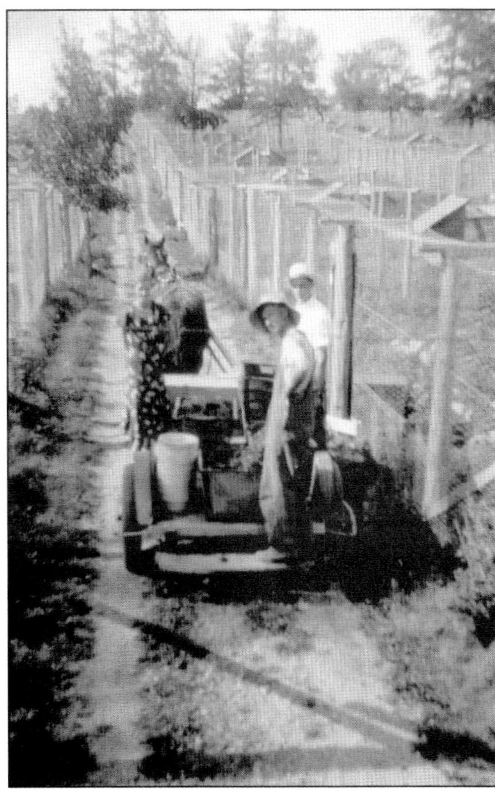

Fox farms were a source of needed employment during the days of the Great Depression. The first fox farm in the area was started by the Fromm family in Mequon, who built one of the largest fur farming operations in the world. A second fox farm emerged when Erna Fromm married Edwin Nieman. He joined the business, opening a fox farm in Cedarburg. During the most challenging economic times, it is said pay was down to 75¢ a day. Here, workers feed the animals at the Cedarburg fox farm in 1934. (Courtesy of Harold Pfohl.)

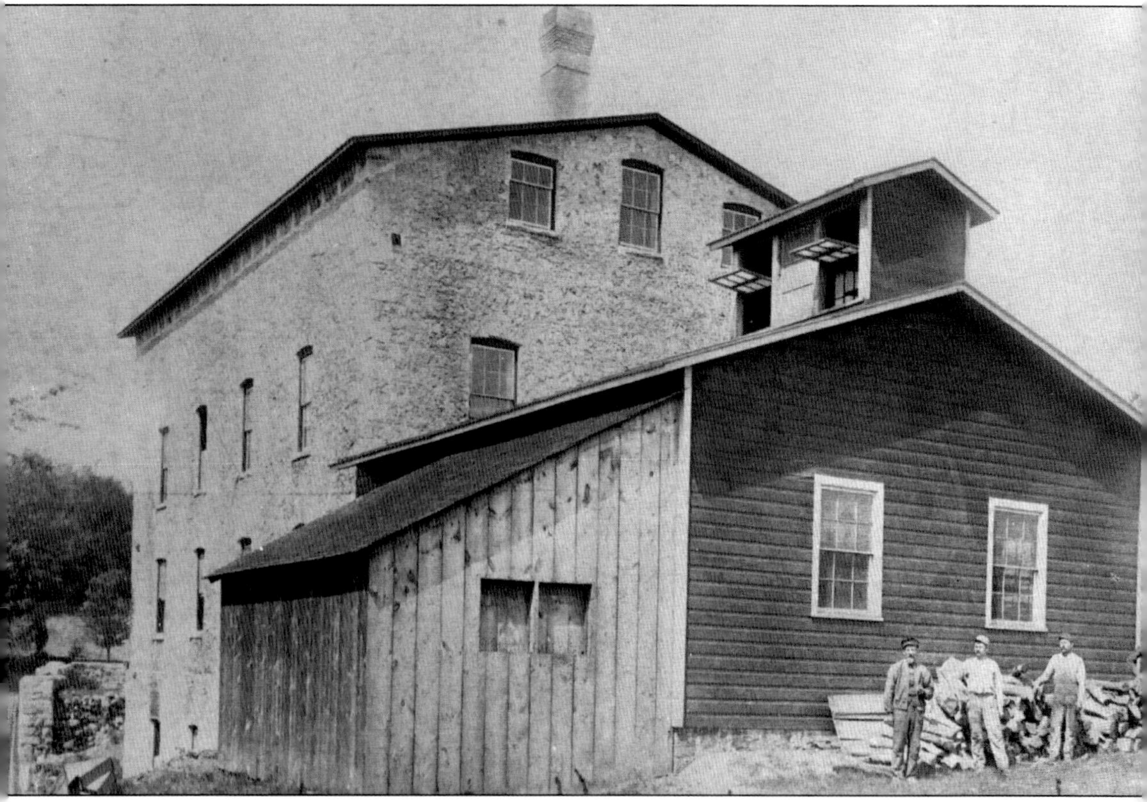

Another mill was built on the east side of Cedarburg around 1871 by the H. Wehausen Company. It was four stories tall and called the Excelsior Company. The original structure was built of stone, but a wooden addition, pictured here, was constructed in 1875. Sometime in the late 1800s, fire consumed the wooden sections of the building. The plant sat empty until John Weber, E.G. Wurthmann, and two others bought it around 1890 and renamed it the Cedarburg Nail and Wire Factory. "Mr. Wurthmann travelled to New York to study firsthand the exciting round nail industry," according to Rita Edquist's essay on industry and transportation in Cedarburg. (Courtesy of the Ozaukee County Historical Society.)

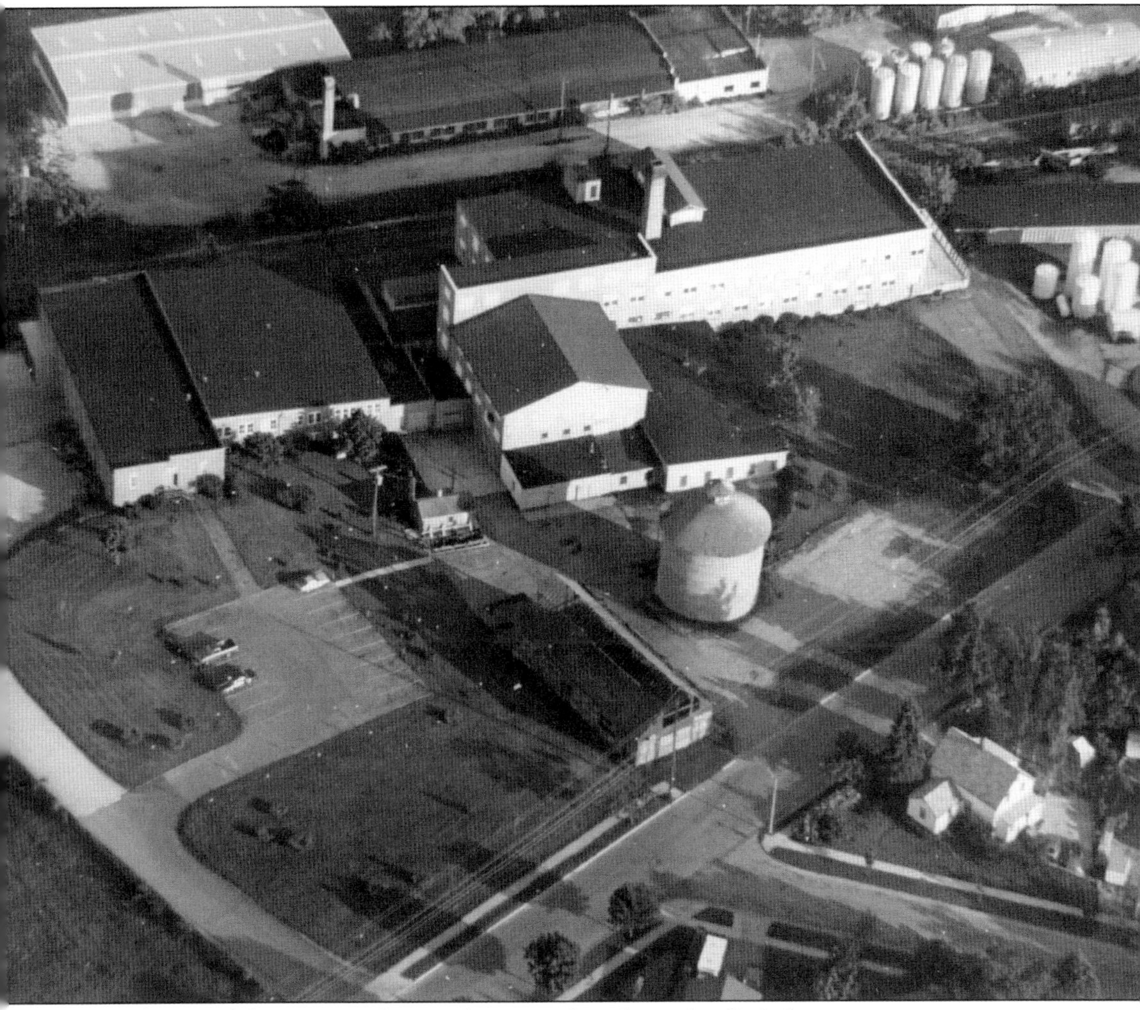

An aerial view of the canning factory shows just how large the Cedarburg cannery operations were. The buildings consisted of about 100,000 square feet of space, some of which was rented to other manufacturers. In addition to canning vegetables, the cannery experimented with a tomato juice cocktail called Ting Tang and also made dog and cat food. (Courtesy of the Ozaukee County Historical Society.)

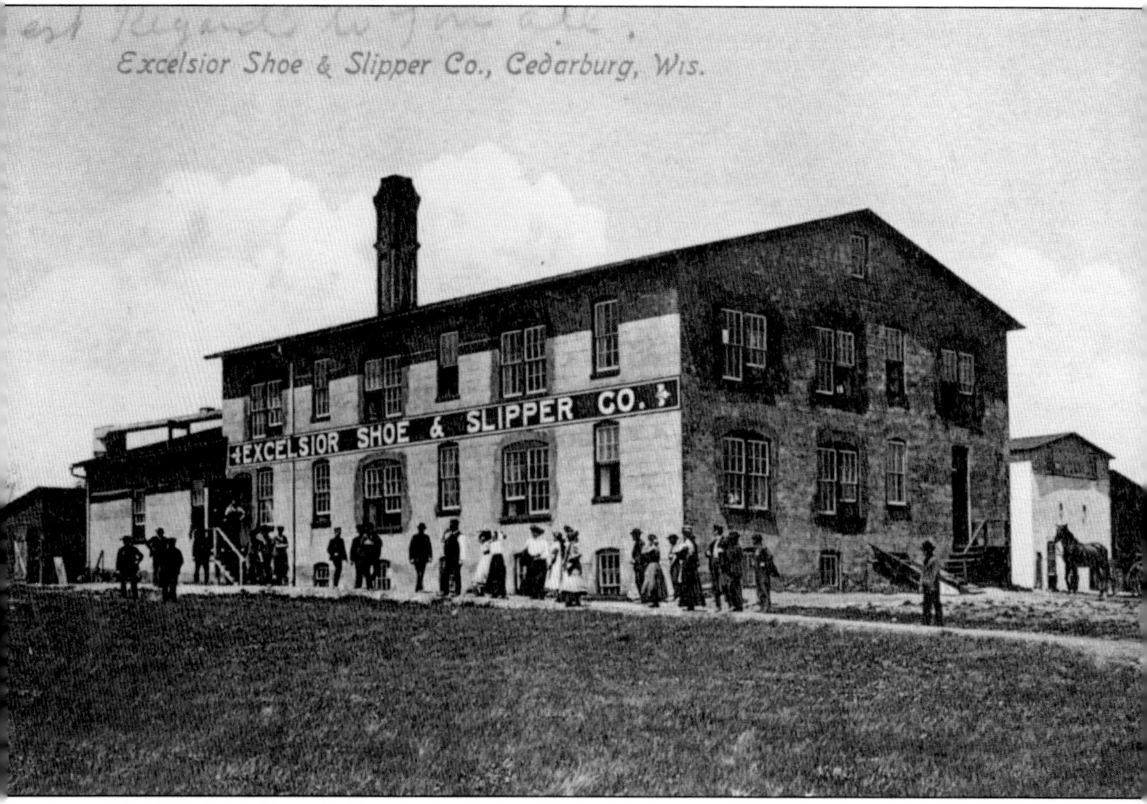

The Excelsior Shoe & Slipper Company was located on Hilbert Street and operated in the late 1800s and the first half of the 1900s. During World War II it manufactured pants for soldiers. One woman recalls that her sister put a note in the pants and received a letter from one of the soldiers. Another shoe company, the Cedar Shoe Company, was housed in Turner Hall in the 1950s. (Courtesy of Vivian Scherf Laabs and Arnold Laabs.)

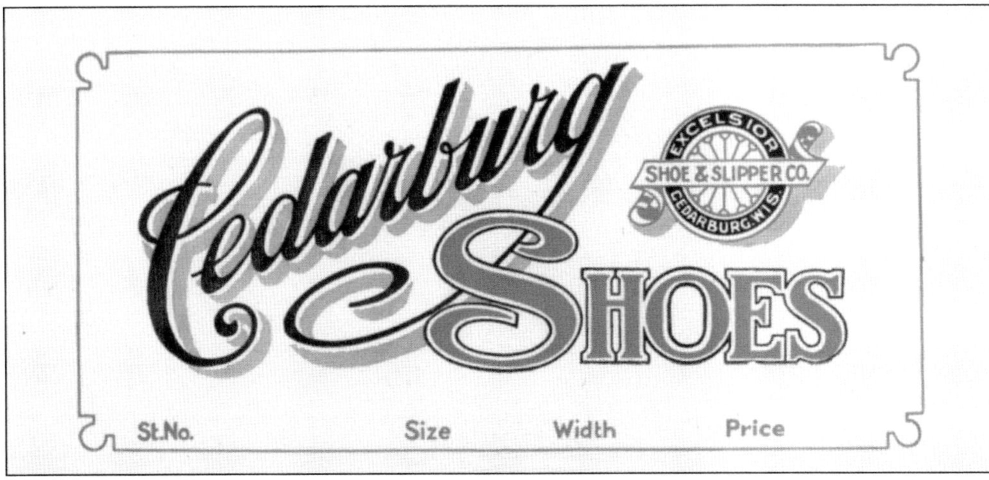

This is an original, unmarked label for a shoebox from the Excelsior Shoe & Slipper Company. The company manufactured shoe styles such as the badger boy, big chief, Cedarburg seamless, kant-wear-out, pioneer, rough rider, and of course, the excelsior. The company employed about 70 people, nearly half of whom were laid up in April 1891 with *la grippe*, according to the *Cedarburg Weekly News* at the time. (Courtesy of Vivian Scherf Laabs.)

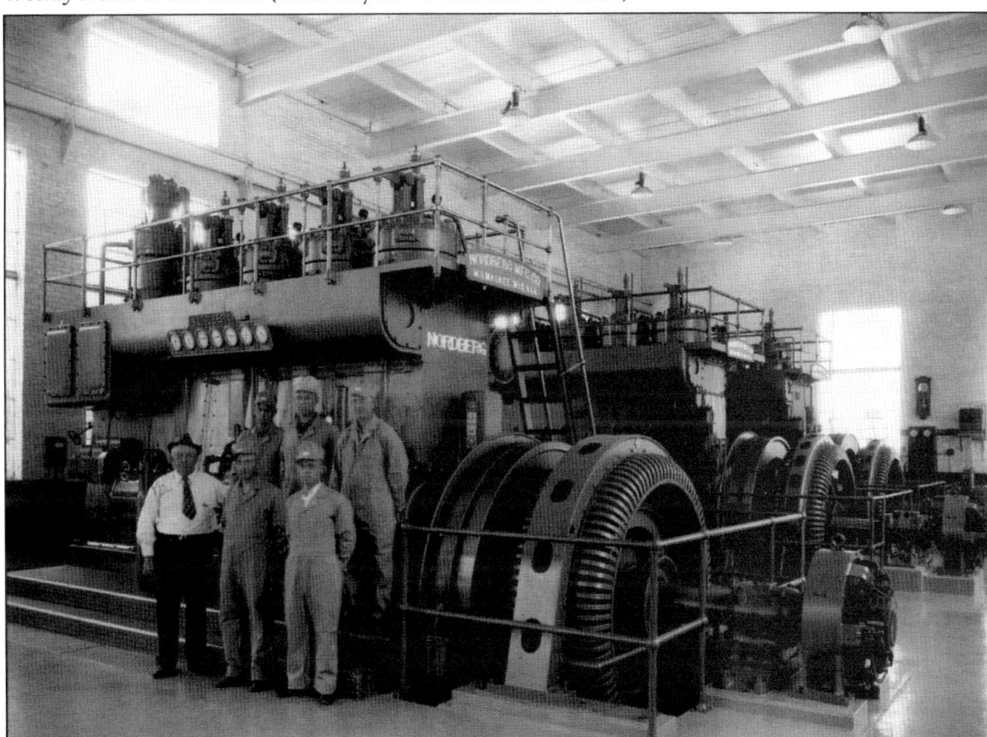

By 1930, Cedarburg Light & Water had 845 electric customers, 138 streetlights, and 456 water customers. Gone were the days of paying a lamplighter to light the oil lanterns on the downtown streets. The utility installed a third Nordberg diesel engine to keep up with demand. Pictured from left to right are (first row) Ernst Schneider, Ray Taque, and Wilmer Boerner; (second row) Philip Schumacher, John Buth, and Palmer Schneider. (Courtesy of Cedarburg Light & Water.)

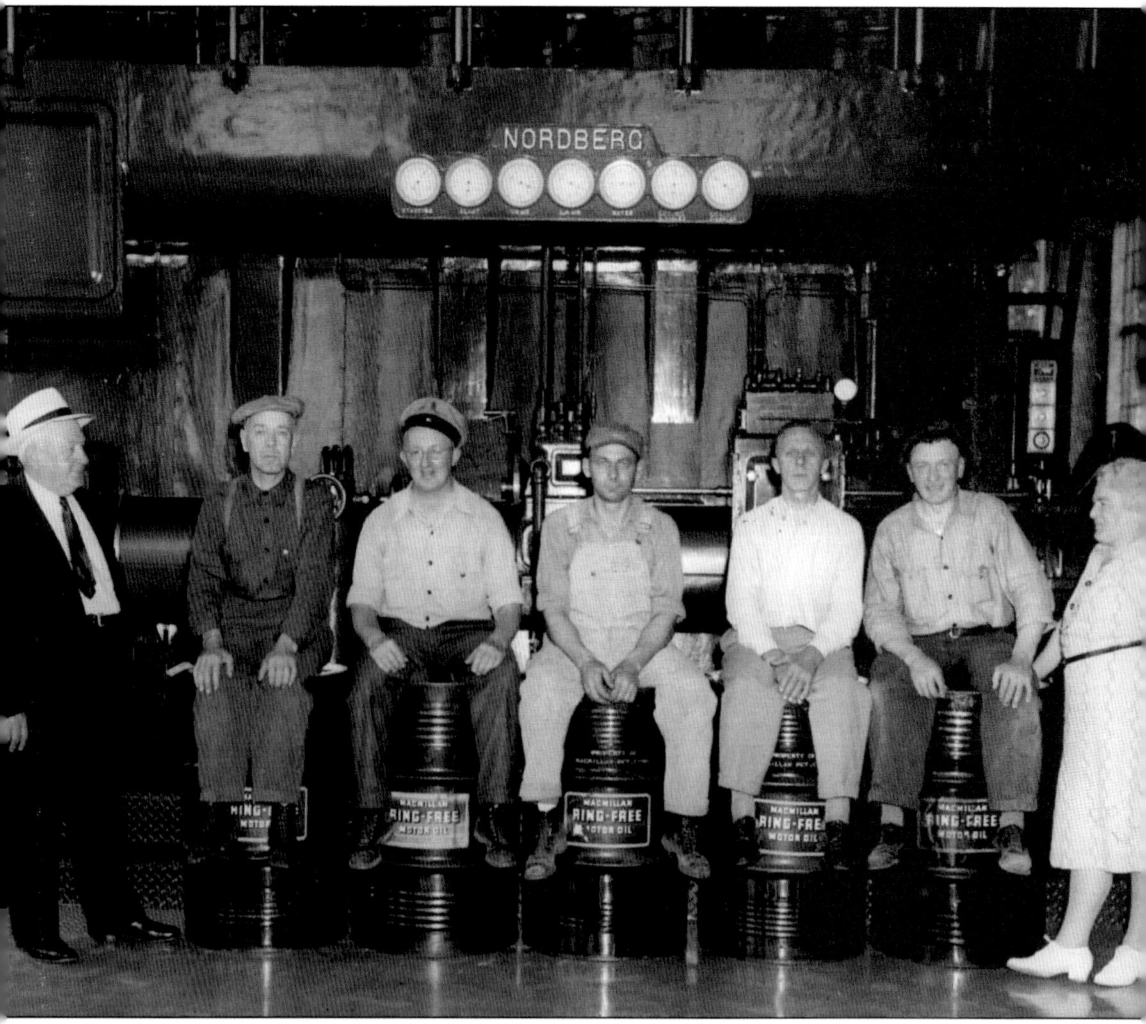

Though it may appear that utility employees are taking a break at a tavern, they are actually sitting atop barrels of oil. Pictured from left to right are Ernst Schneider, John Buth, Palmer Schneider, Philip Schumacher, Wilmer Boerner, Ray Taque, and Blache Kuhefuss. Boerner was killed in 1942 when a generator exploded. (Courtesy of Cedarburg Light & Water.)

Five

WORSHIPPING

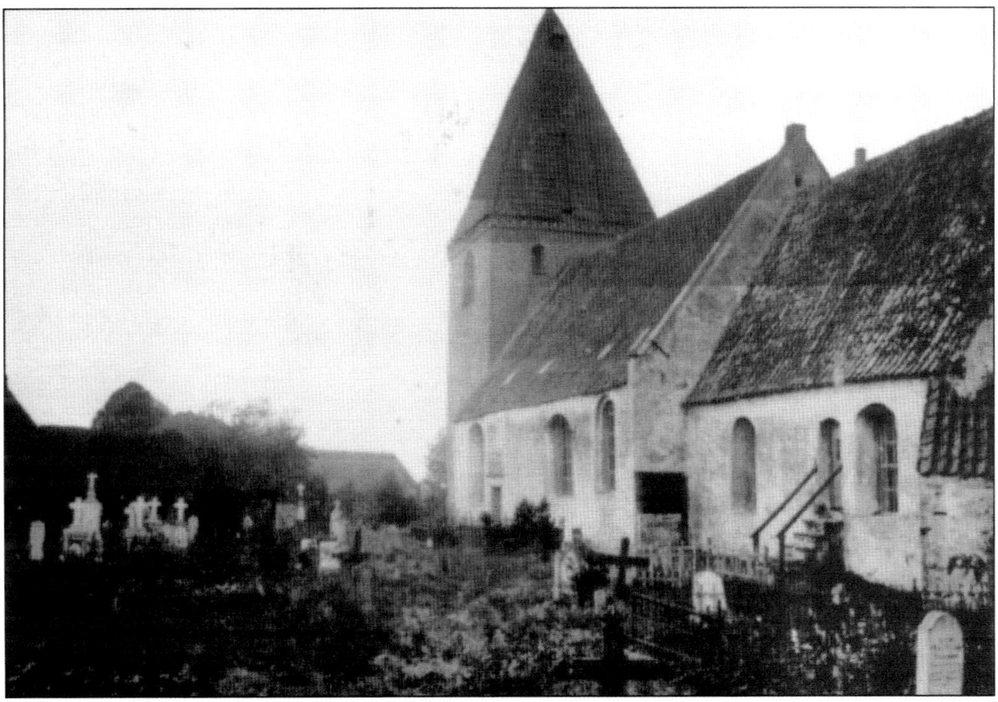

Settler Christoph Friedrich Boerner and his family were members of this Lutheran church in Kirchhatten, Germany, before fleeing to America for religious freedom. Germany in the early 1800s was a confederation of some 300 states that were linked in few ways. The Lutheran Church was controlled by the state, though two strong factions existed within: the Reformed and the Confessional Lutherans, who considered the Reformed ways to be watered down. So when an edict came from the German government that the two groups become one Union Church of Germany, many of Lutherans left for America. (Courtesy of Denise Boerner.)

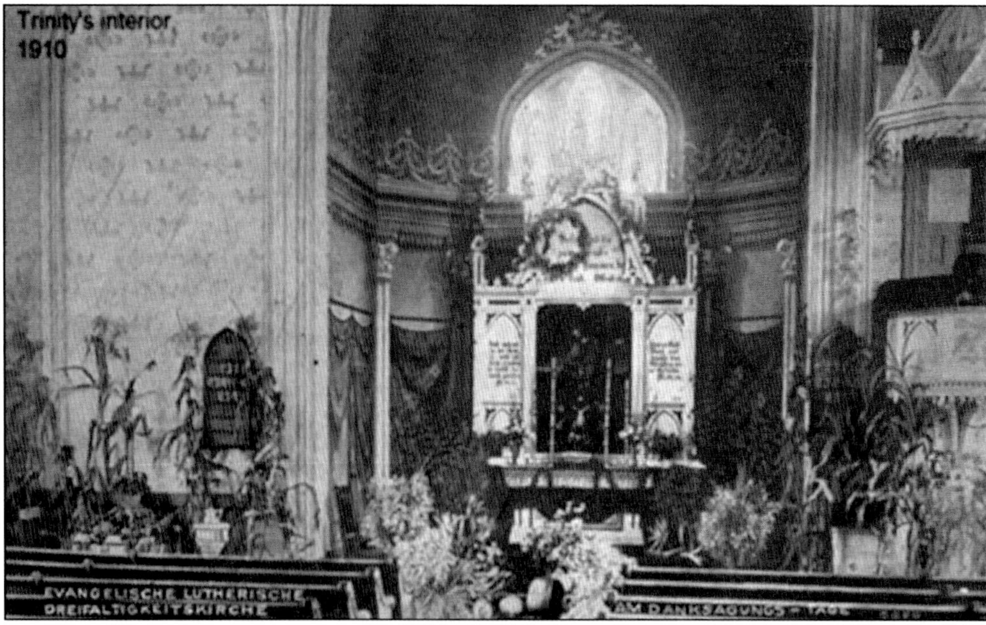

The founders of Trinity Lutheran Church made their way to Wisconsin from Kamin in Pomerania, Germany, after the unification of the Lutheran Church. In 1838, a contingent traveled to Wisconsin, where they separated. One group went to Cedarburg, where it founded Trinity Lutheran Church. The first pastor was Rev. Johann Kindermann, who served from 1843 to 1855. The first church was built on what is now Western Avenue on property contributed by both Ludwig Groth and Carl Dobberpuhl. The present church was constructed in 1891 on Columbia Avenue. The interior of the church is pictured. (Courtesy of Mark Anderson.)

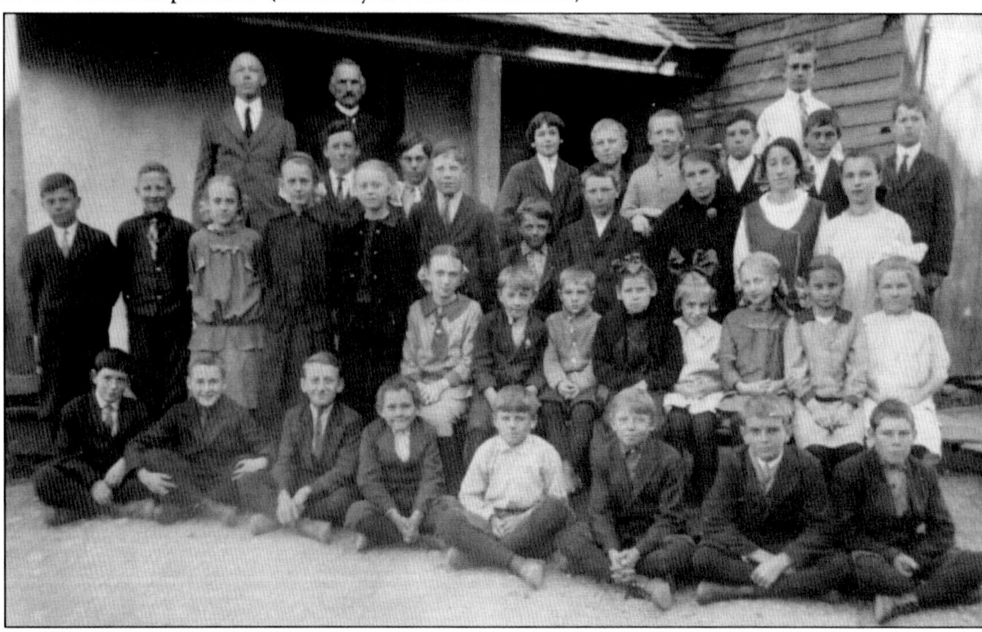

Schoolchildren and teachers are pictured outside of the former Trinity Lutheran School in 1914. Trinity Lutheran School was the first school in Cedarburg. It was located on what is now Washington Avenue. Students learned in both English and German. (Courtesy of Mark Anderson.)

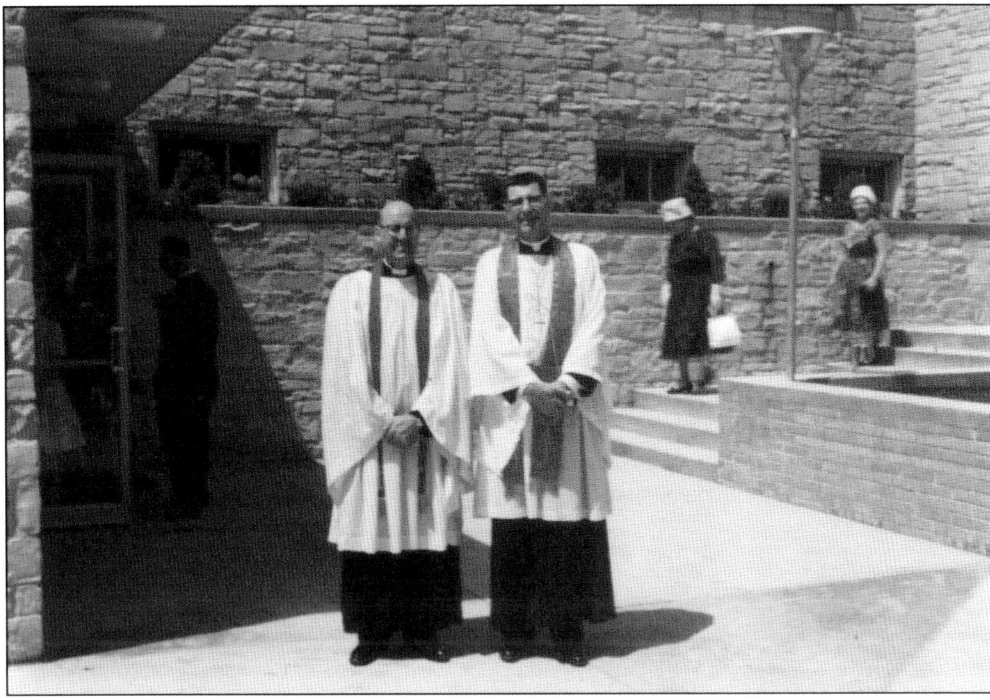

Trinity Lutheran Church continued to grow at its Columbia Avenue home, and a parish hall was added. In 1961, the church celebrated the completion of its education wing, which today sees youth as well as adults pass through for spiritual education and social fellowship. Pictured are pastors Eugene Leschensky (left) and Karl Bracker at the dedication of the education wing on July 11, 1961. (Courtesy of Mark Anderson.)

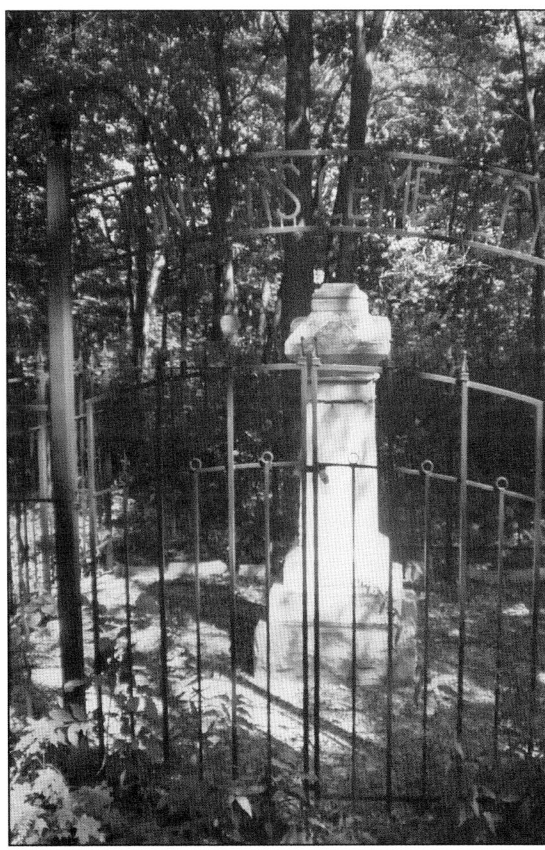

The original members of Trinity Lutheran Church are buried in what is known as Founders Cemetery. Burial was discontinued as early as 1844 because the earth was too rocky to continue. It is said that it took two men two days to blast through the rock with dynamite in order to prepare one grave. This monument was erected in 1877 and still stands in tribute to those laid to rest in Founders Cemetery. Although 26 names are listed on the monument, no one knows for sure how many are buried in Founders Cemetery. (Courtesy of the *News Graphic*.)

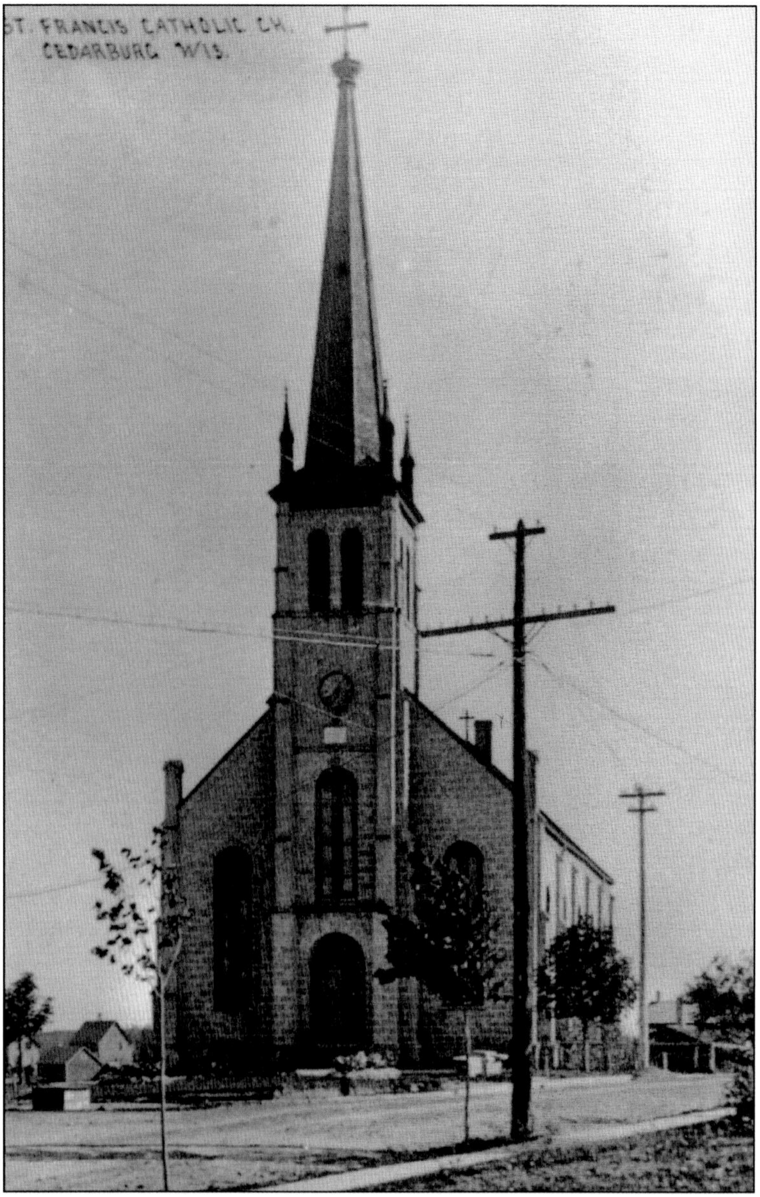

The first Catholic church in Cedarburg was constructed in 1844 in a log structure on what is now Pioneer and Wauwatosa Roads in a small town known as Newland. Irish Catholics were living in the area in the late 1830s and had likely held church services in members' homes. The New Church of Newland was serviced by Fr. Martin Kundig, a Milwaukee Jesuit who visited many churches to conduct services. Kundig is credited with helping to develop parishes throughout southeast Wisconsin in the mid-1800s. As early as 1843, the parish was called the St. Francis Congregation of Cedarburg. By the mid-1860s, membership was increasing at a tremendous pace, and church leaders again found themselves faced with a need for a larger church. Rather than rebuild on the current site, they chose a triangular parcel where Washington Avenue intersected with the old plank road. It was the German Protestants who helped the Catholics raise money for construction of the now iconic Catholic church that is the cornerstone of downtown Cedarburg. (Courtesy of the Edward A. Rappold Photograph Collection, Cedarburg Cultural Center.)

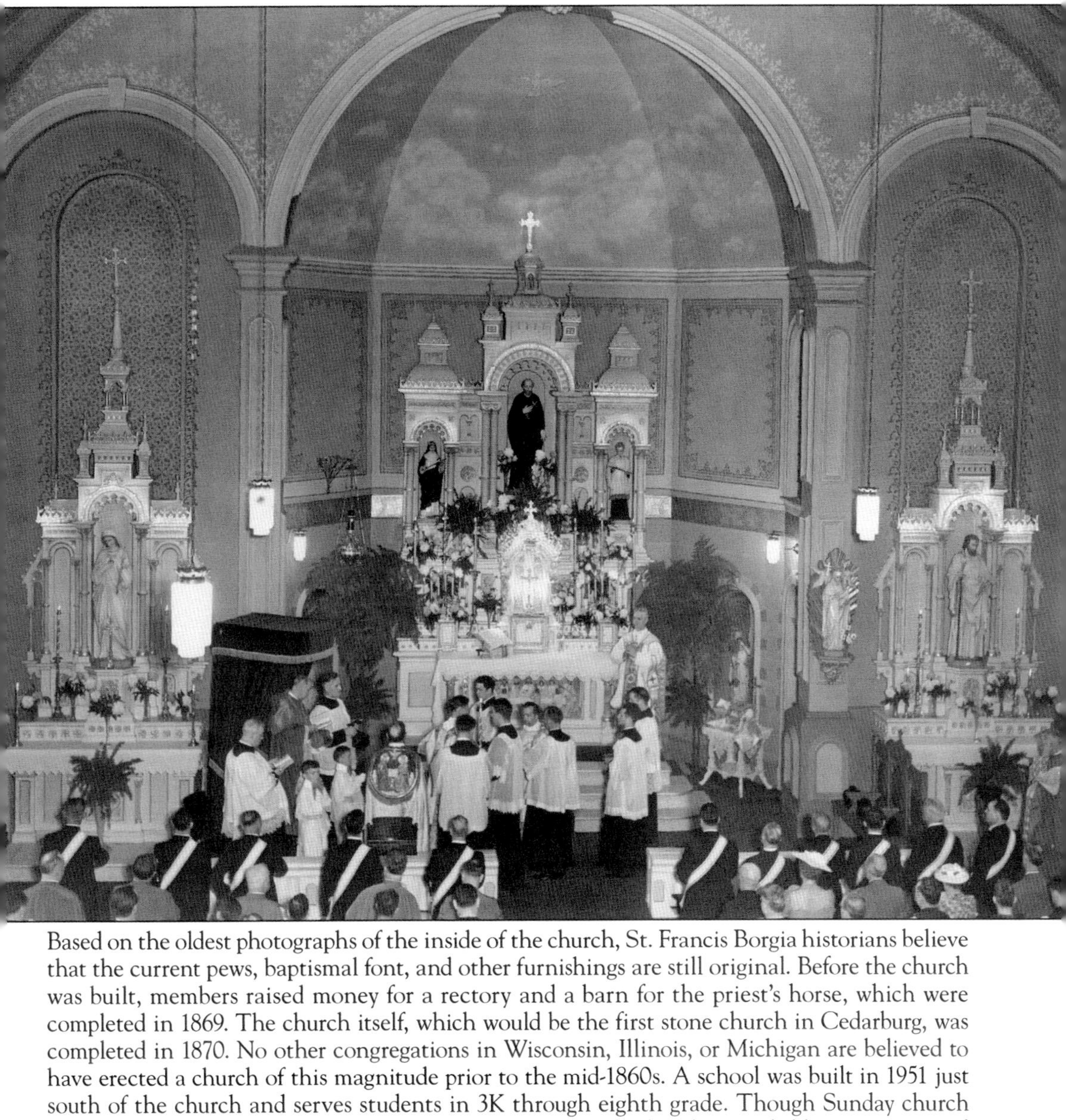

Based on the oldest photographs of the inside of the church, St. Francis Borgia historians believe that the current pews, baptismal font, and other furnishings are still original. Before the church was built, members raised money for a rectory and a barn for the priest's horse, which were completed in 1869. The church itself, which would be the first stone church in Cedarburg, was completed in 1870. No other congregations in Wisconsin, Illinois, or Michigan are believed to have erected a church of this magnitude prior to the mid-1860s. A school was built in 1951 just south of the church and serves students in 3K through eighth grade. Though Sunday church services and church activities now take place at the north church site, children's masses and weekday morning masses are still said at the St. Francis Borgia south church. (Courtesy of St. Francis Borgia Church.)

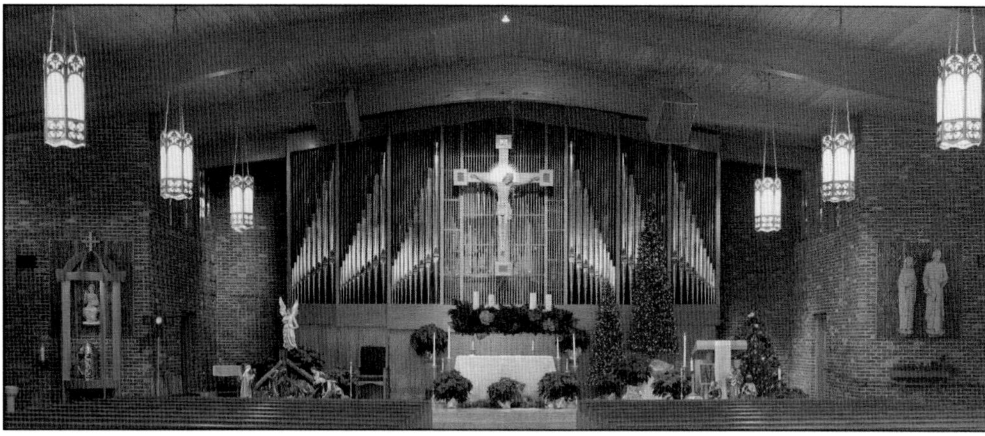

For a period of some 30 years, Cedarburg was home to two Catholic churches: St. Francis Borgia on the south and Divine Word Savior, just north of Five Corners. In 2002, however, Catholics in Cedarburg learned that they would have only one priest to serve the city. So the parish councils of both churches formally requested that the parishes be merged. Pictured is the inside of the St. Francis Borgia North church. The church serves an estimated 2,000 households and families in Cedarburg and the surrounding area. (Courtesy of Tom Ingrassia.)

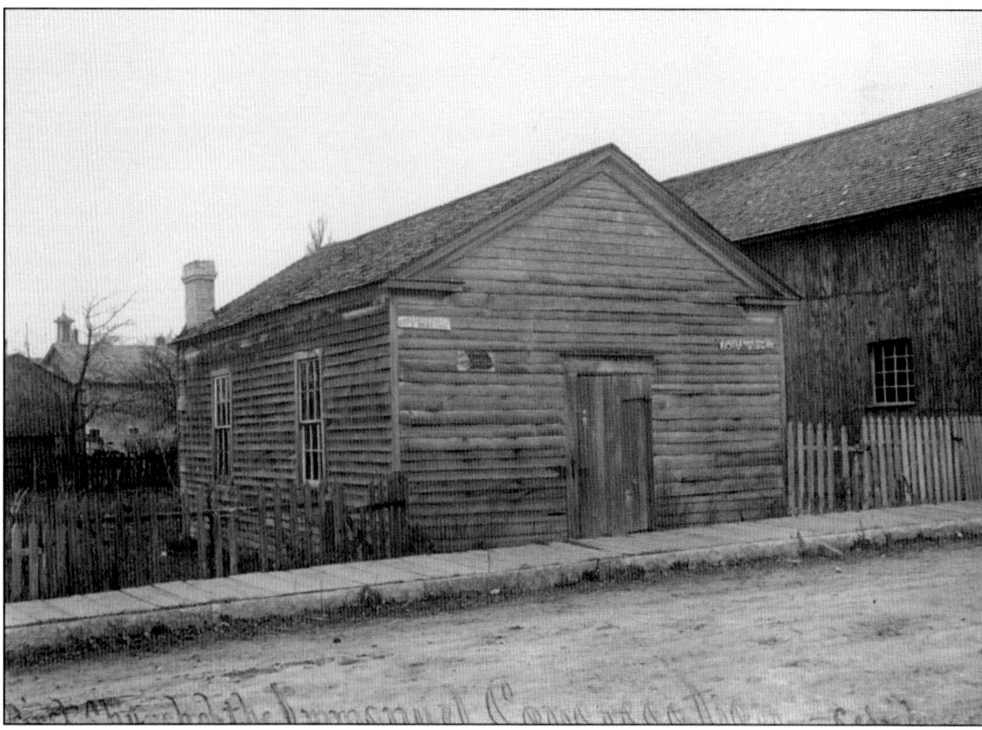

A second Lutheran church was organized in Cedarburg in 1852, after a Milwaukee transplant to Cedarburg named Karl Zeige asked the minister from his Milwaukee church to come to the Cedarburg-Grafton area and preach. The pastor, Friedrich Lochner, organized a church in Grafton and one in Cedarburg called Immanuel Lutheran. The first services were probably held in homes, but it was not long before a small church measuring just 28 feet long and 18 feet wide was built on Western Road. (Courtesy of Harold Pfohl.)

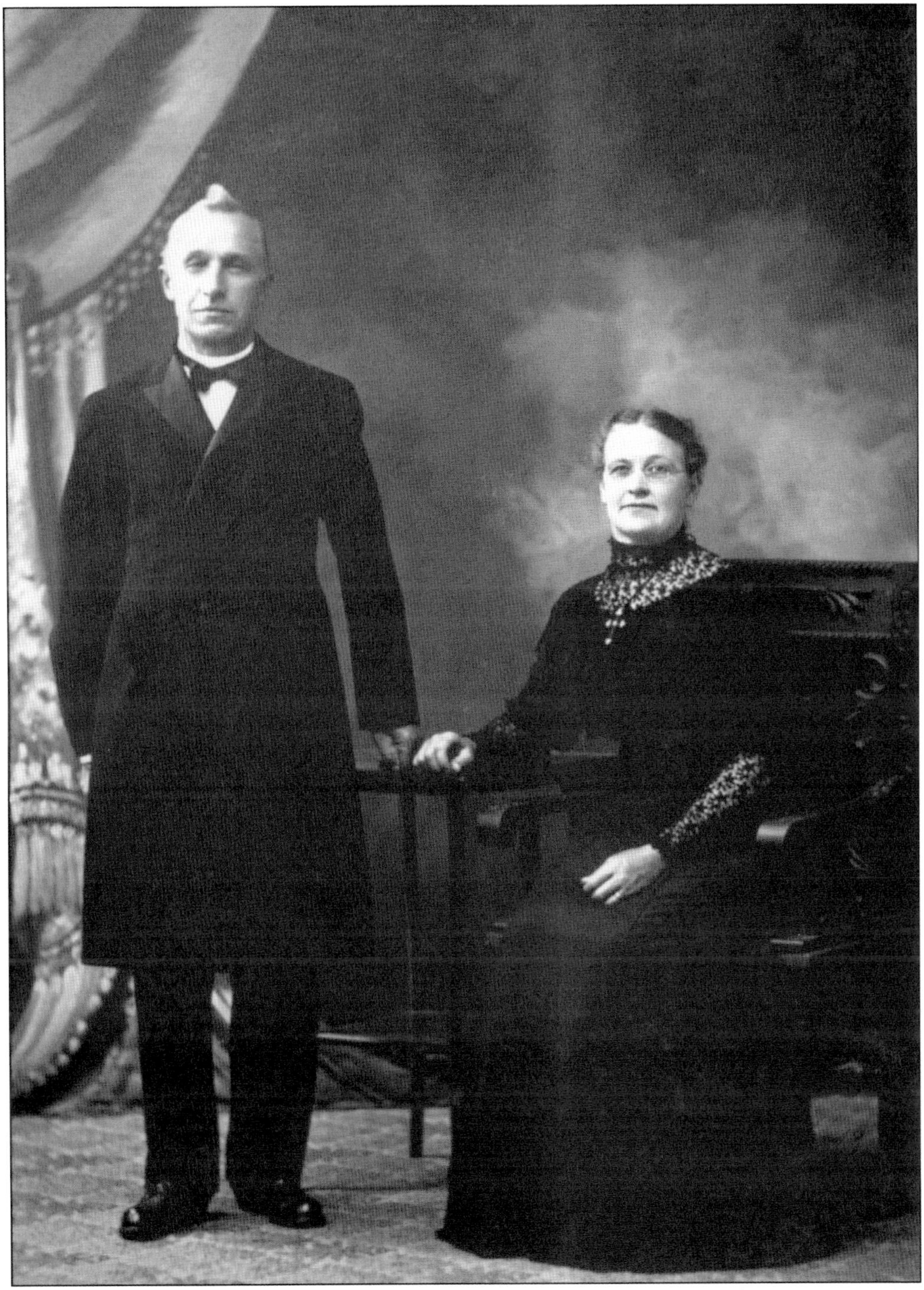

E.G. Strassburger was a 24-year-old graduate student at Wartburg Theological Seminary in 1873, when he became Immanuel Lutheran's first assistant pastor. He held the position for only a few months when senior pastor Ludwig Habel, ailing from injuries sustained in a fall from his buggy, died. Strassburger spent his entire pastoral career at Immanuel Lutheran, serving until 1919. Strassburger is pictured with his wife, Freda Behrens Strassburger. (Courtesy of Harold Pfohl.)

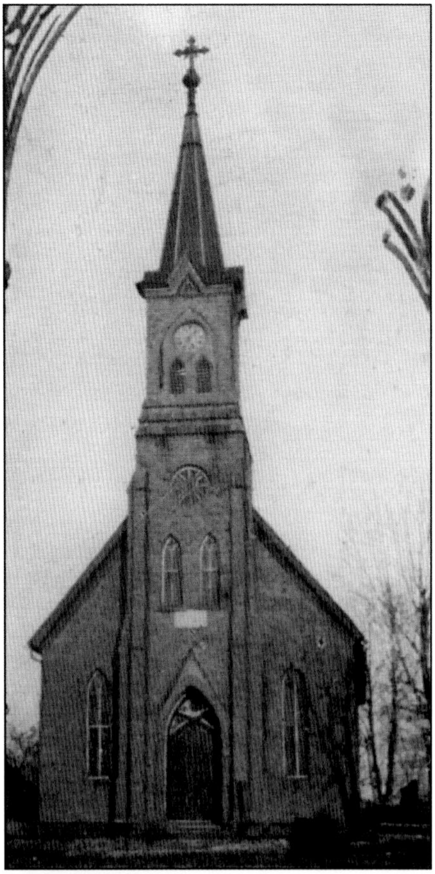

By 1881, the Immanuel Lutheran congregation had outgrown its space on Western Road and set about planning for a new one that would serve generations to come. A committee of four men was formed to raise money for the venture. By the end of that year, they had collected $3,000 of the $7,745 it cost to build the church. The new church, pictured here, was dedicated in 1883 on what is now Washington Avenue. (Courtesy of Immanuel Lutheran Church.)

In its early years, Immanuel Lutheran Church provided a parochial school for its younger members. The second church property on Western Road served as the school from 1896 until 1926, when a parish hall was built in the new church and served as classrooms. At one point, there were as many as 120 students at the school. But by the end of 1922, attendance was so low that the school was closed. Teacher Arthur Dauss is pictured with students. (Courtesy of Harold Pfohl.)

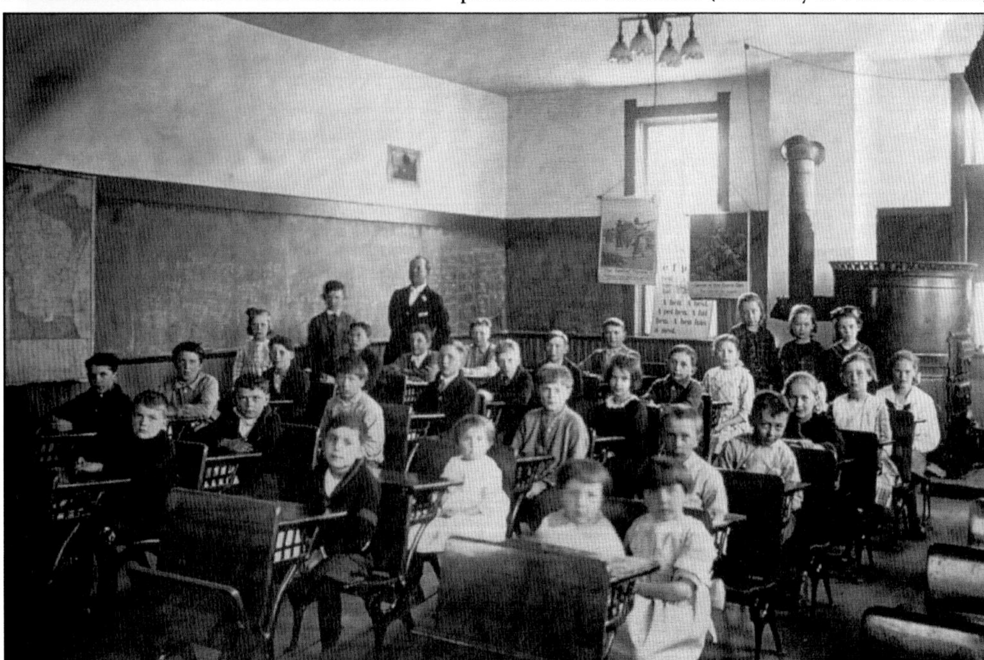

Until 1902, Immanuel Lutheran Church did not have a chancel, which is the vaulted area containing the altar. Instead, the altar had simply been tucked into a niche in a whitewashed wall. Eventually, the wall was removed and the chancel was built. (Courtesy of Immanuel Lutheran Church.)

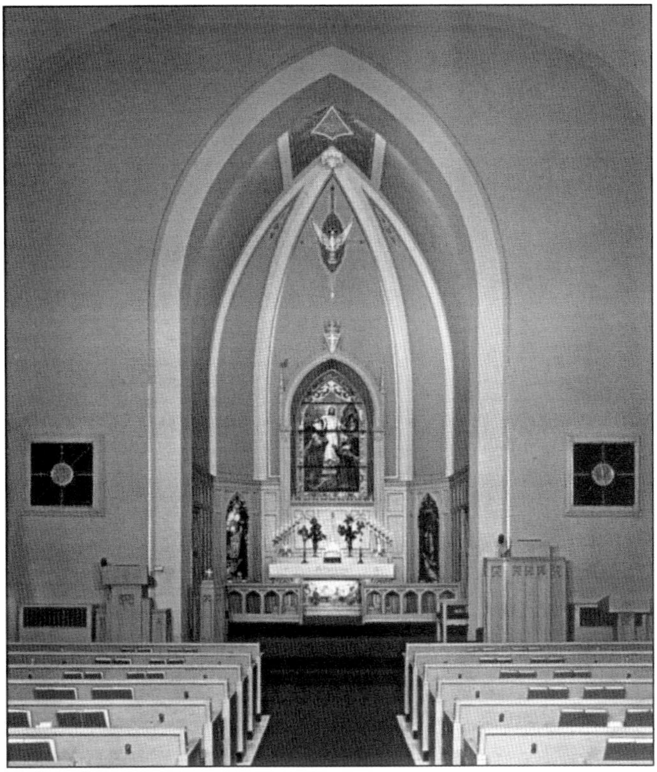

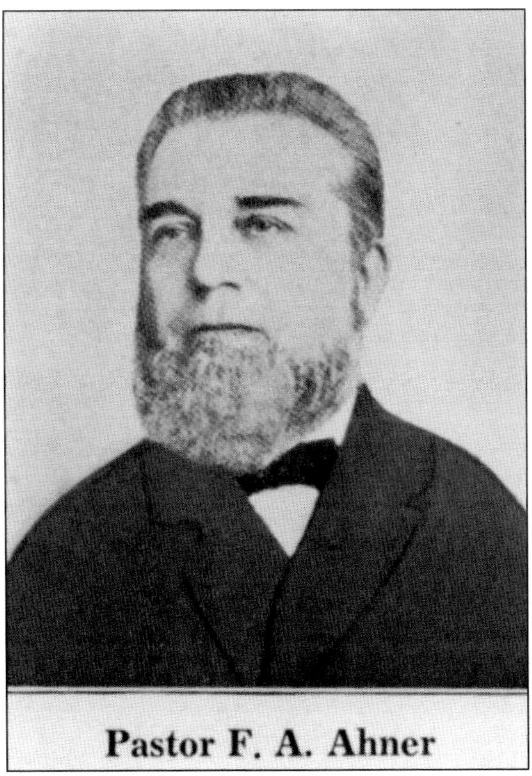

In 1862, a disagreement over dancing led to a rift at Immanuel Lutheran Church that would give rise to another Lutheran congregation in Cedarburg. Accounts indicate that Pastor Frederick Ahner was a strict conformist when it came to immoral acts, such as dancing or playing cards. Offenders were said to be locked out of the church. Factions formed, and the dispute erupted to the point that pastors from outside churches were called in to mediate. Finally, Pastor Lochner and his group left and formed another church, which was called First Immanuel. They remained affiliated with the Lutheran Church-Missouri Synod. (Courtesy of First Immanuel Lutheran Church.)

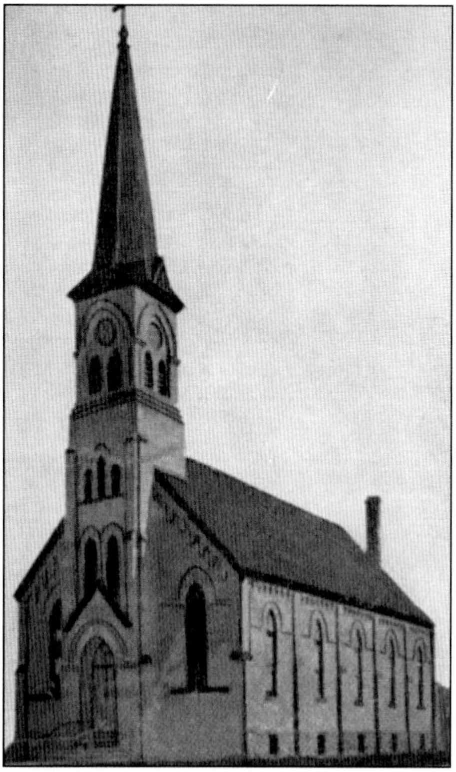

During First Immanuel Lutheran Church's early years, the congregants met in a church on what is now Washington Avenue and Mill Street. In 1891, members celebrated the dedication of a new, Gothic-style church on Cleveland Street and St. John Avenue. Bricks were hauled more than 10 miles from Port Washington by horse and buggy. Rev. Paul Wiechmann was the pastor during this time. He was known as the building pastor, not only because of the new church but because he suggested that some school subjects be taught in English. (Courtesy of First Immanuel Lutheran Church.)

In 1990, First Immanuel Lutheran Church members chose to build a new church to house its growing congregation. There was some consideration given to expanding the stone church, but in the end, the property on Evergreen Boulevard allowed room for both a church and a combined elementary and middle school. Ground was broken in November 1991, and a dedication was held in February 1993. The former stone church is now home to St. Nicholas, an Orthodox church. (Courtesy of First Immanuel Lutheran Church.)

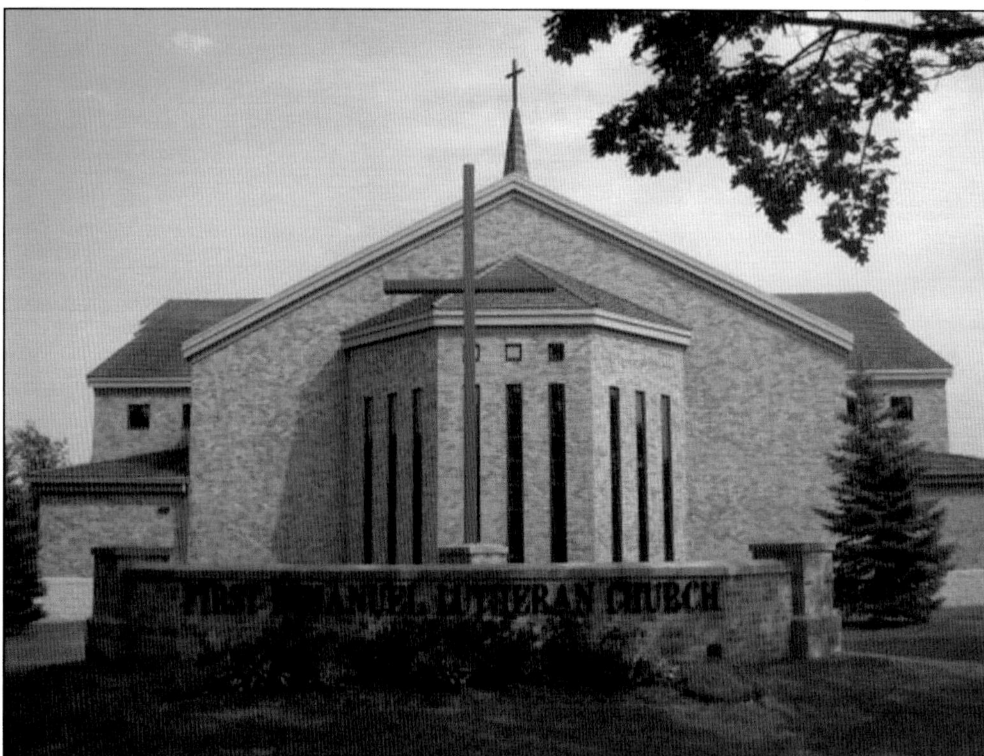

Betty Kroening has been the secretary at First Immanuel Lutheran Church since 1969 and is widely known throughout Cedarburg. In addition to working at the church, Kroening works as a hostess at an area restaurant. (Courtesy of First Immanuel Lutheran Church.

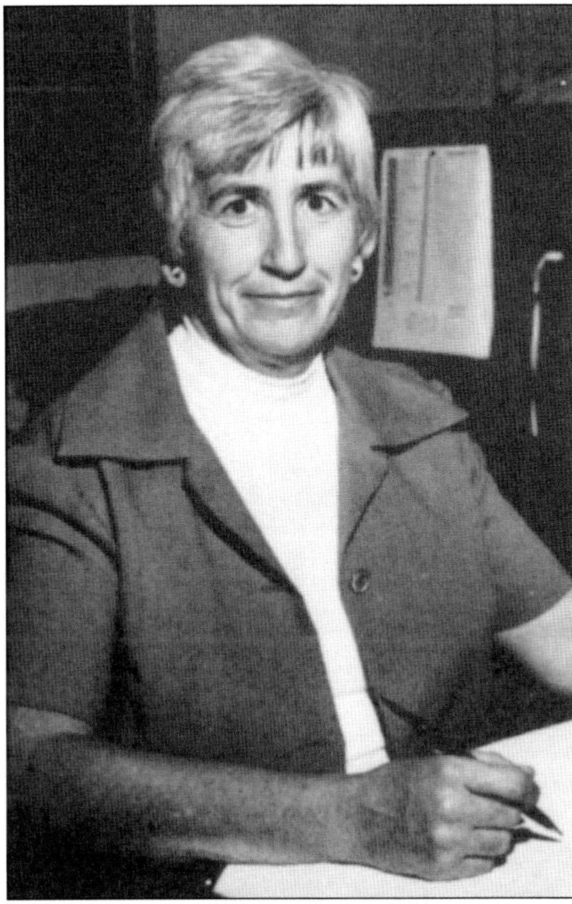

The church with the Gothic, arched windows, gabled entrance, and three-story bell tower, located on what is now Portland Road, was built in 1905. For many years it served as Community Methodist Church. When the Methodists outgrew the church, they built a new one on Evergreen Boulevard. Around 1960, Ozaukee Baptist Church occupied the church on Portland Road. That congregation moved out around 2005, and today the church is home to New Life Community Church. (Courtesy of Mark Anderson.)

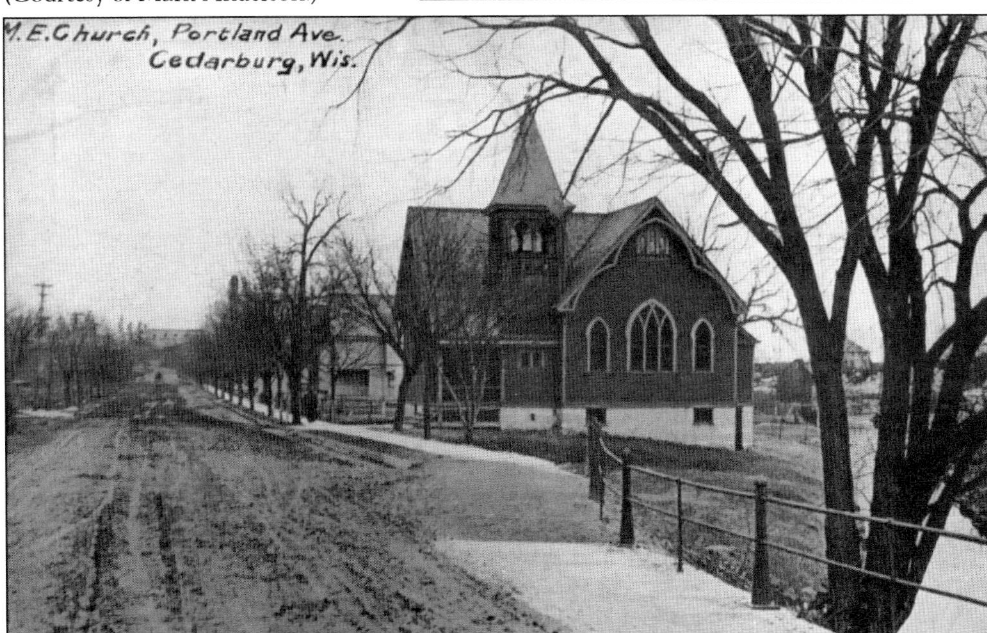

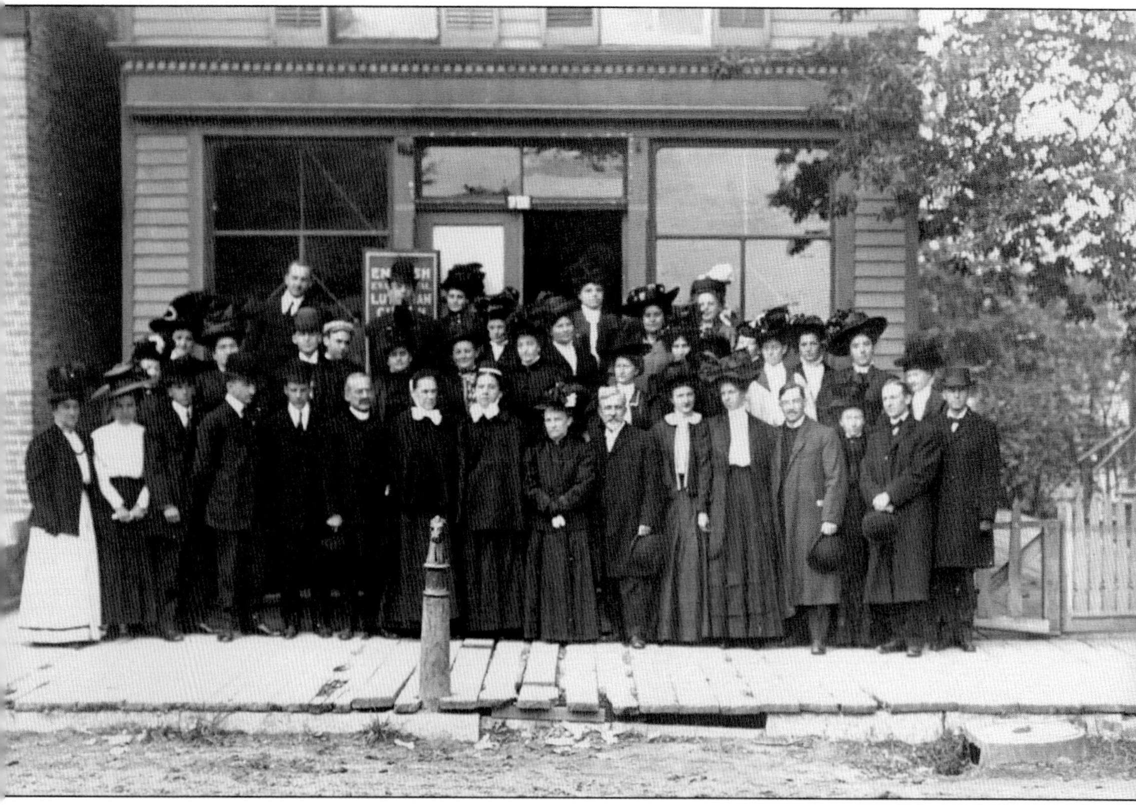

The first English-language Lutheran church service took place in an old millinery store on Washington Avenue using rented chairs, benches, an old pump organ, and a dry goods box as the altar. The Reverend A.C. Anda, western field secretary of the Evangelical Lutheran Church, canvassed the territory and found there was a strong need for an English-speaking Lutheran church in Cedarburg. An organizational meeting was held in the high school and, driven by a desire to teach children in the English language, Advent Lutheran Church was born in 1903. Pictured are the members of a joint conference meeting standing in front of the old storefront church. (Courtesy of Advent Lutheran Church.)

Sunday school classes preceded formation of the mission church later known as Advent Lutheran Church. Classes and worship services were held in Immanuel Lutheran School. The first sermon of Advent Lutheran was said by Pastor William Keller Frick. These are members of the church guild in front of the home of Charles Meinicke. (Courtesy of Advent Lutheran Church.)

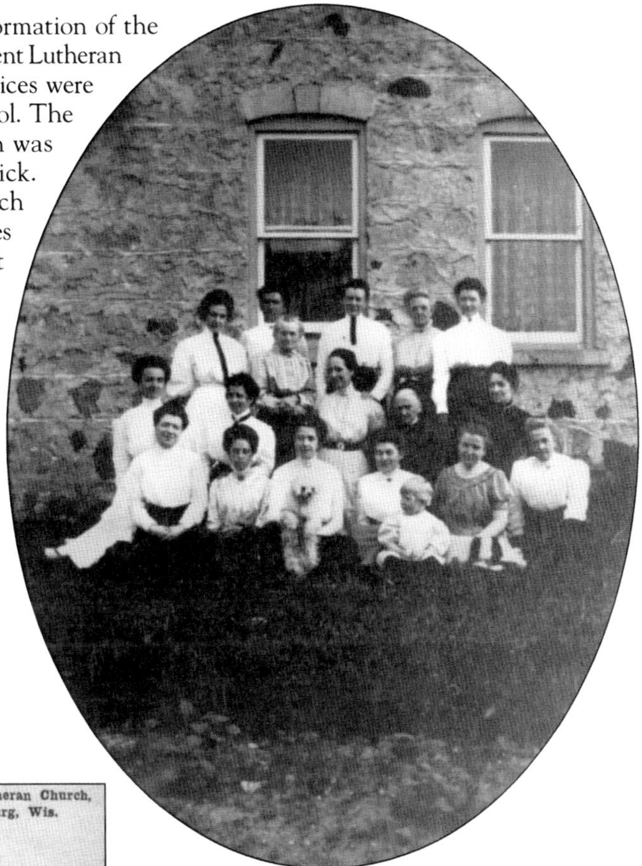

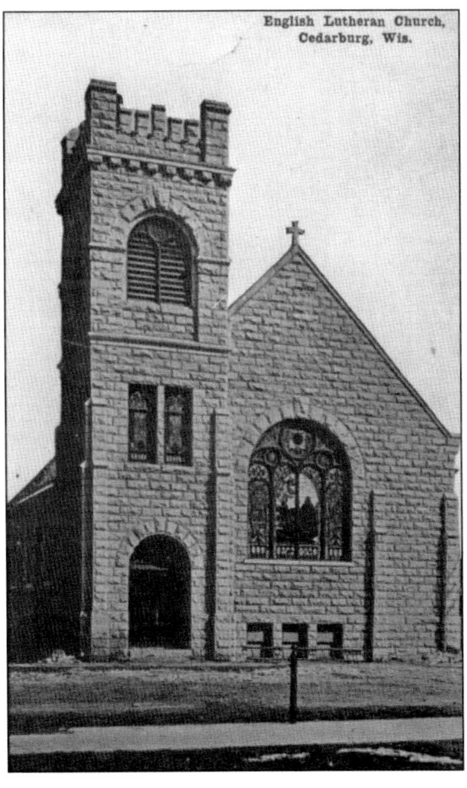

Advent Lutheran Church grew rapidly, cramping the storefront church by 1908. Church officials had been discussing the need for a larger church when member G. A. Boerner stepped forward and offered to donate a lot he owned on Washington Avenue. His only stipulation was that the church build an edifice valued at not less than $5,000. The church was completed in 1909. (Courtesy of Advent Lutheran Church.)

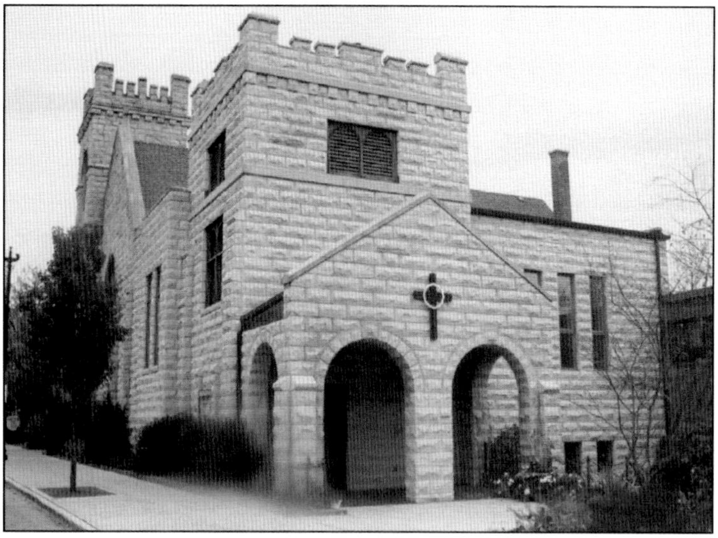

Members of the church chose the name Evangelical Lutheran Church of the Advent. Rev. Dr. Janis Kinens accepted the call to become Advent's pastor in 1998. He is a Vietnam veteran and collector of die-cast model cars. His 1958 Cadillac is frequently parked outside the church, which is adjacent to the interurban bridge. (Courtesy of Advent Lutheran Church.)

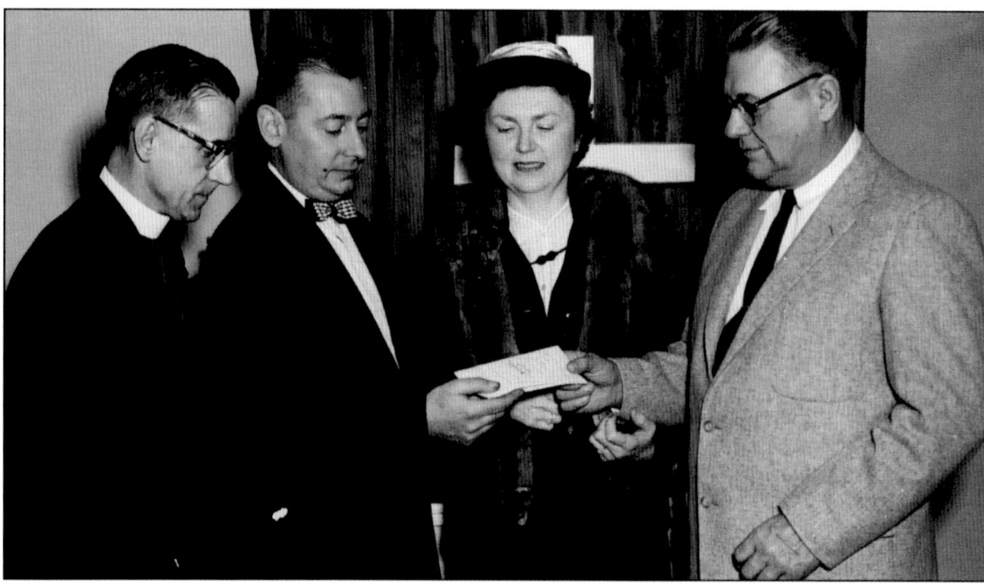

Faith Lutheran Church was founded in 1956 through a historic effort by its members, who left Immanuel Lutheran when the congregation grew too big for its many worshippers. Much debate had occurred within Immanuel Lutheran on whether to expand the current church, but ultimately the members opted to start a "mission church," which became Faith Lutheran Church. Ronald Stephenson and his wife, who donated 12 acres for the new church, are pictured handing over the deed to the property. From left to right are Pastor C.A. Becker, Ed Rappold, and Alice and Ronald Stephenson. (Courtesy of Faith Lutheran Church.)

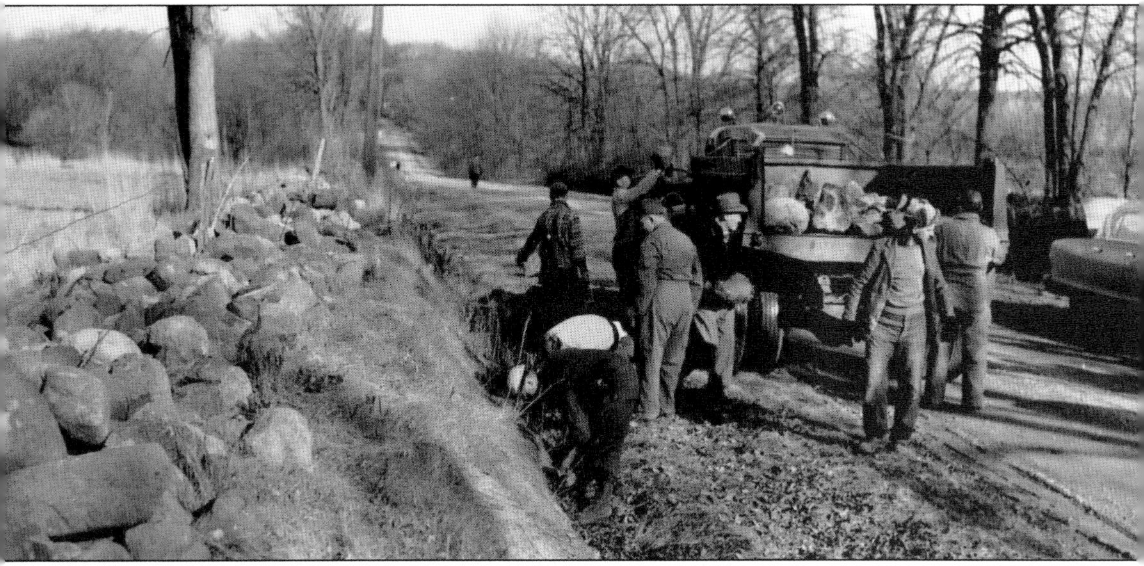

Much like the early Cedarburg pioneers who mined stone from the creek to build the mills, the members of Faith Lutheran Church collected the fieldstone—some 590 tons—needed to build their new church. The church members held so-called splitting parties to break the stones apart. (Courtesy of Faith Lutheran Church.)

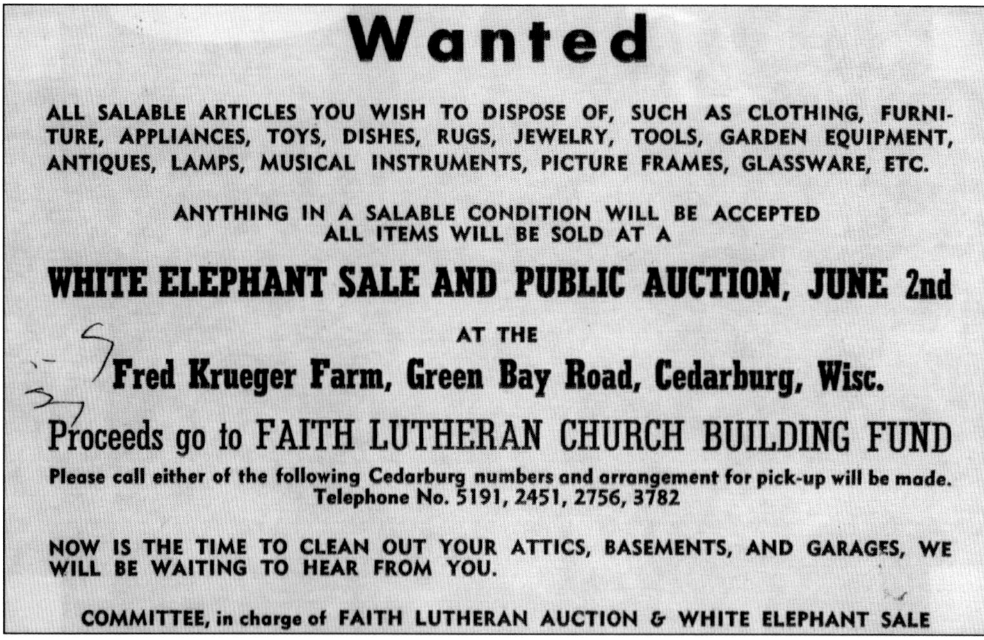

Wanted

ALL SALABLE ARTICLES YOU WISH TO DISPOSE OF, SUCH AS CLOTHING, FURNITURE, APPLIANCES, TOYS, DISHES, RUGS, JEWELRY, TOOLS, GARDEN EQUIPMENT, ANTIQUES, LAMPS, MUSICAL INSTRUMENTS, PICTURE FRAMES, GLASSWARE, ETC.

ANTHING IN A SALABLE CONDITION WILL BE ACCEPTED
ALL ITEMS WILL BE SOLD AT A

WHITE ELEPHANT SALE AND PUBLIC AUCTION, JUNE 2nd

AT THE

Fred Krueger Farm, Green Bay Road, Cedarburg, Wisc.

Proceeds go to FAITH LUTHERAN CHURCH BUILDING FUND

Please call either of the following Cedarburg numbers and arrangement for pick-up will be made.
Telephone No. 5191, 2451, 2756, 3782

NOW IS THE TIME TO CLEAN OUT YOUR ATTICS, BASEMENTS, AND GARAGES, WE WILL BE WAITING TO HEAR FROM YOU.

COMMITTEE, in charge of FAITH LUTHERAN AUCTION & WHITE ELEPHANT SALE

Everything needed for construction of Faith Lutheran Church was donated, but money was still badly needed. Bake sales, bird feeder sales, festivals, smorgasbords, and spaghetti suppers were held to raise funds. This is an example of a flyer distributed to members seeking "all salable items" for a public auction. (Courtesy of Faith Lutheran Church.)

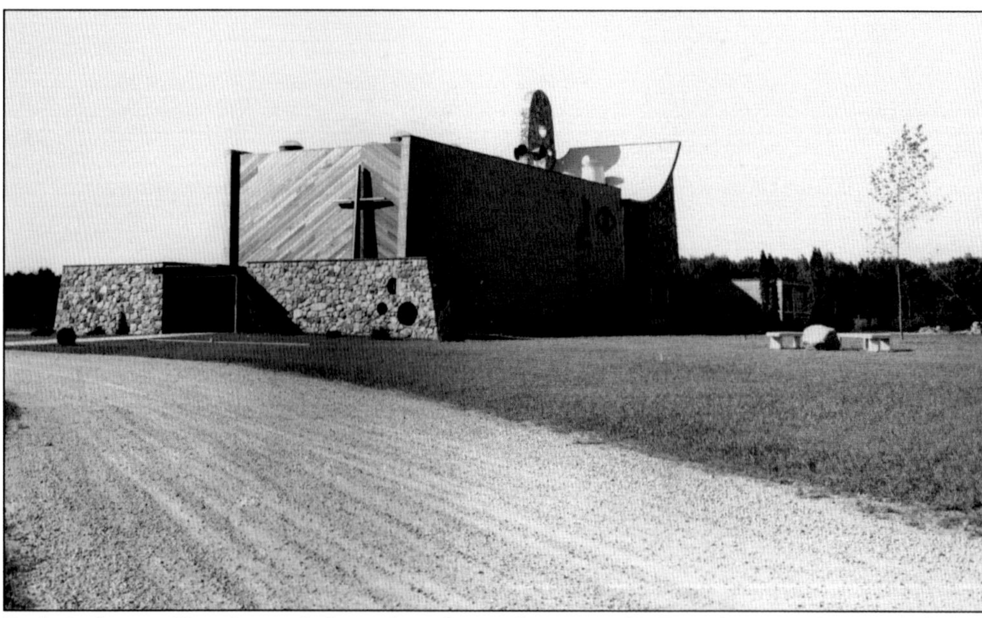

Faith Lutheran Church was dedicated on September 14, 1958. Founding members included Ed and Ken Rappold, Allen Wollner, Le Roy Hoffmann, and Wallace Hoffmann. Great care was taken to include religious themes and symbols in the exterior and interior, including the symbolic eye and hand on the outside. (Courtesy of Faith Lutheran Church.)

Six

RECREATION

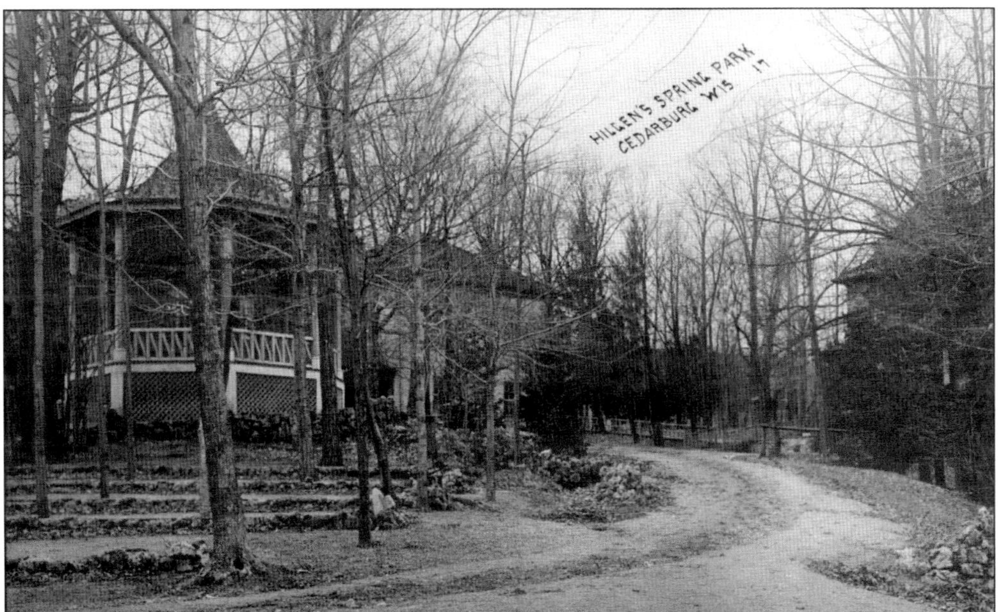

One of the most popular attractions in the Midwest was Hilgen's Spring Resort, built in 1852 by Frederick Hilgen on 72 acres east of downtown Cedarburg. The complex was the spa of its time, using the water from Cedar Creek to provide an artesian spring fountain and bathhouses. It is said that locals could pay a fee to take a bath there on Saturdays, saving themselves the labor of collecting clean water from the creek. Hilgen's Spring Resort also boasted two hotels with dining rooms, a tavern, bandstand, a bowling alley, and dance hall. (Courtesy of Kathy Lanser.)

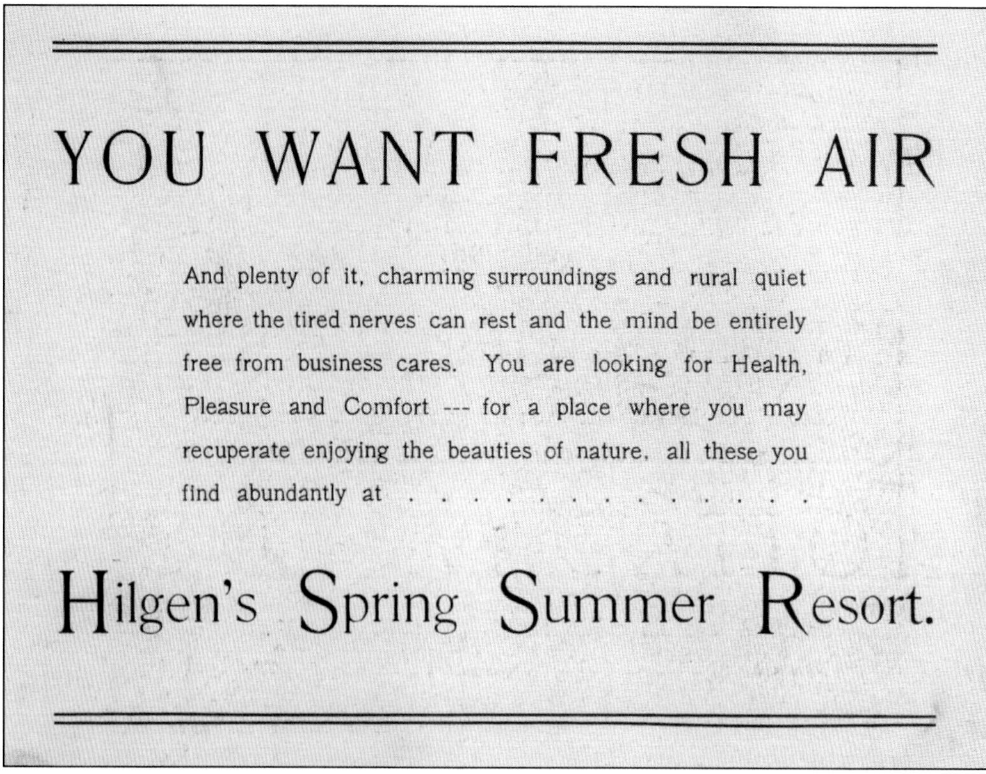

Hilgen's Spring was not just popular with Milwaukee-area residents. Visitors from Chicago, St. Louis, and Kansas City descended on the park during the summer and early autumn months that it was open. The park also served as a venue for local dances, wedding, picnics, and balls. (Courtesy of the Ozaukee County Historical Society.)

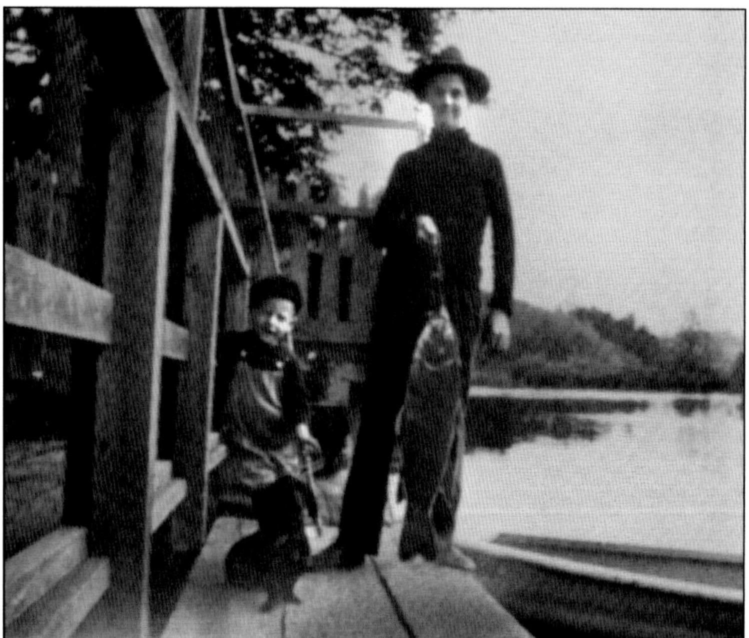

Hilgen's Spring Resort also included a spring-fed fish pond, which was a popular fishing spot for locals. Fred W. Hilgen and his son Frederick are pictured with a big catch. (Courtesy of the Ozaukee County Historical Society.)

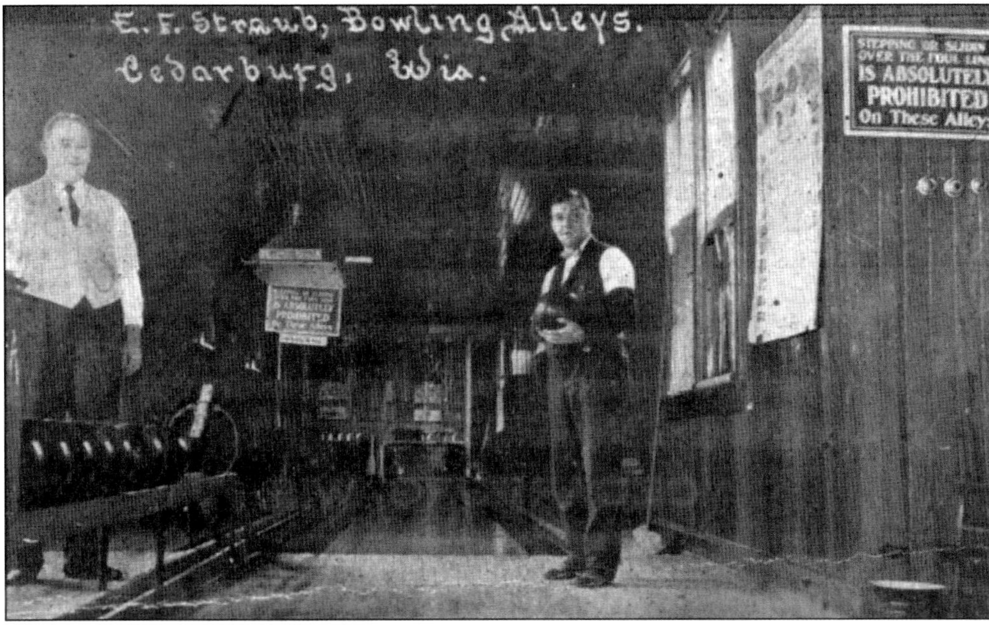

An early bowling alley in Cedarburg was the E.F. Straub Bowling Alley. It was located near the train tracks on what is now Portland Road. It was later the Carrie Jo Inn, which also had several bowling lanes. The L&G Express Bar now sits on the spot. (Courtesy of Vivian Scherf Laabs and Arnold Laabs.)

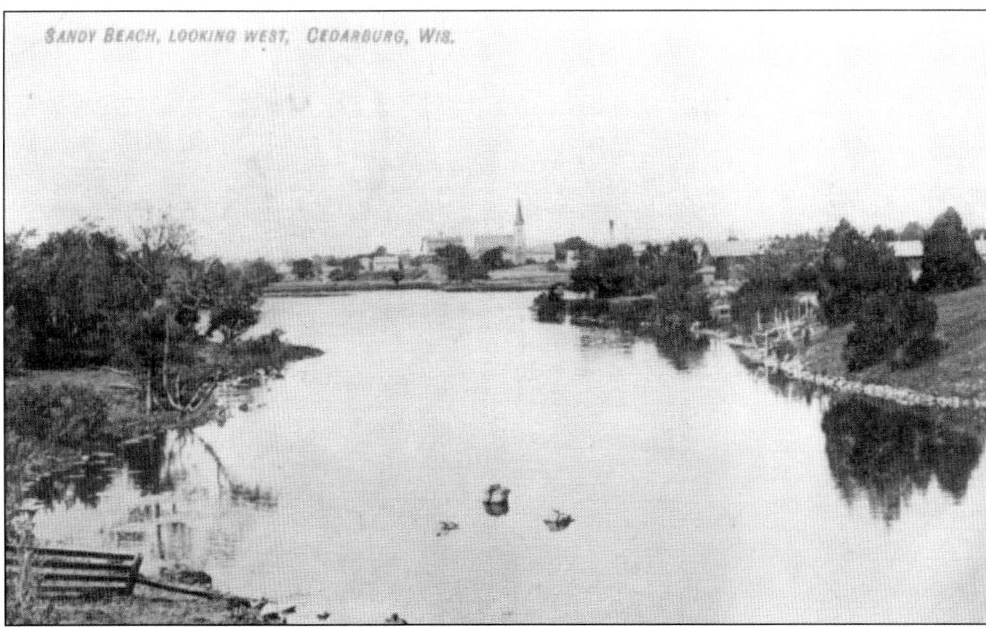

Cedar Creek, seen here from what is now the Highland Drive area, served as a watery playground for the youth of Cedarburg. In the summer, kids spent their days fishing and swimming in the creek. In the winter, they ice-skated and sledded across it. Before indoor plumbing, swimming was contained to the millraces when the water was low to avoid waste disposed from outhouses. (Courtesy of Mark Anderson.)

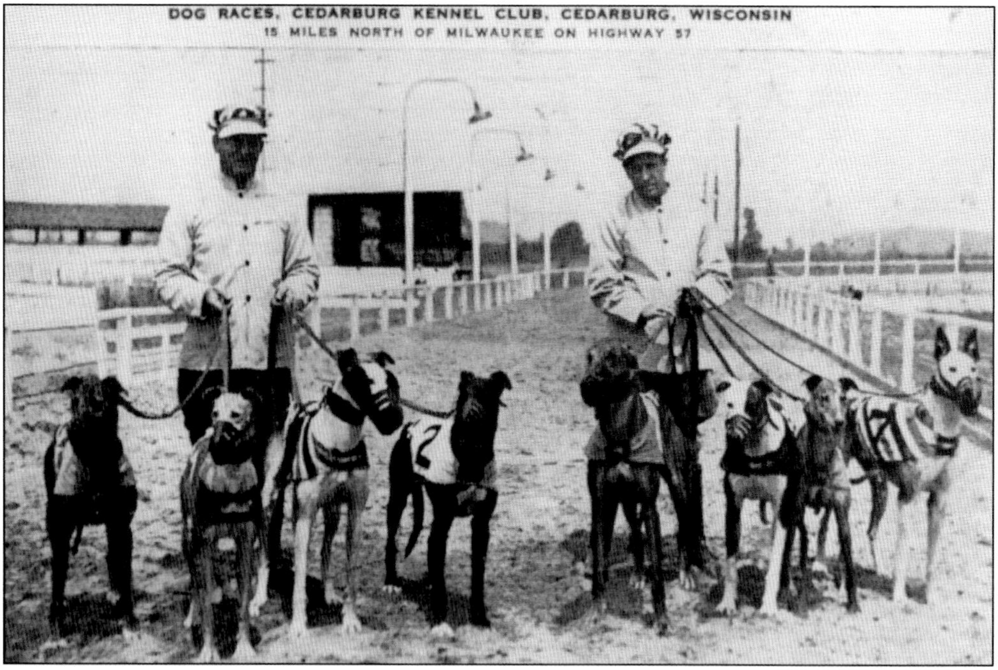

The Cedarburg fairgrounds have held many different attractions over the decades. In the early part of the 19th century, it was dog racing, held rain or shine, according to the advertisements of the time. Newspaper accounts indicate that people were drawn to Cedarburg because they could bet on dogs and horses. Patrons would place bets of $2, $5, and $10 at booths located under the grandstands. Dog racing ended in Cedarburg in 1928. (Courtesy of the Edward A. Rappold Photograph Collection, Cedarburg Cultural Center.)

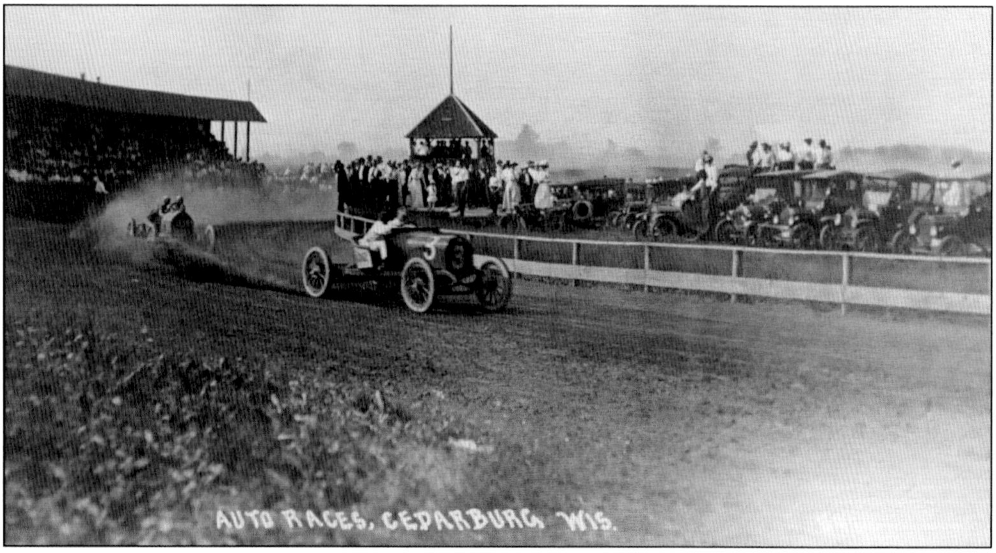

Another big draw to the fairgrounds was the automobile races. Almost as soon as there were automobiles, there were races. This photograph was likely taken before 1920. In 1947, after the Cedarburg Volunteer Fire Department bought 23 acres of the fairgrounds, they built a quarter-mile oval track inside the original half-mile track. Stock car races were held at the park through 1979. (Courtesy of the Edward A. Rappold Photograph Collection, Cedarburg Cultural Center.)

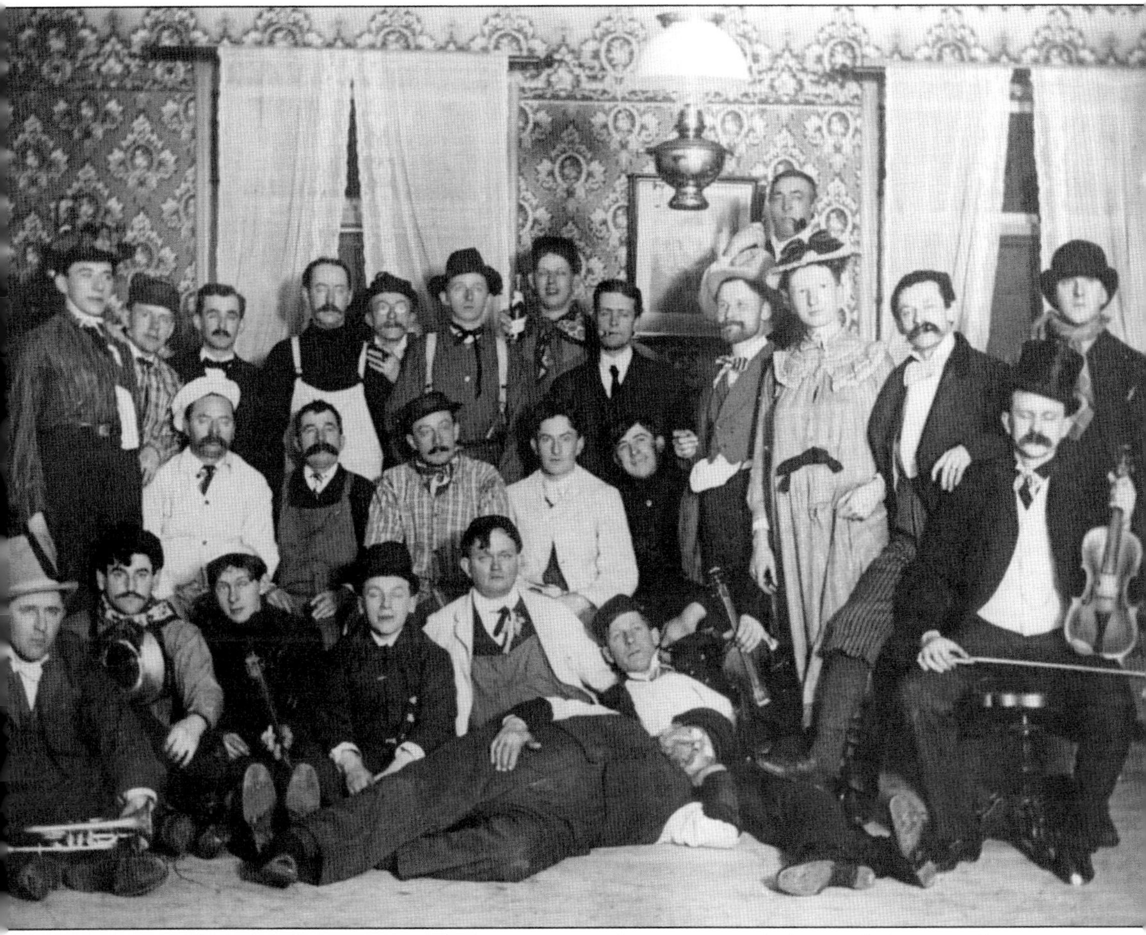

Sometimes called "hard times parties," these social gatherings provided a needed respite during challenging times. In this photograph, revelers attend a party at the Bodendoerfer home in 1903. (Courtesy of the Edward A. Rappold Photograph Collection, Cedarburg Cultural Center.)

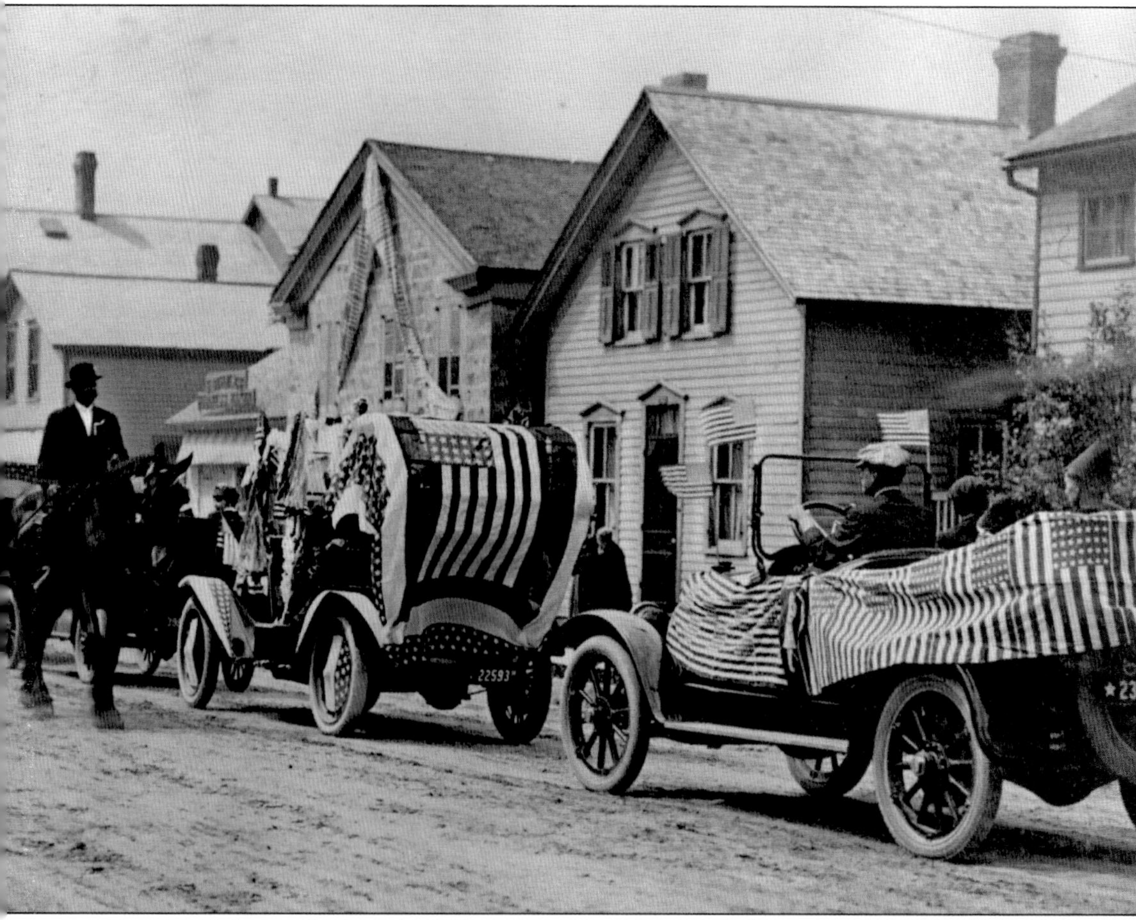

Fourth of July parades have been an important part of Cedarburg throughout the generations. Here, a parade in 1916 takes the same route of the 21st-century parades. Note how close the homes are to the street; that was to make room for barns and other structures behind them. (Courtesy of the Ozaukee County Historical Society.)

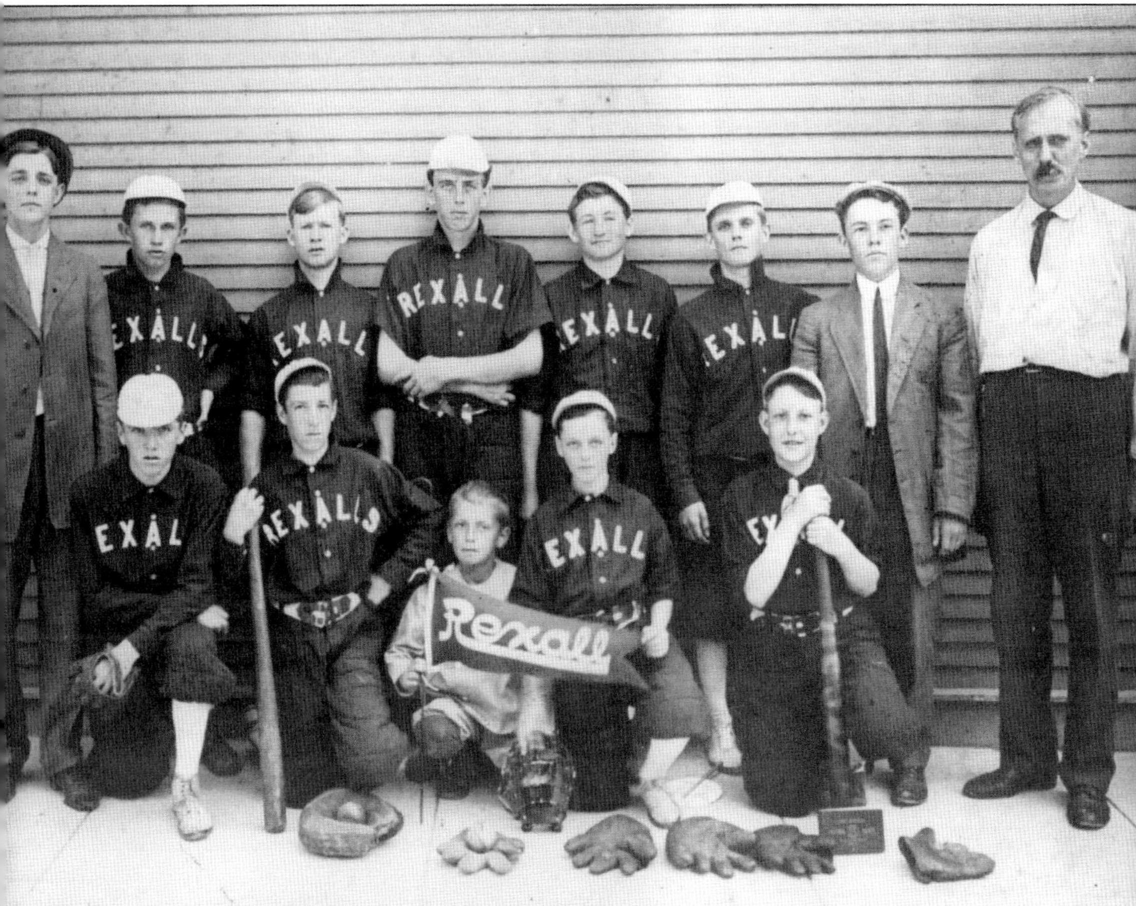

This 1912 baseball team was sponsored by Gerrit's Rexall Drug Store, possibly because it was the only one to sell baseball bats at the time. While basketball may have dominated early sports in Cedarburg, baseball would grow in popularity by the 1950s. (Courtesy of Robert Armbruster.)

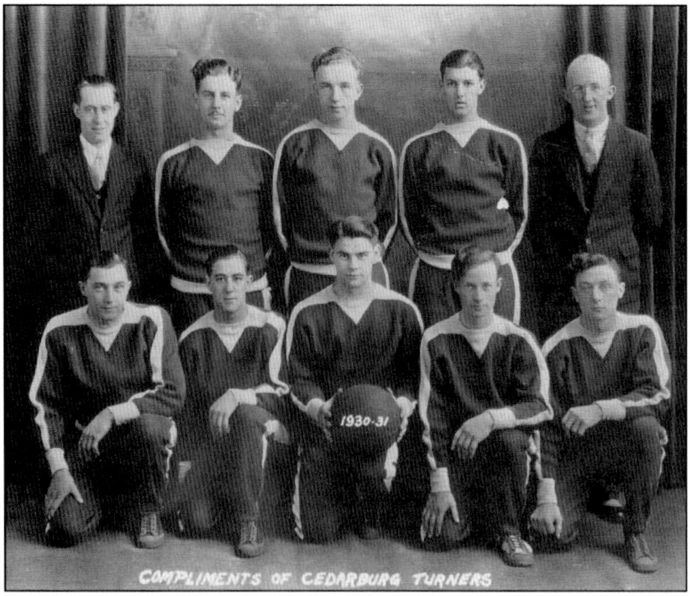

The 1930–1931 Turners basketball team is pictured here. Under coach Melvin Maronde, it was one of the legends of amateur basketball at the time. The team won 19 of 23 games that year, winning 18 straight. They traveled throughout Ozaukee, Washington, Sheboygan, and Waukesha Counties to play different teams. At home, they played at Turner Hall. The team was the north division champion in 1935. (Courtesy of Robert Armbruster.)

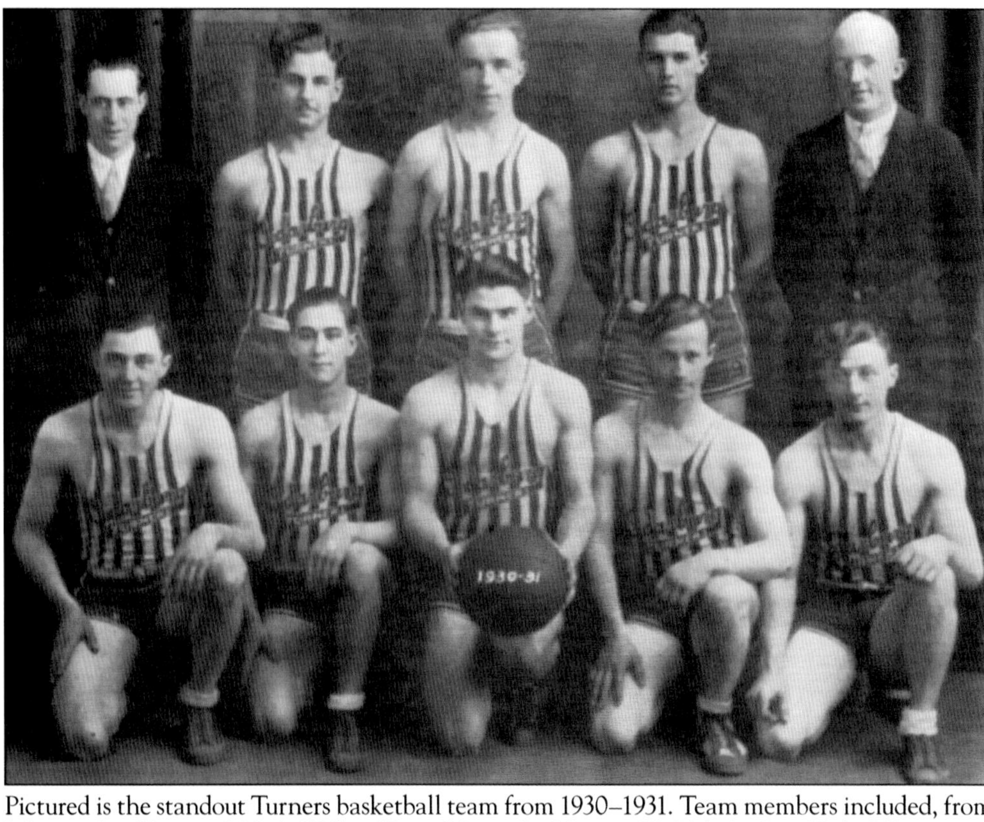

Pictured is the standout Turners basketball team from 1930–1931. Team members included, from left to right, (first row) Herb Wilke, Harry Maronde, Monroe Kafehl, Arthur "Babe" Friess, and Ralph Bodendorfer; (second row) coach Melvin Maronde, Howard Roebken, Ed Schneider, Ed Nicolaus, and manager Palmer Schneider. (Courtesy of Robert Armbruster.)

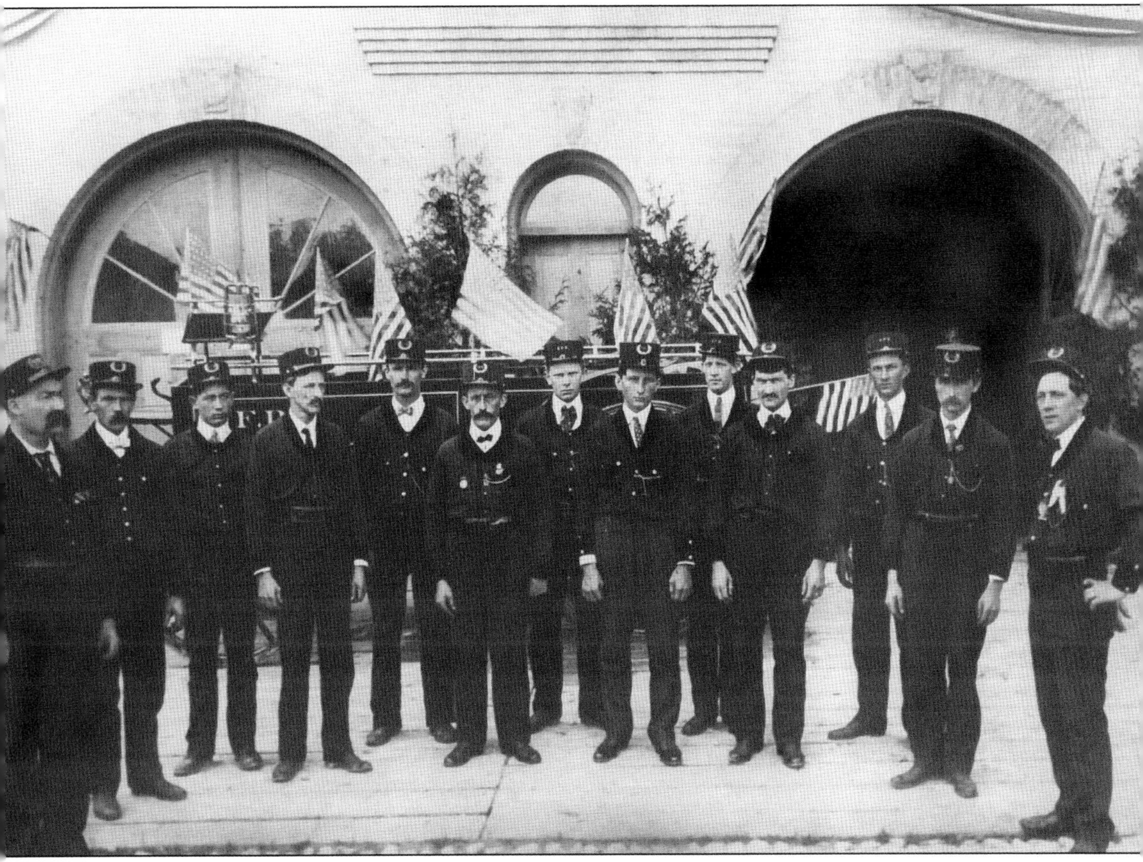

Members of the Cedarburg Volunteer Fire Department are pictured before a parade on July 4, 1904. Parades began at the firehouse on what is now Mequon Avenue and traveled north through the city. Floats consisted of elaborately decorated carriages or wagons outfitted with streamers and pulled by horses. For many years, Hilgen's Spring Resort had a float. (Courtesy of the Cedarburg Fire Department.)

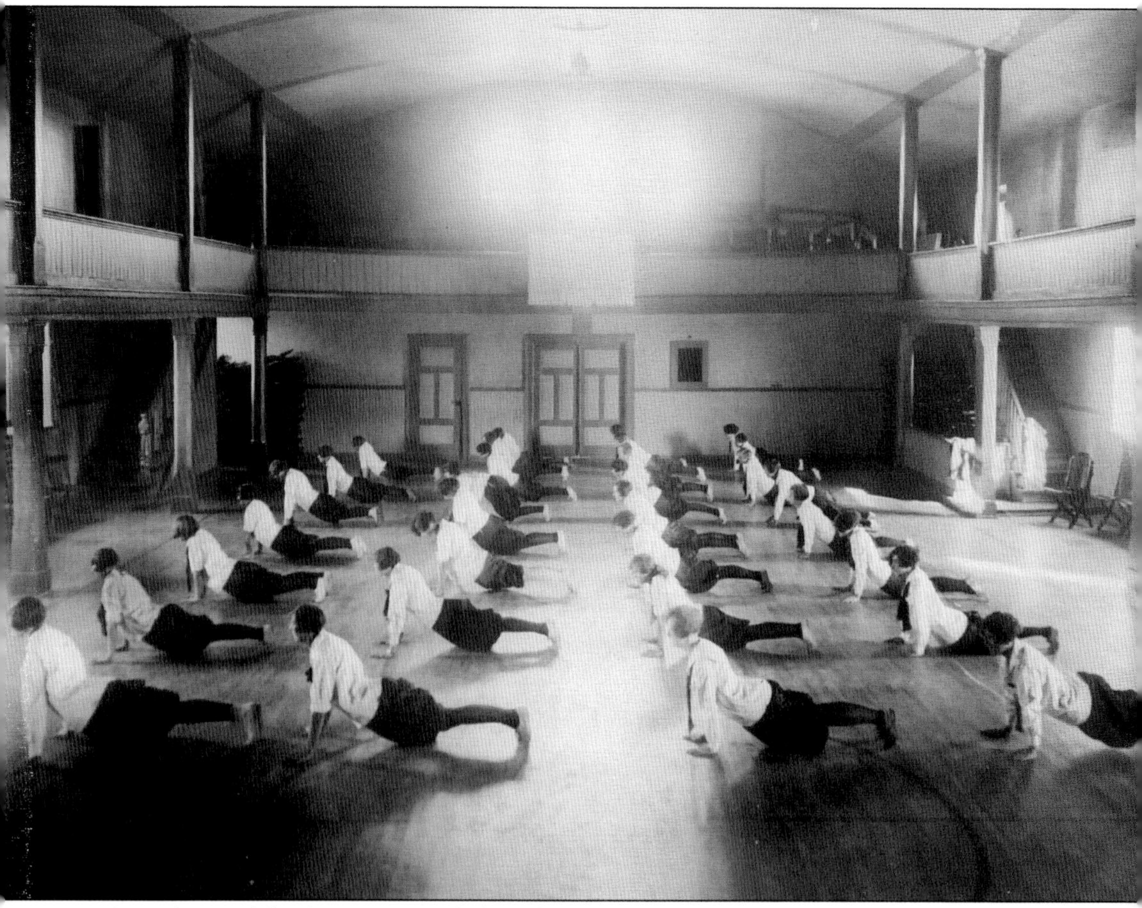

A vital part of the downtown Cedarburg landscape and recreational life in the city was Turner Hall. The German word *turnen* means "gymnastics," and Turner Hall provided gymnastics classes for children and adults of both genders. For many years, gym classes were held in the hall, as well as grand balls, dances, theater productions, school plays, and other activities. (Courtesy of the Ozaukee County Historical Society.)

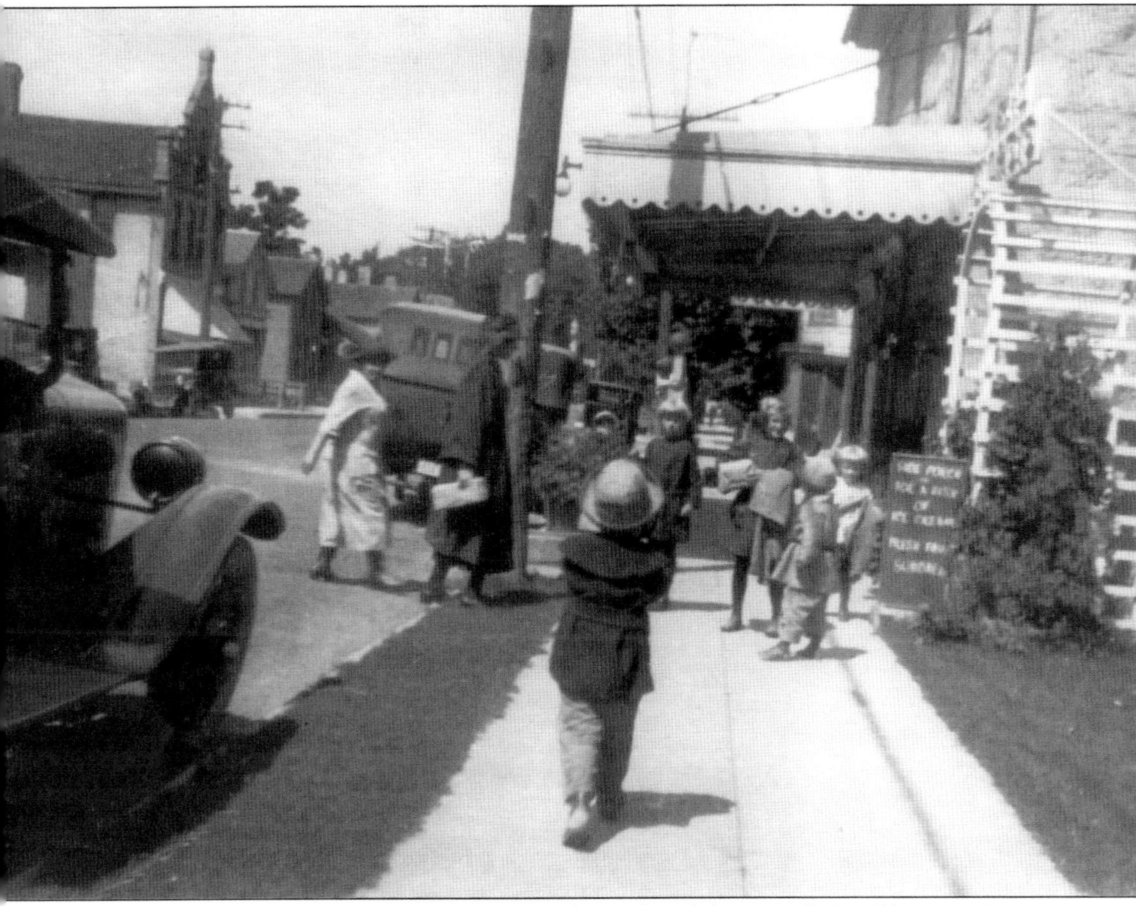

Wirth's Store was the destination for the group in this undated photograph. In addition to shoes, dry goods, and other items, the store offered ice cream and sun-dried fresh fruit. (Courtesy of Brook and Liz Brown.)

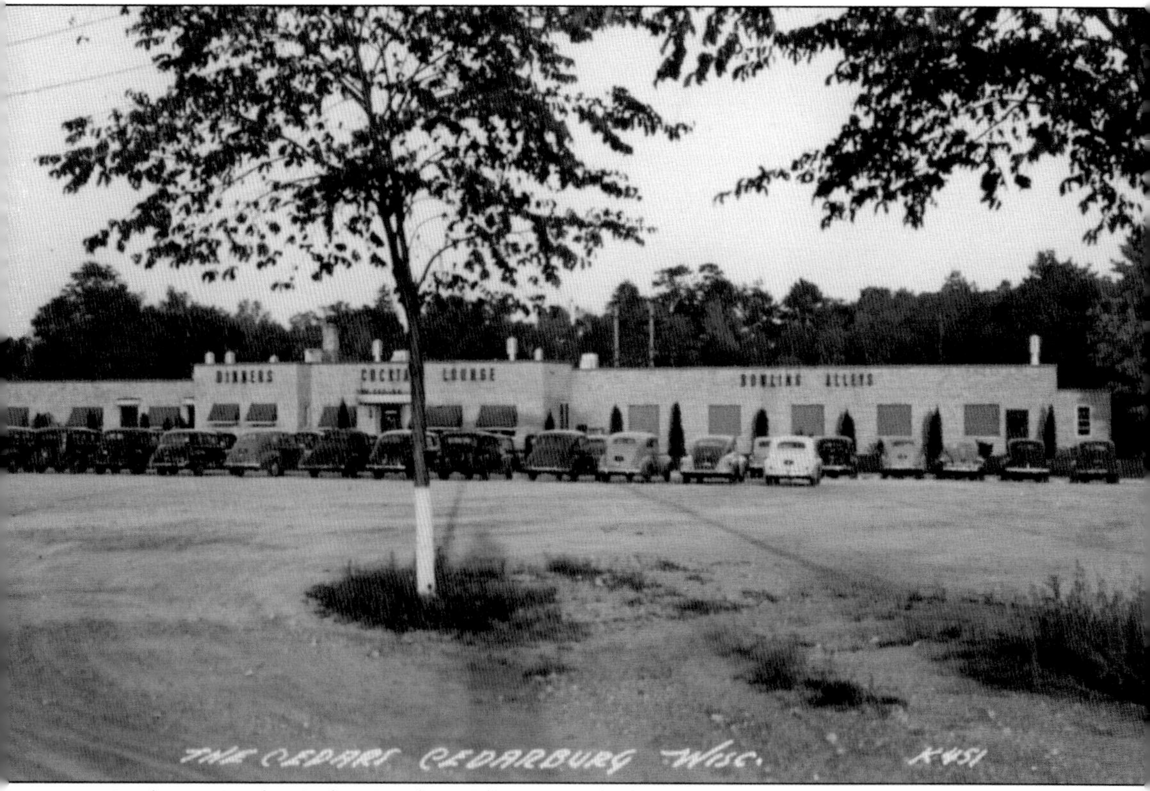

In the 1940s, the Cedars Bowling Alley opened where the popular Hilgen's Spring Resort once stood. James Hilgen had operated Hilgen's Spring until his death in 1923. Walter Barth and Edward Straub managed the park through the difficult years of Prohibition and the Great Depression until 1941, when they sold the property. The once-popular springs were covered with gravel and the land was subdivided. (Courtesy of Vivian Scherf Laabs and Arnold Laabs.)

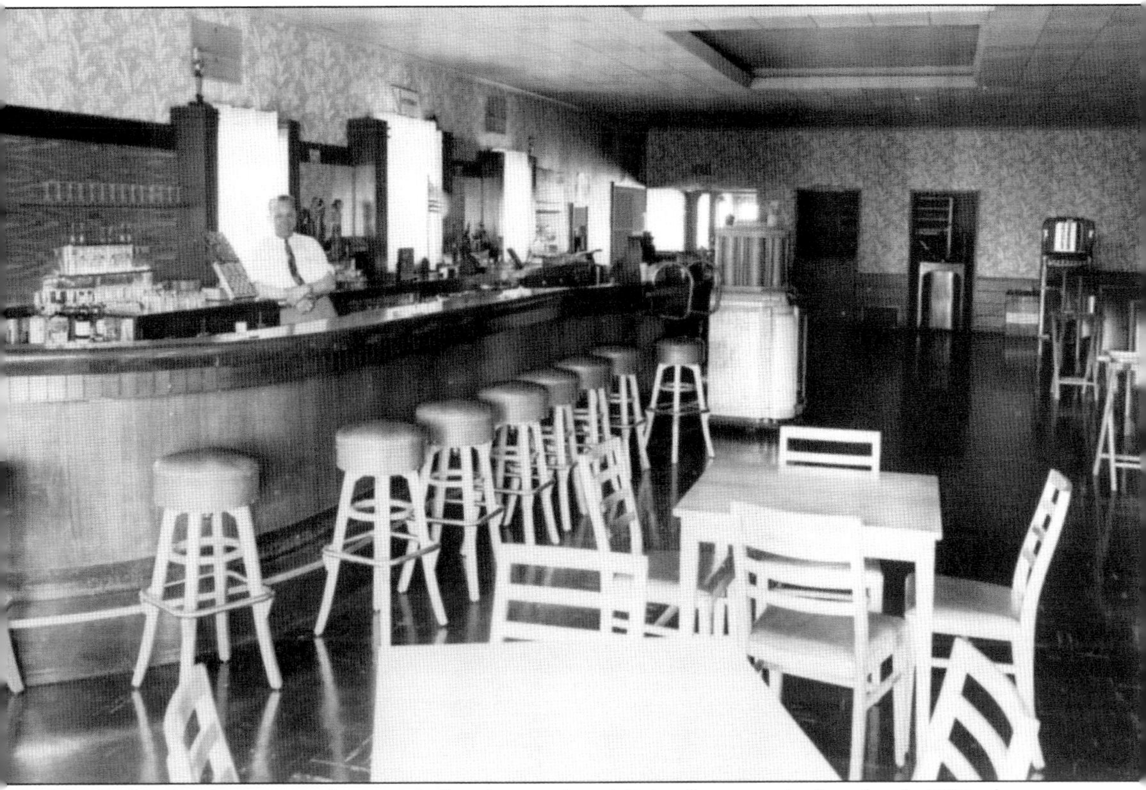

The Cedars has been a popular spot for bowling and socializing for some six decades. In 2010, three friends bought the business and renamed it Cedars III. Large windows were installed throughout to allow patrons to overlook the creek and see an occasional deer walk by. The Cedars III is now the venue for the popular Mel's Pig Roast, which is held each year to raise thousands of dollars for Special Olympics. (Courtesy of Vivian Scherf Laabs and Arnold Laabs.)

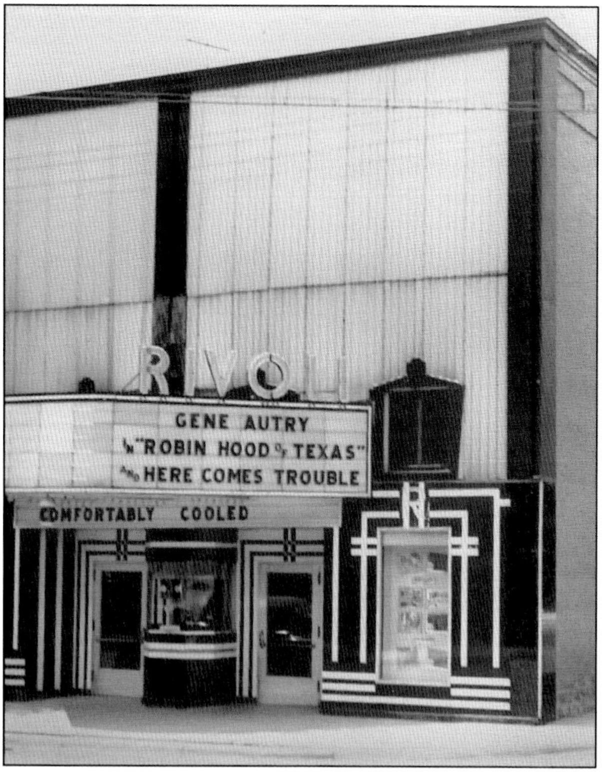

Moving pictures came to Cedarburg in January 1936 thanks to the efforts of Ann and Mark Morgan, who purchased the former Boerner Bros. Store building on the corner of Washington Avenue and Center Street. The Rivoli Theatre opened with the showing of *A Tale of Two Cities* for 25¢ per ticket. One of the first employees of the theater, Pearl Strege Blaisdell, was 91 years old in 2009 and remembered that more than 100 people lined up outside the ticket booth on opening day. (Courtesy of Vivian Scherf Laabs.)

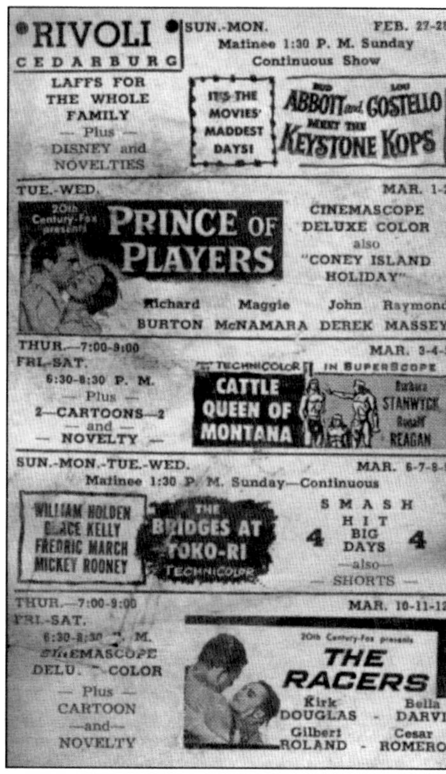

This Rivoli Theatre flyer from the mid-1950s shows the types of films shown at the time. Westerns were very popular in this era, but moviemakers also began to cater more to younger viewers as older people stayed home more to watch television. An estimated 10.5 million homes had a television by 1950. (Courtesy of Vivian Scherf Laabs.)

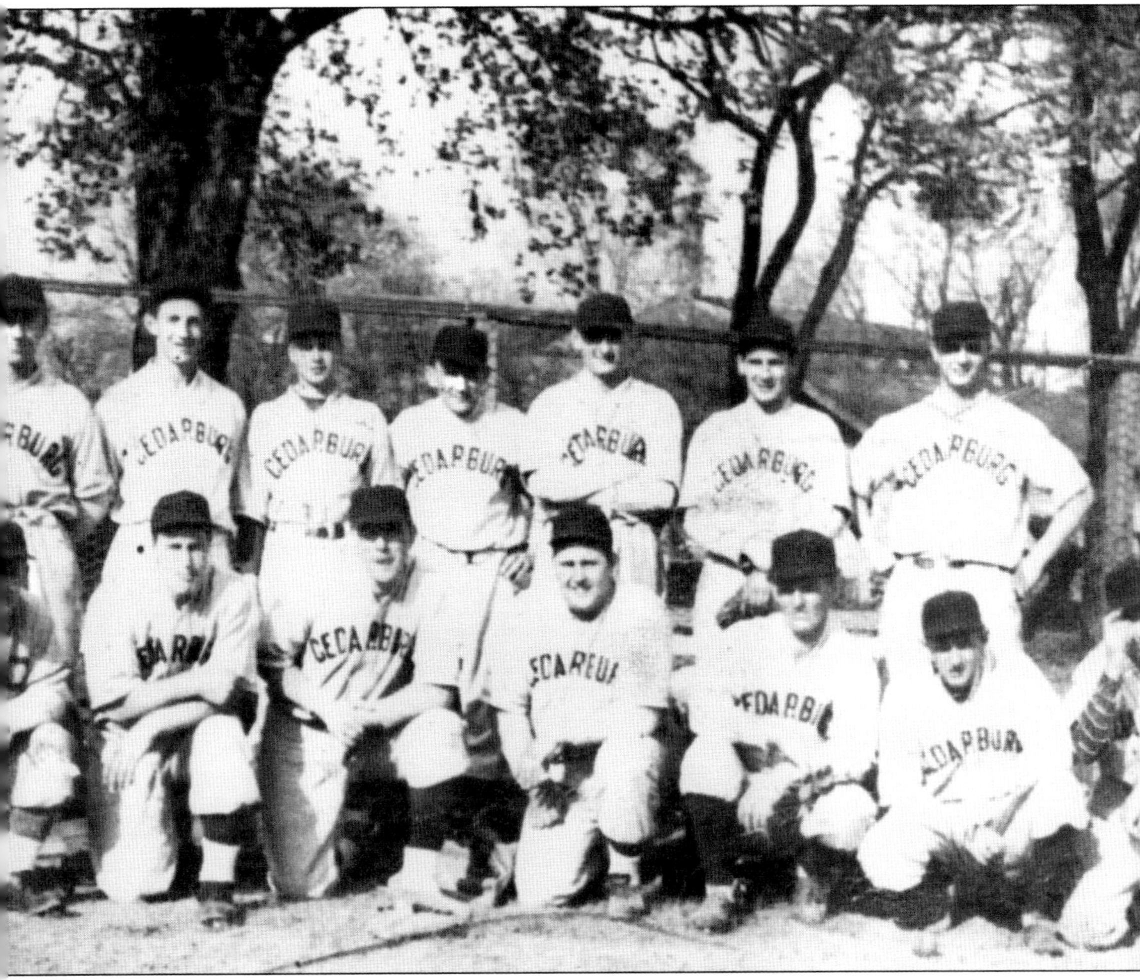

Cedarburg got its own amateur baseball team in the early 1950s, with Kiekhaefer Cedarburg Mercury as its sponsor. In 1972, the company, which had become Mercury Marine, dropped sponsorship in Cedarburg to devote its resources to its Fond du Lac team. The team became simply the Cedarburg Baseball Team, until adopting the nickname "the Mercs" in 1990. They are now part of the Land O' Lakes Baseball League Northern Division. Pictured, from left to right, are (first row) Hugo Regnitz, John Regnitz, Mel Kuehl, Lester Retzlaff, Roy Eggert, Clarance Behling, and unidentified; (second row) Ralph Krueger, Kid Behling, J. Borleske, Chester Scherf, Jigger Behling, Harold Reuter, and Marty Jaeger. (Courtesy of the Ozaukee County Historical Society.)

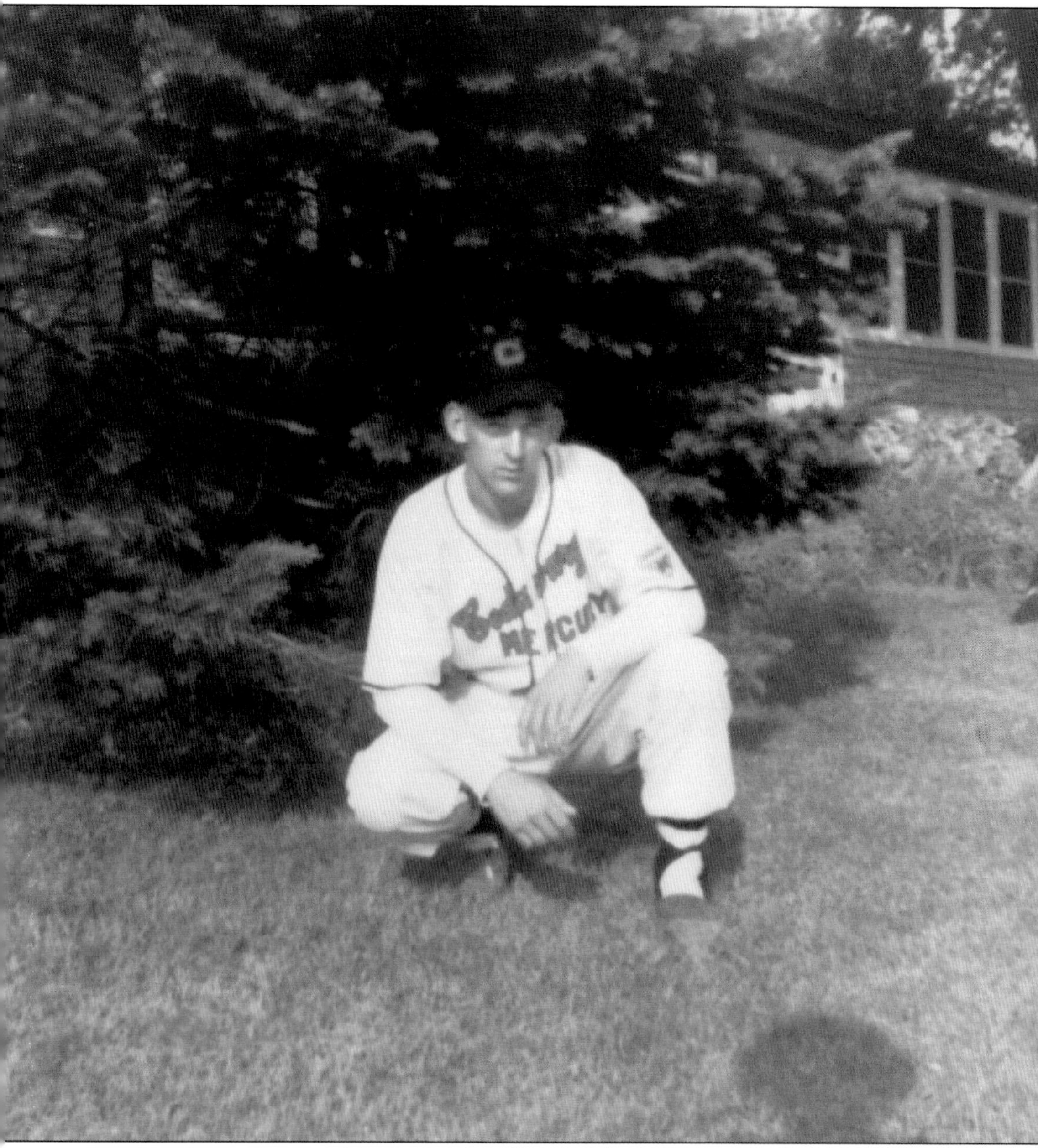

Cedarburg standout pitcher Stewart Scherf is pictured above. Scherf is said to have had two shutout games. During his athletic career at Cedarburg High School, he earned 12 varsity letters while competing in baseball, basketball, and football. As a quarterback for the school football team, Scherf threw 16 touchdown passes in his senior year alone. He was one of the inaugural inductees into the Cedarburg High School Hall of Fame in 2011. (Courtesy of Vivan Scherf Laabs.)

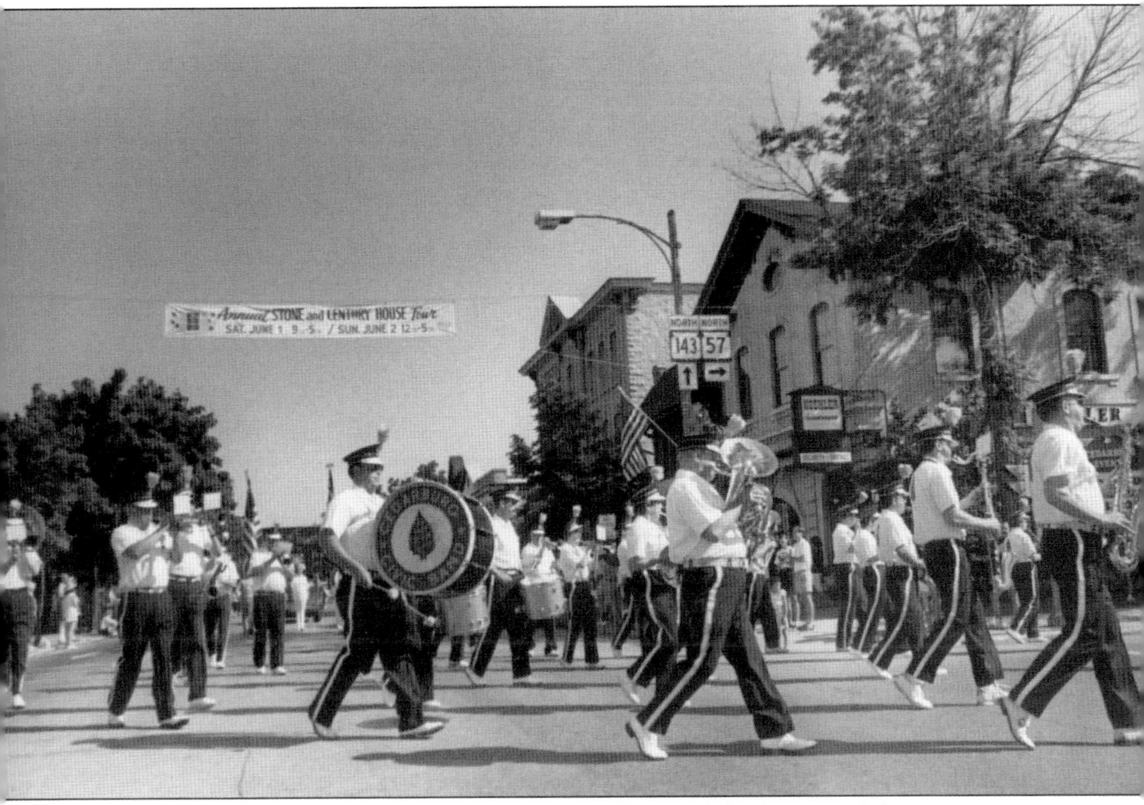

Music has long been a part of Cedarburg's history, and one of the fixtures of the music scene is the Cedarburg Civic Band, a mainstay of city parades and festivals for more than 110 years. Generations of families, like the Butts and the Boergers, have been a part of the band since its early days. In the summer, visitors to Cedarburg can hear the band as it plays on the lawn in front of city hall on Sunday afternoons. (Courtesy of the *News Graphic*.)

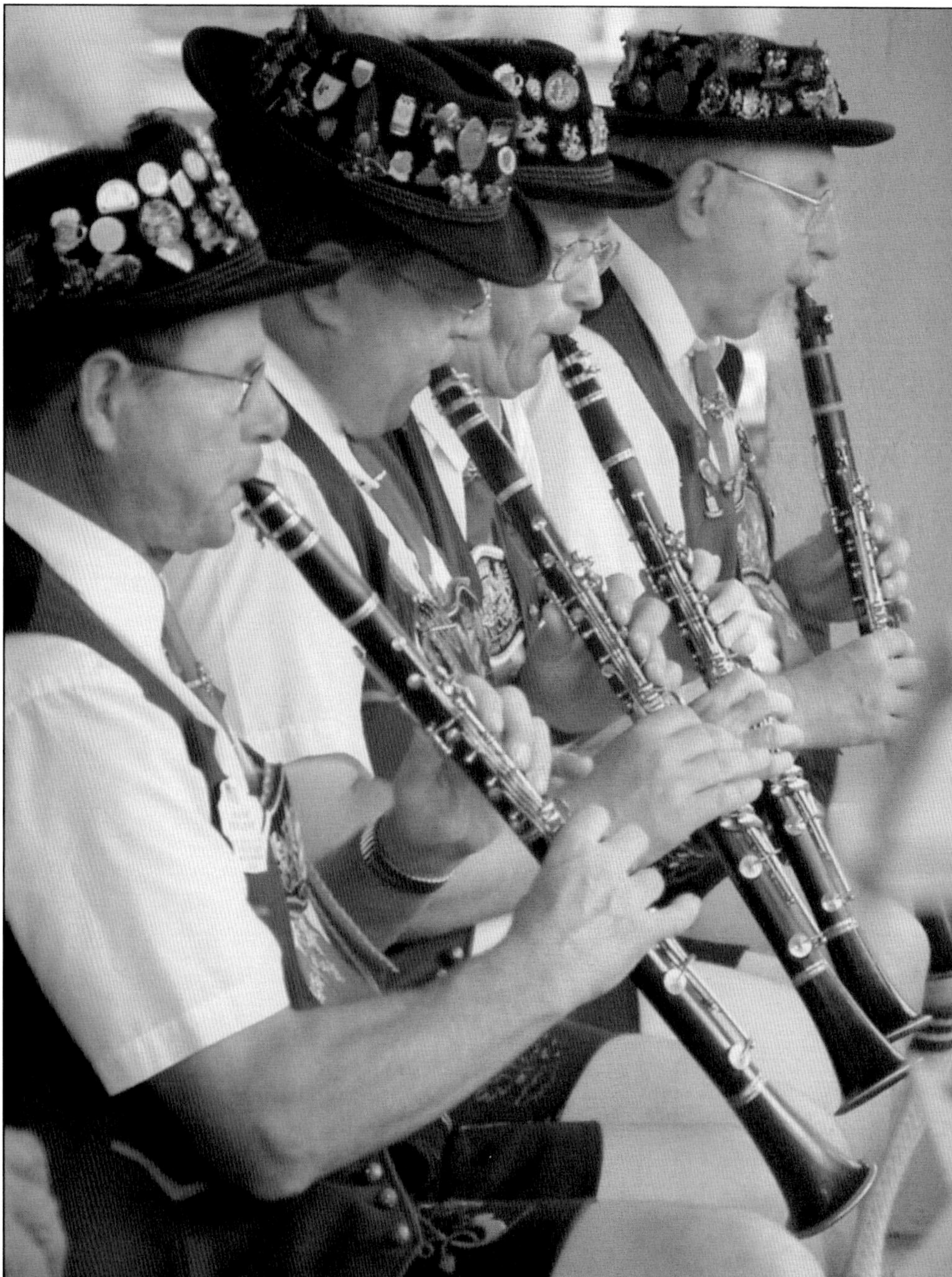

Many of Cedarburg's German descendants eagerly became a part of the Freistadt Alte Kameraden Band when it was formed in 1942 to bring authentic German-style music to the area and to demonstrate their deep feelings of patriotism during World War II. Originally called the Victory Band, it was formed by a group of about 10 friends from the Lindenwood 4-H Club. Still going strong today, Alte Kameraden has played numerous venues in Germany, including the Munich Oktoberfest, and at the Smithsonian Institute's Festival of American Folk Life. The band, still playing in their lederhosen, is a staple of Cedarburg's German Festival. (Courtesy of the *News Graphic*.)

Seven

Preservation

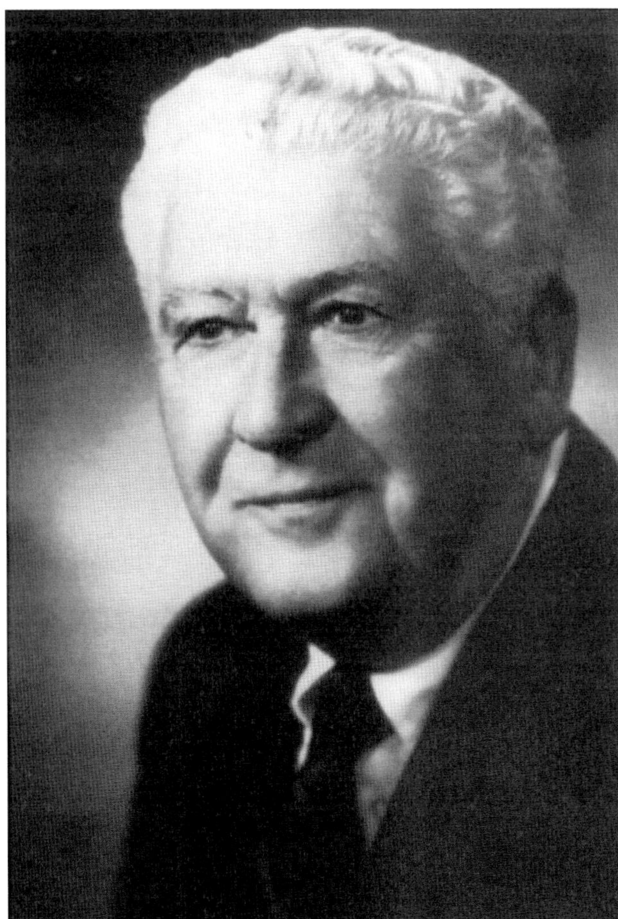

E. Stephan Fischer, born in Yugoslavia in 1908, is recognized as the leading champion of saving Cedarburg's historic buildings. First elected in 1946, and again in 1952, Fischer saw the old buildings as works of beauty that could also attract tourists to the city. But he lost the 1958 mayoral race to Merlin Rostad, who favored contemporary architecture. Prompted by talk that St. Francis Borgia church officials wanted to raze the church to build a new one, Fischer ran again in 1966 and won, serving until 1982. Twelve years later, Fischer was recognized for his preservation efforts when he received the Historic Preservation Achievement Award from the Wisconsin Historical Society. (Courtesy of the *News Graphic*.)

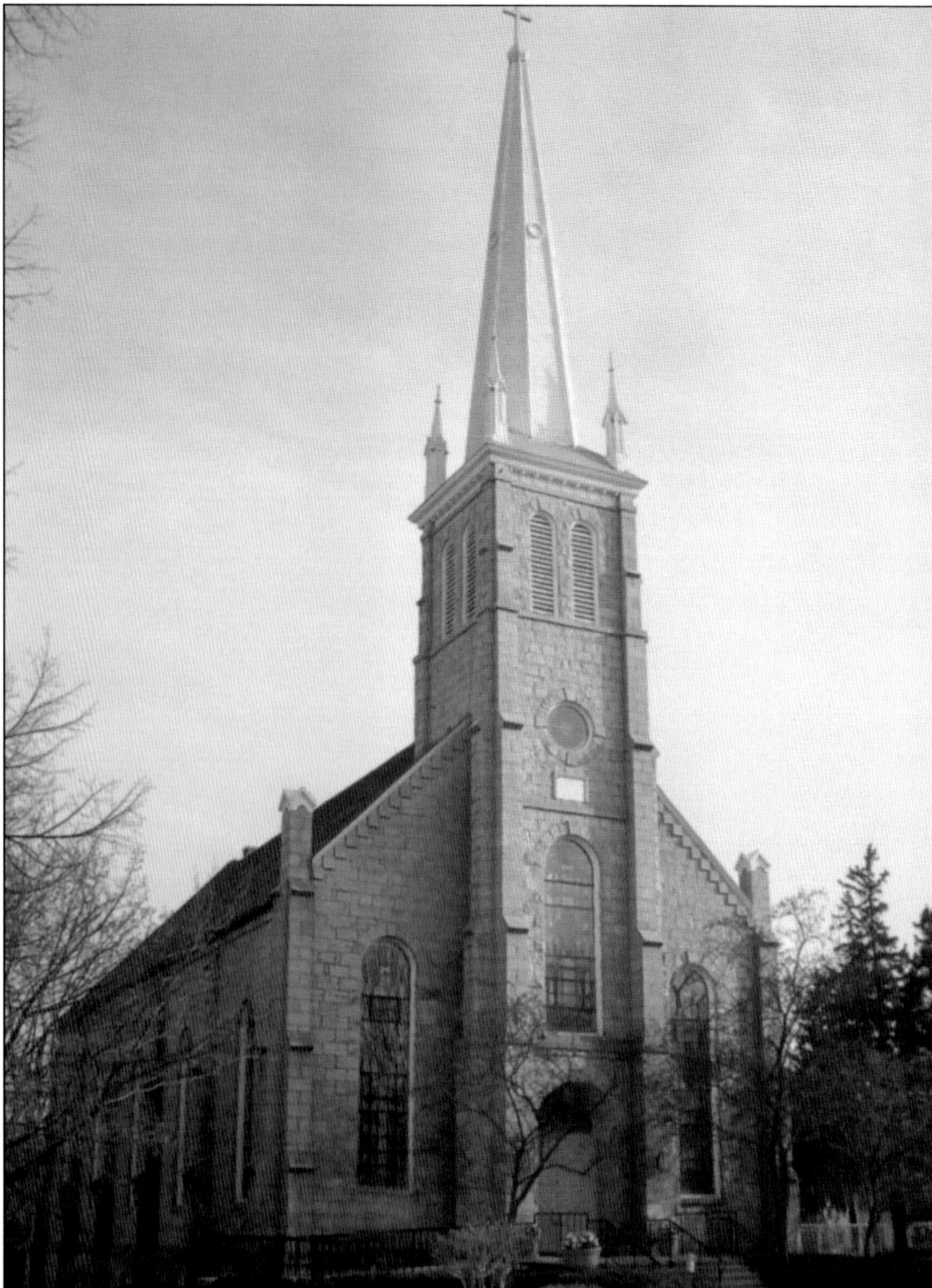

Called "the ornament of our city," St. Francis Borgia Church on the south end of downtown Cedarburg was nearly destroyed in 1966 when church officials sought to raze it and build a new one for their growing congregation. The plan was enough to bring former mayor E. Stephan Fischer back into politics. He ran and won office in 1966, and he promptly stopped the city's demolition order for the church. (Courtesy of the *News Graphic*.)

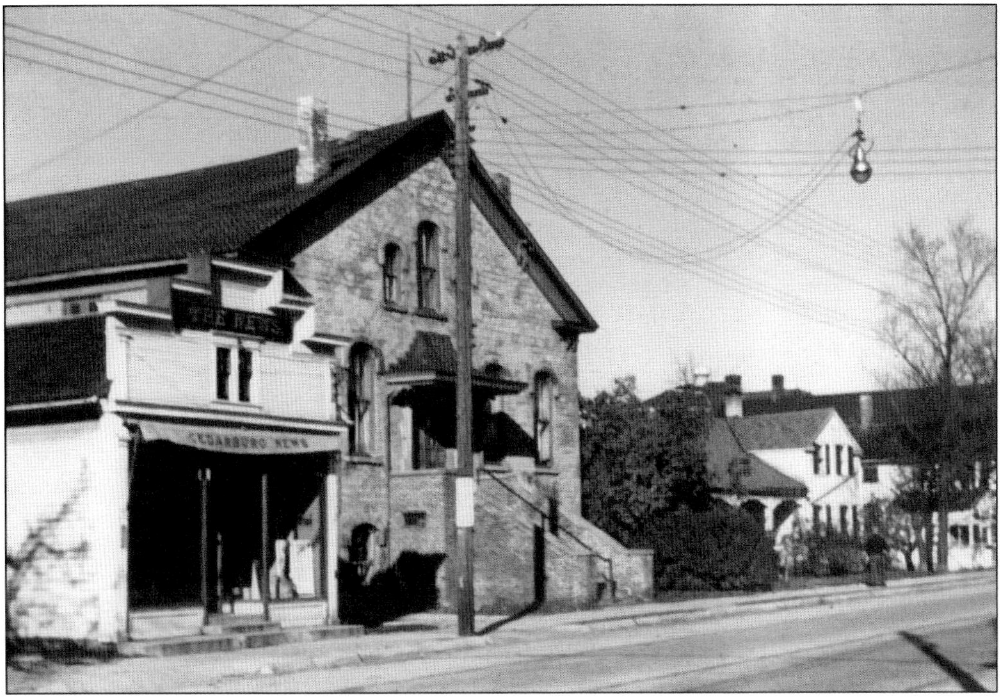

Built in 1868, Turner Hall served generations of Cedarburg residents as a gathering place, gym, classroom, and ballroom. But its purposefulness ran out as new recreational facilities were built. In 1960, Cedarburg State Bank, which owned Turner Hall, announced it would demolish it to build a new bank. There was an effort by some citizens to save it, but it was not enough. The building was demolished on February 7, 1961. (Courtesy of the Ozaukee County Historical Society.)

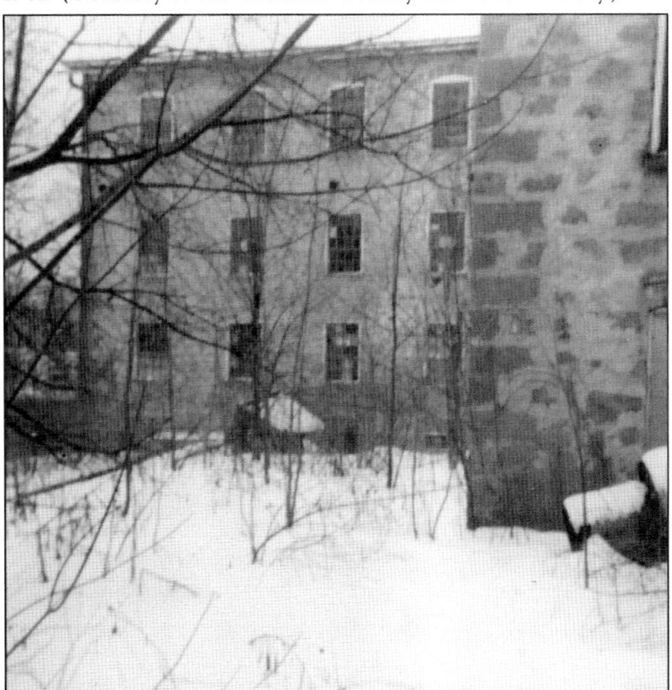

The iconic woolen mill that had held so much of Cedarburg's early history was in danger of destruction after it closed in 1968, when the owners sought to raze it and build a gas station and mini-mart on the spot. The building sat vacant for several years, with broken windows and quiet rooms filled with old, giant water tanks. This is the condition of the building when Jim and Sandy Pape of Milwaukee bought it in 1971. (Courtesy of Jim and Sandy Pape.)

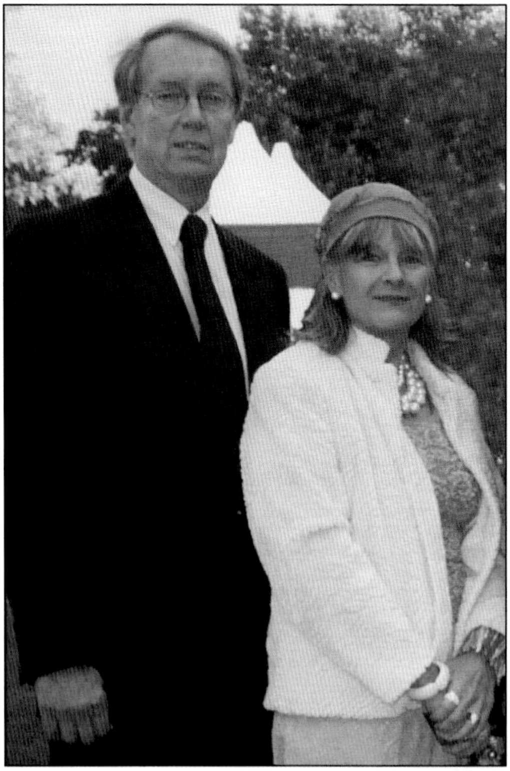

Jim Pape and his wife, Sandy, owned a small winery on the east side of Milwaukee in the late 1960s. Jim had considered buying the old woolen mill in 1969 for a condominium development, but he did not pursue it at that time. He came back in 1971, and with developer Bill Welty, bought the mill and its surrounding buildings for $110,000. The Papes took the main mill structure while Welty took a smaller building just west of the mill, which he operated as a general store and gift shop. (Courtesy of the *News Graphic*.)

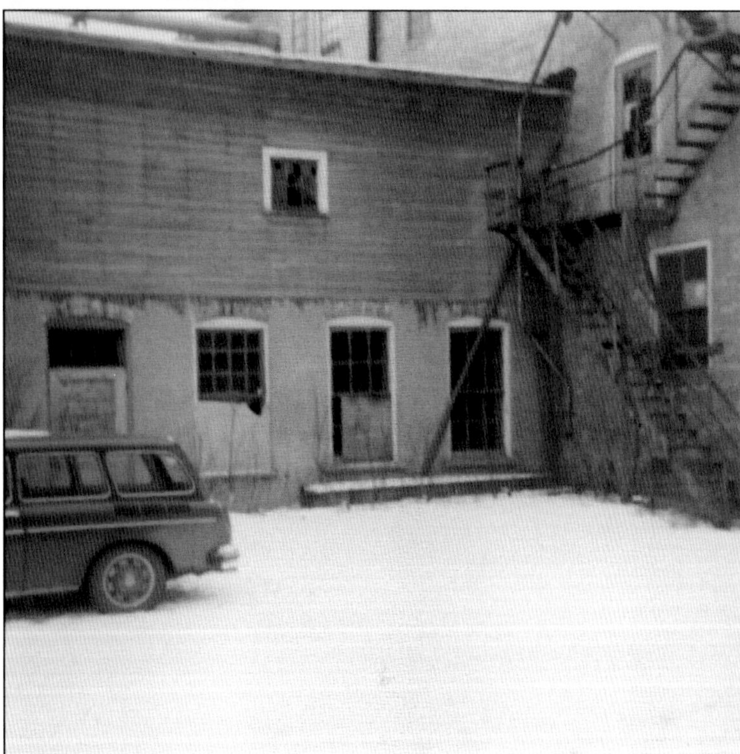

The first task of the Papes was restoring the portion of the mill where the winery would be located. Bricks that were used to line the boiler room were recycled for use as the winery tasting room floor. The boilers were used in the kiln to make wine bottles. The Cedar Creek Winery opened in May 1972. (Courtesy of Jim and Sandy Pape.)

When the Papes bought the 107-year-old woolen mill in 1971, the structure was in considerably sound shape for its age, with the exception of a leaky roof and debris-filled rooms. Other work was needed, too, such as filling the drains (pictured) which were used to channel the water after washing wool. Pape completed the renovation of the mill's first floor in 1973 and opened it up to shopkeepers. The second floor opened in 1974 and the third in 1978. Today, the mill is known as the Cedar Creek Settlement. (Courtesy of Jim and Sandy Pape.)

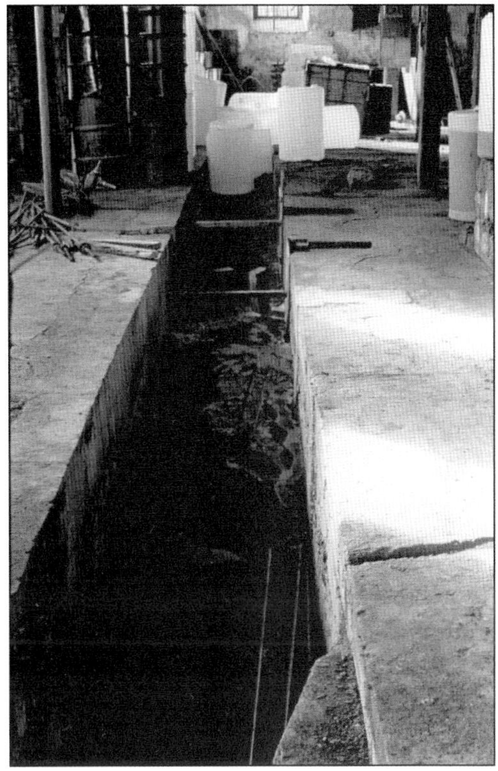

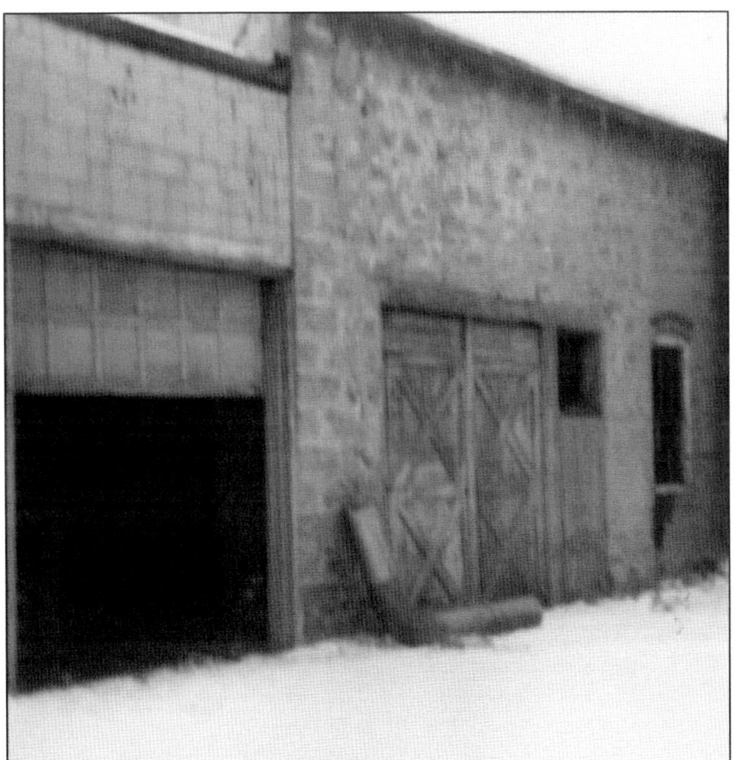

The portion of the mill pictured here housed the boilers, which heated different structures. It was the location for the Bighorn Forge blacksmith shop in the 1970s through 2007. When blacksmith Dan Nauman moved out, the building was renovated and made into a restaurant, capturing the elements of an old blacksmith shop. Today, it is the Anvil Pub & Grille, known for its charm and rustic dining experience. (Courtesy of Jim and Sandy Pape.)

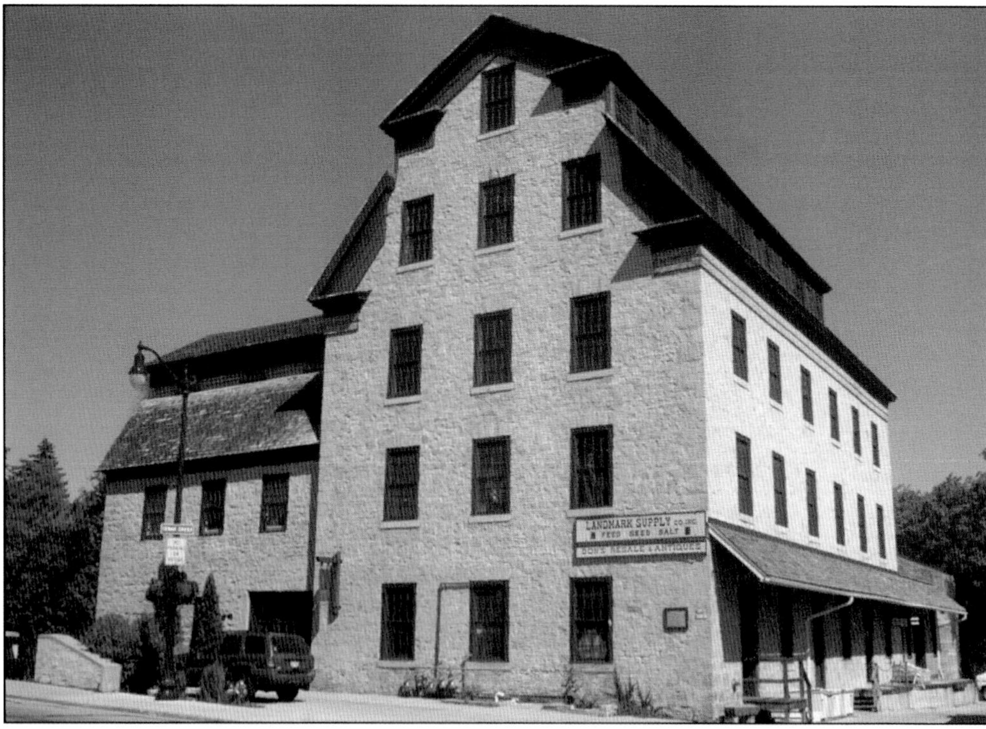

Another mill that received new life in the 1970s was the iconic gristmill on Columbia Road. Though it remained in operation through the years as a feed store run by the Cedarburg Supply Company, the Cedarburg Landmark Preservation Society bought the mill in 1981 and now leases space to an animal feed and seed shop, an architectural firm, and a popular brewpub overlooking the Cedar Creek. (Courtesy of the *News Graphic*.)

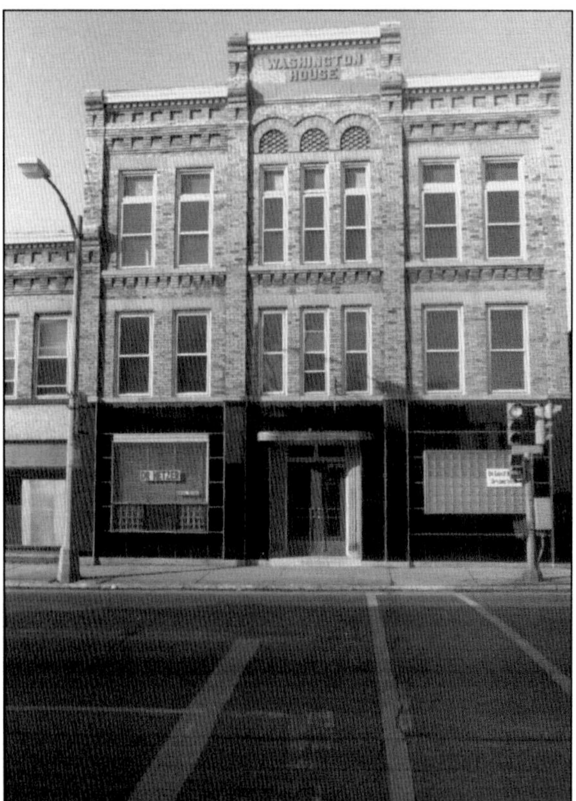

After the Papes completed restoration of the woolen mill, they set their sights on the historic Washington House Inn in 1983. Built in 1886 as one of Cedarburg's earliest hotels, it was being used in the late 20th century to house a vacuum cleaner shop, a law firm, and a dental office on the first floor and apartments on the second floor. (Courtesy of Jim and Sandy Pape.)

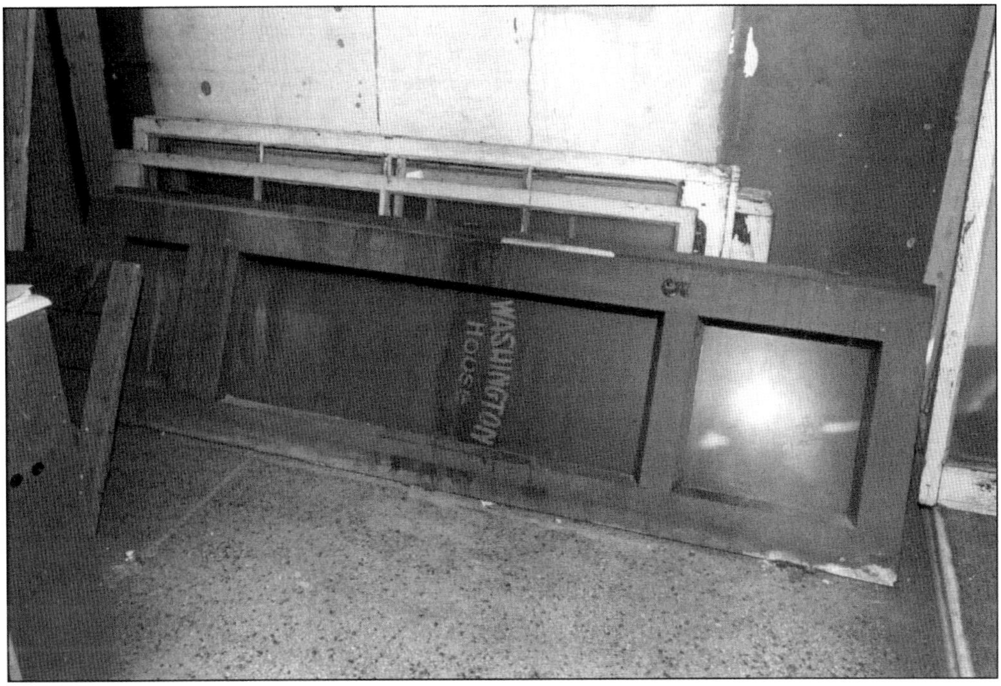

The Papes took this photograph of an unused door lying among the items stored in the old hotel. They put the door to use in the restored inn. They also studied old photographs of the hotel to restore the hotel to the look of its original facade. (Courtesy of Jim and Sandy Pape.)

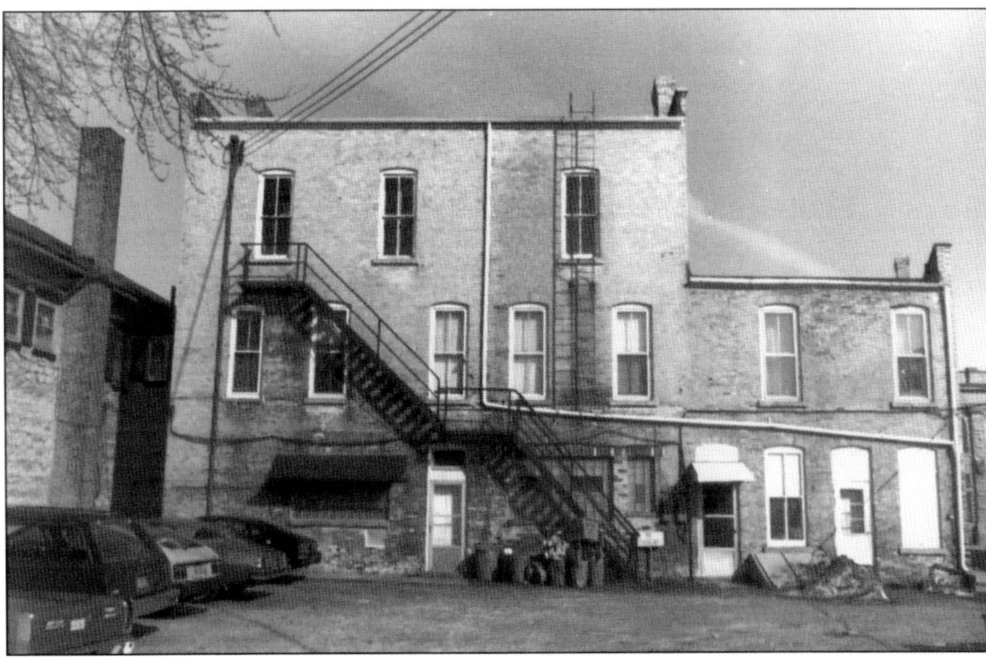

This photograph shows the back of the old Washington House Inn before its restoration in the early 1980s. The outside staircase was removed and the building's exterior was renovated as the back entrance to the inn. The rooms are now named after the city's pioneers, including the William Schroeder Room and the Frederich Roebken Room. (Courtesy of Jim and Sandy Pape.)

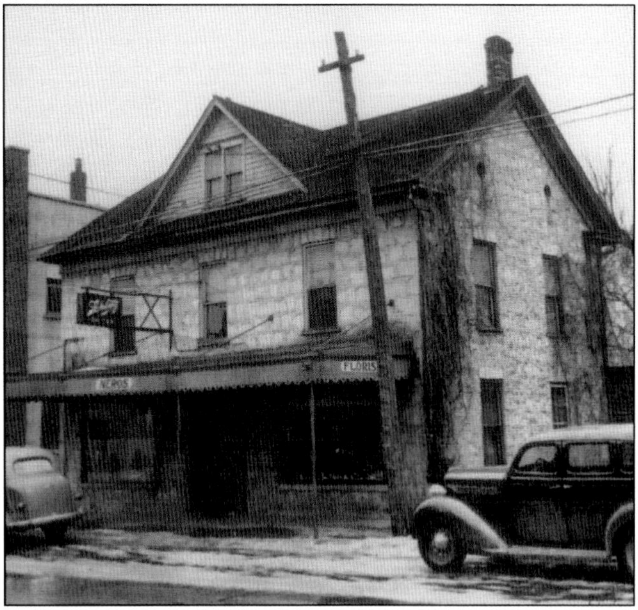

Cedarburg's other inn is also a restored old hotel. Originally called the Central House Hotel, it boasted fine liquors and fine cigars. Of course, the hotel's tavern was only for men in its early days. The inn changed hands in the 1880s when the Neros bought it and renamed it Nero's Tavern and Hotel. The Nero family bought it in the 1880s and kept it through the 1980s. For many years, the Nero family was also in the floral business. They maintained a greenhouse on the site where a medical building now sits on Mill Street. (Courtesy of Brook and Liz Brown.)

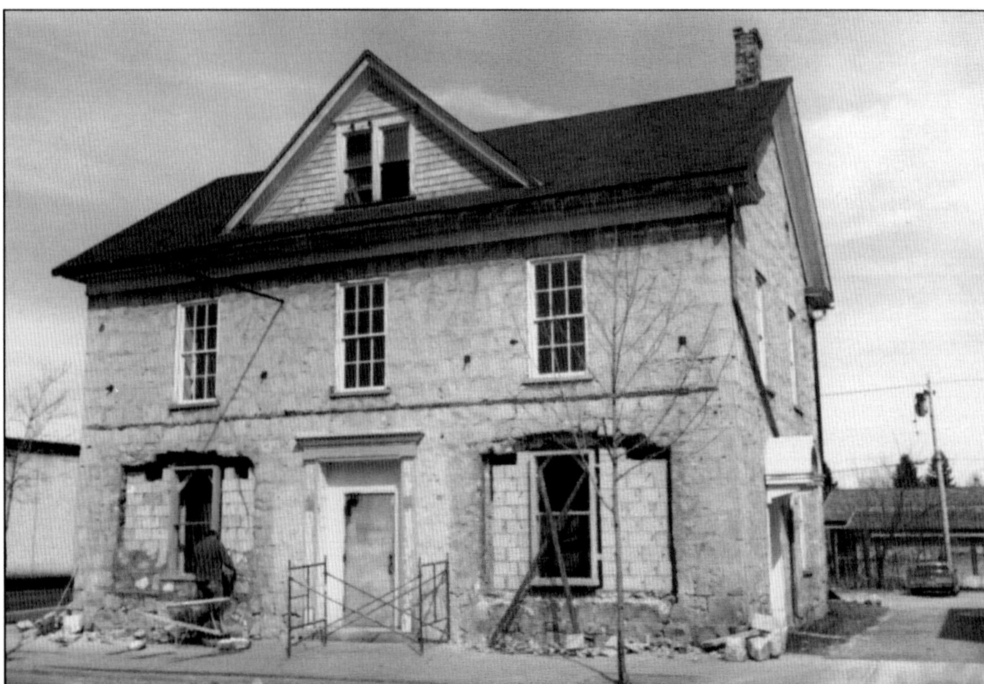

When Brook and Liz Brown bought the old Nero Hotel in 1983, the city held five-and-a-half pages of condemnation notices on the building because of the numerous code violations. Nero's Tavern was the main operation at the time, and the hotel was essentially a flop house, renting rooms for cheap. In this image, restoration begins on the old hotel, which the Browns renamed the Stagecoach Inn. (Courtesy of Brook and Liz Brown.)

Most of the improvements to the Stagecoach Inn were done by the Browns themselves, even though both held full-time jobs as teachers at the time. They studied historical photographs as reference points during the restoration. Most of the hallways, doors, stairs, and woodwork are original today. In this photograph, Liz Brown paints one of the rooms. (Courtesy of Brook and Liz Brown.)

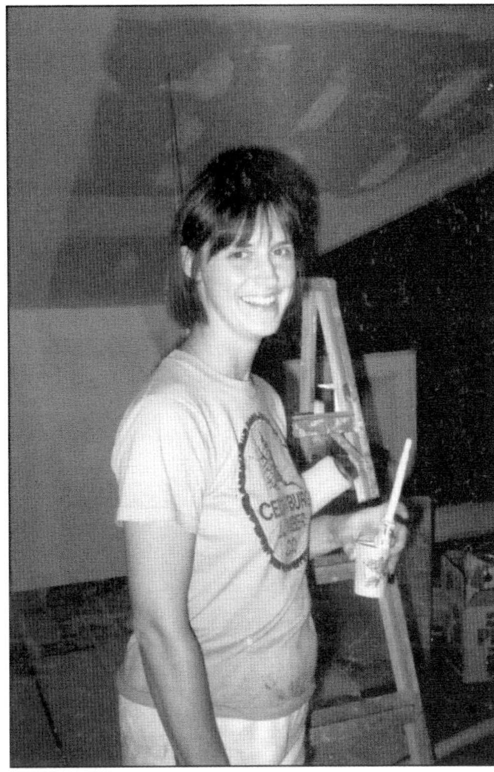

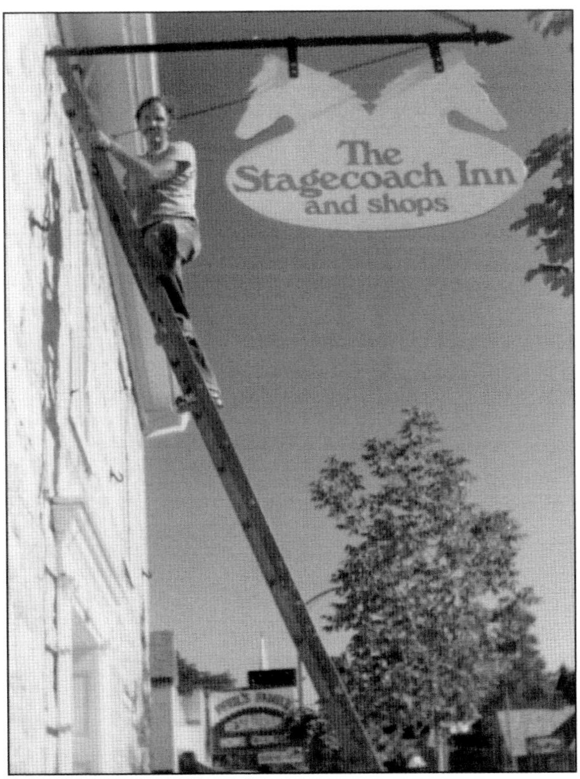

The Browns are only the third owners in the building's 153-year-history. When they first opened it to guests, they had four rooms. The Browns kept working on the building, continuing to the third floor. Today, the inn has 13 rooms and a garden in the back. A candy store is also located in the Stagecoach building. Here, Brook Brown makes repairs to the roof during restoration. (Courtesy of Brook and Liz Brown.)

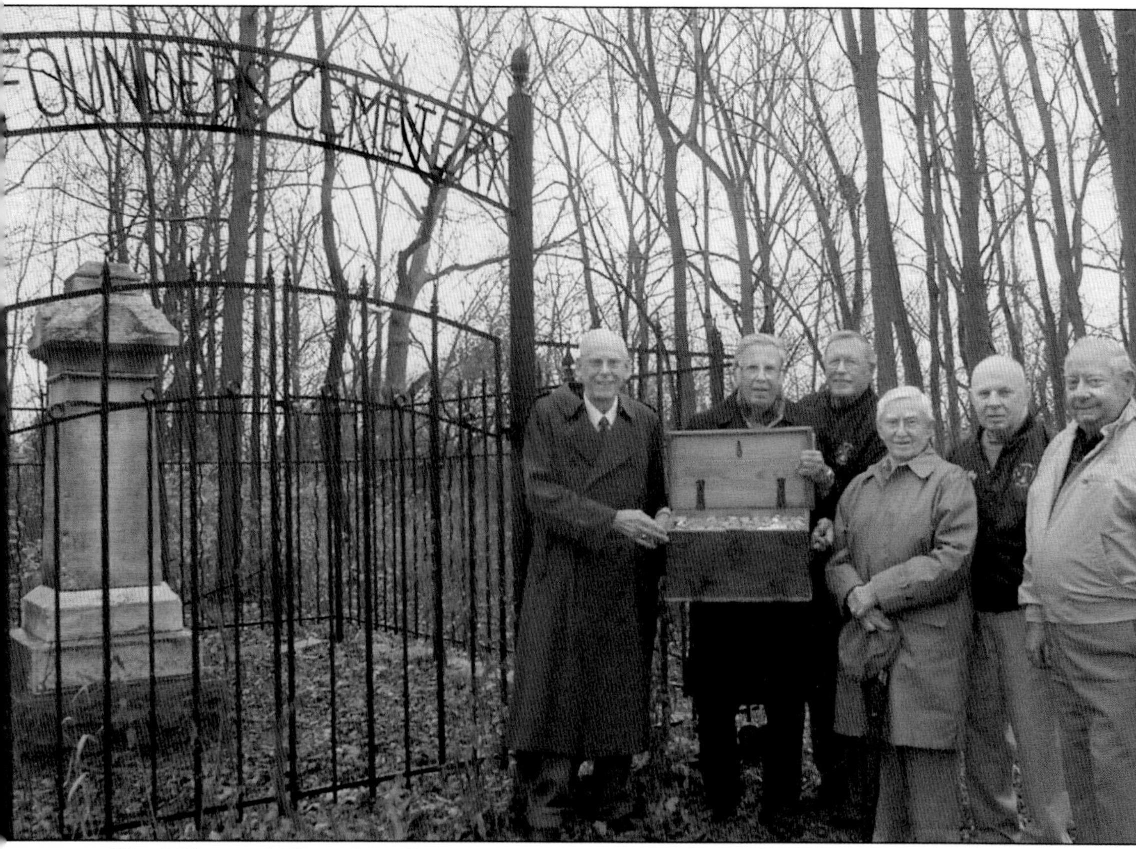

The 167-year-old Founders Cemetery was overrun with weeds in 1966 when the Cedarburg Landmarks Commission decided the city's earliest residents needed a more dignified burial site. The city purchased it, and concerned residents took to cleaning it up. Founders Park was dedicated on July 3, 1976, as part of the nation's bicentennial celebration. These men, some of those involved in the cleanup, are pictured with a chest of coins the founders brought with them from Germany. Pictured from left to right are Bob Armbruster, Ron Kraft, former mayor Jim Coutts, Palmer Krueger, Allen Boerner, and Ed Rappold. (Photograph by Mark Justesen, courtesy of the *News Graphic*.)

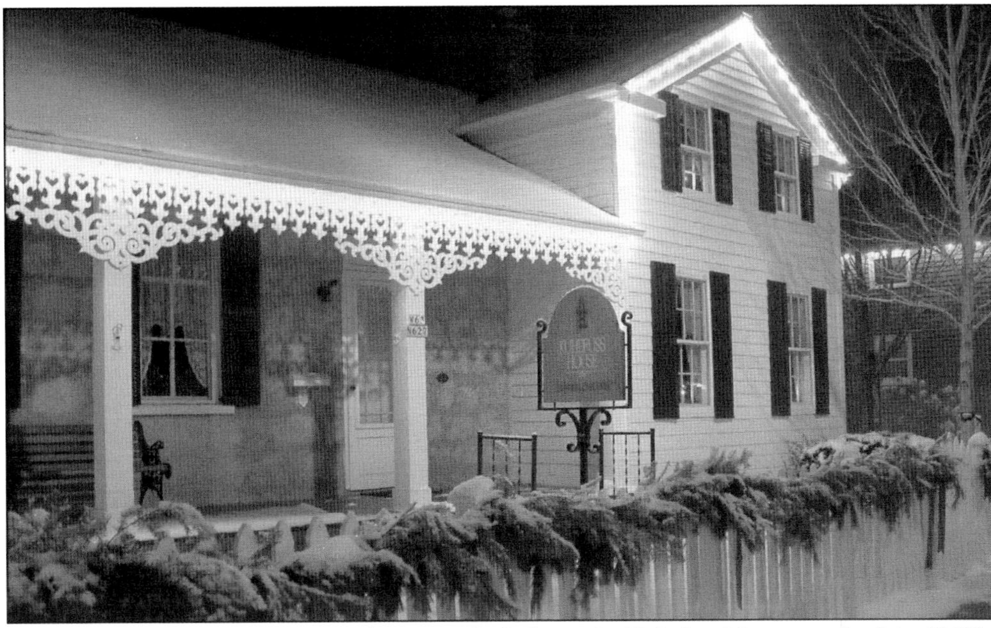

One of the first German American homes in Cedarburg, the Kuhefuss House, was built in 1849 by George Fisher. In 1854, German immigrant Edward Blank purchased the house, and for the next 135 years, five generations of Blank and Kuhefuss families lived there. One of the sole survivors of the families was Marie Kuhefuss, a schoolteacher who never married. When she died in 1989, she left the home and its furnishings to the Cedarburg Cultural Center, which maintains it as a museum today. (Photograph by Deb Kranitz.)

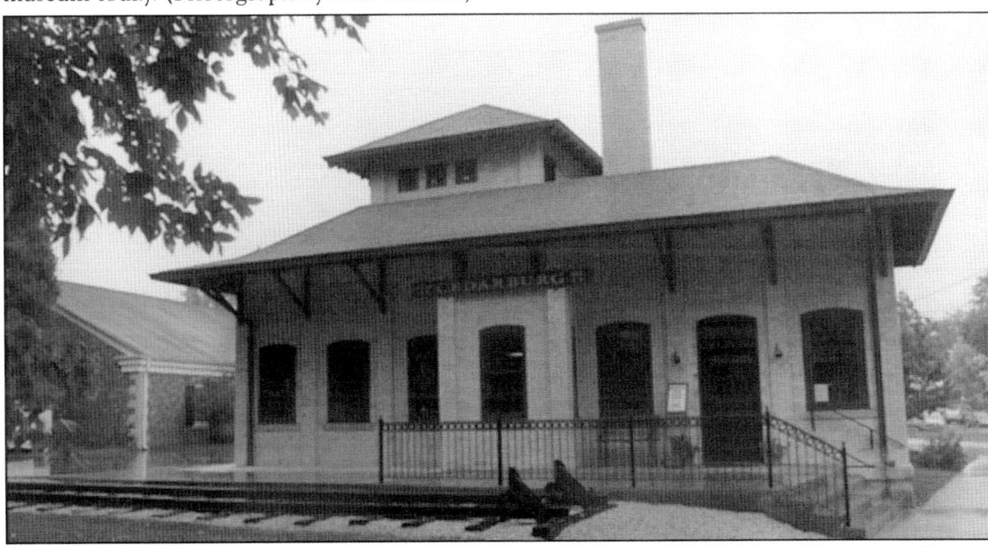

The former interurban railway depot underwent a major renovation in the early part of the 21st century. The building, which was owned by the city of Cedarburg, received a new paint job and new decking. Copper gutters were added, and the interior was restored to its original splendor from the days when passengers waited for the train to take them to points north and south. The city of Cedarburg transferred ownership of the building to the Ozaukee County Historical Society in 2003, and the depot now houses the archives research center for the historical society. (Photograph by Mark Justesen, courtesy of the *News Graphic*.)

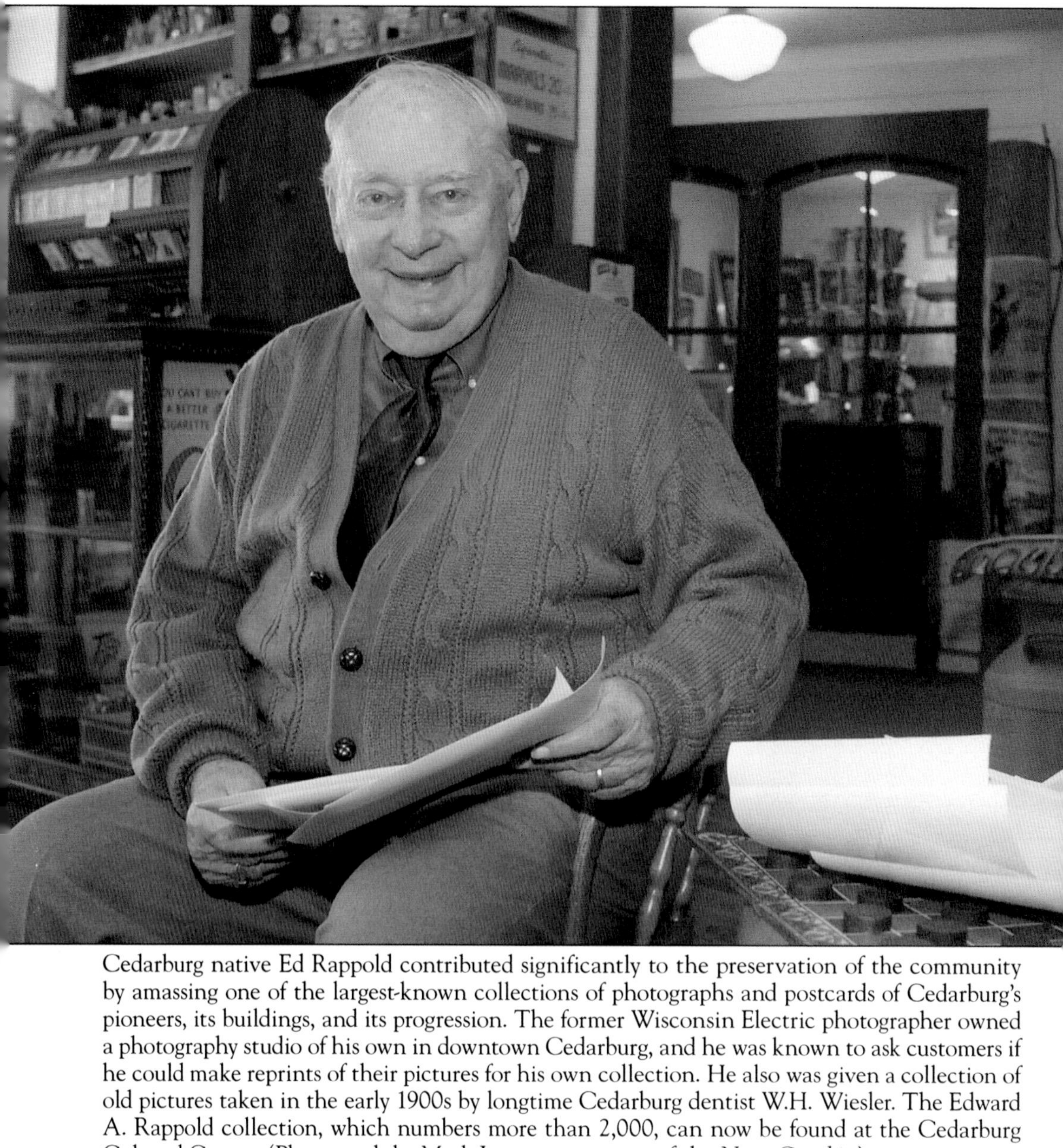

Cedarburg native Ed Rappold contributed significantly to the preservation of the community by amassing one of the largest-known collections of photographs and postcards of Cedarburg's pioneers, its buildings, and its progression. The former Wisconsin Electric photographer owned a photography studio of his own in downtown Cedarburg, and he was known to ask customers if he could make reprints of their pictures for his own collection. He also was given a collection of old pictures taken in the early 1900s by longtime Cedarburg dentist W.H. Wiesler. The Edward A. Rappold collection, which numbers more than 2,000, can now be found at the Cedarburg Cultural Center. (Photograph by Mark Justesen, courtesy of the *News Graphic*.)

Longtime Ozaukee County Clerk Harold C. Dobberpuhl developed a love of photography while in high school in Milwaukee. He later published pictures for various newspapers in Ozaukee County and southeastern Wisconsin, winning first place in the pictorial category of the 1956 photograph contest of the Wisconsin Press Photographer's Association. His hundreds of photographs of Ozaukee County, including many in Cedarburg, were later published in several books. (Courtesy of the *News Graphic*.)

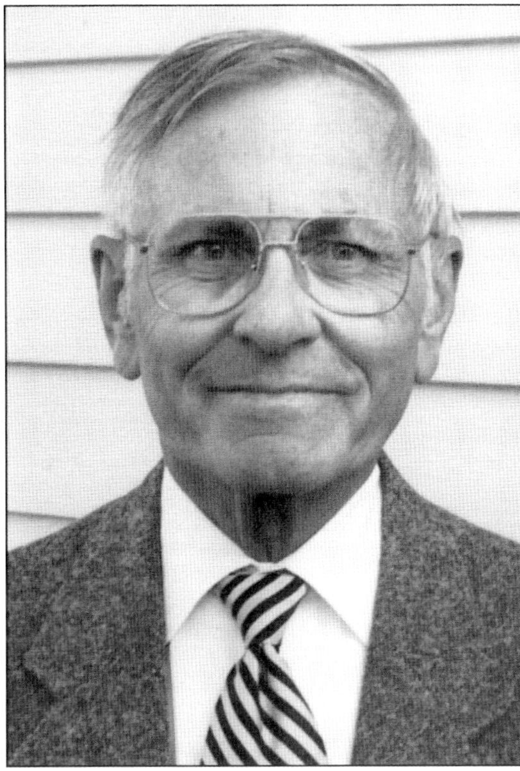

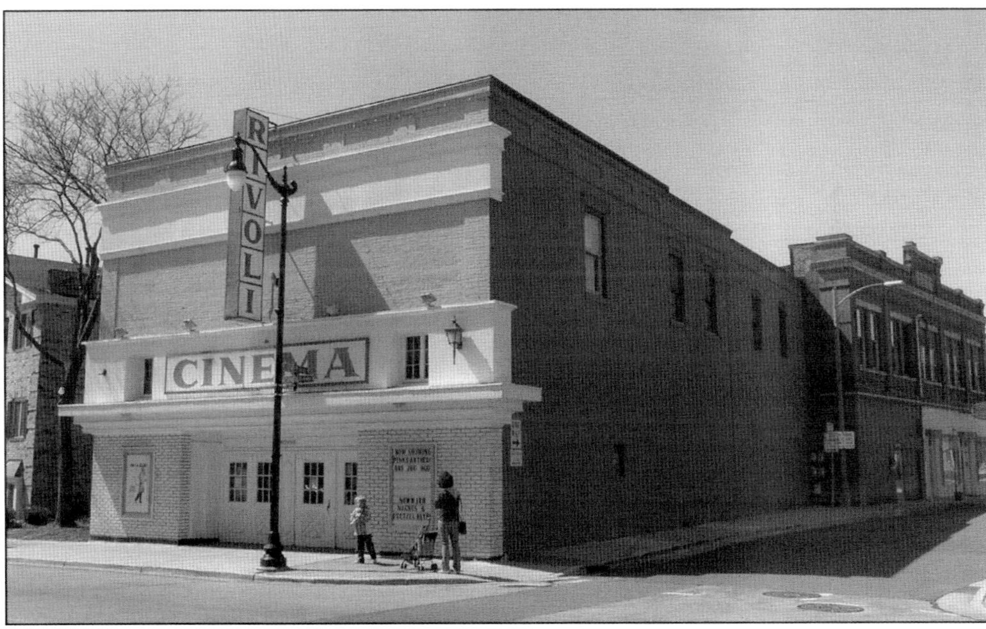

Generations of Cedarburg residents hold fond memories of their visits to the Rivoli Theatre, whether it was the place for a first date or a family outing. Marcus Theatres leased the space for decades, but when there was talk that an investment company might buy the building and turn it into retail space, the Cedarburg Landmark Preservation Society stepped in and bought it in 2005. (Photograph by Mark Justesen, courtesy of the *News Graphic*.)

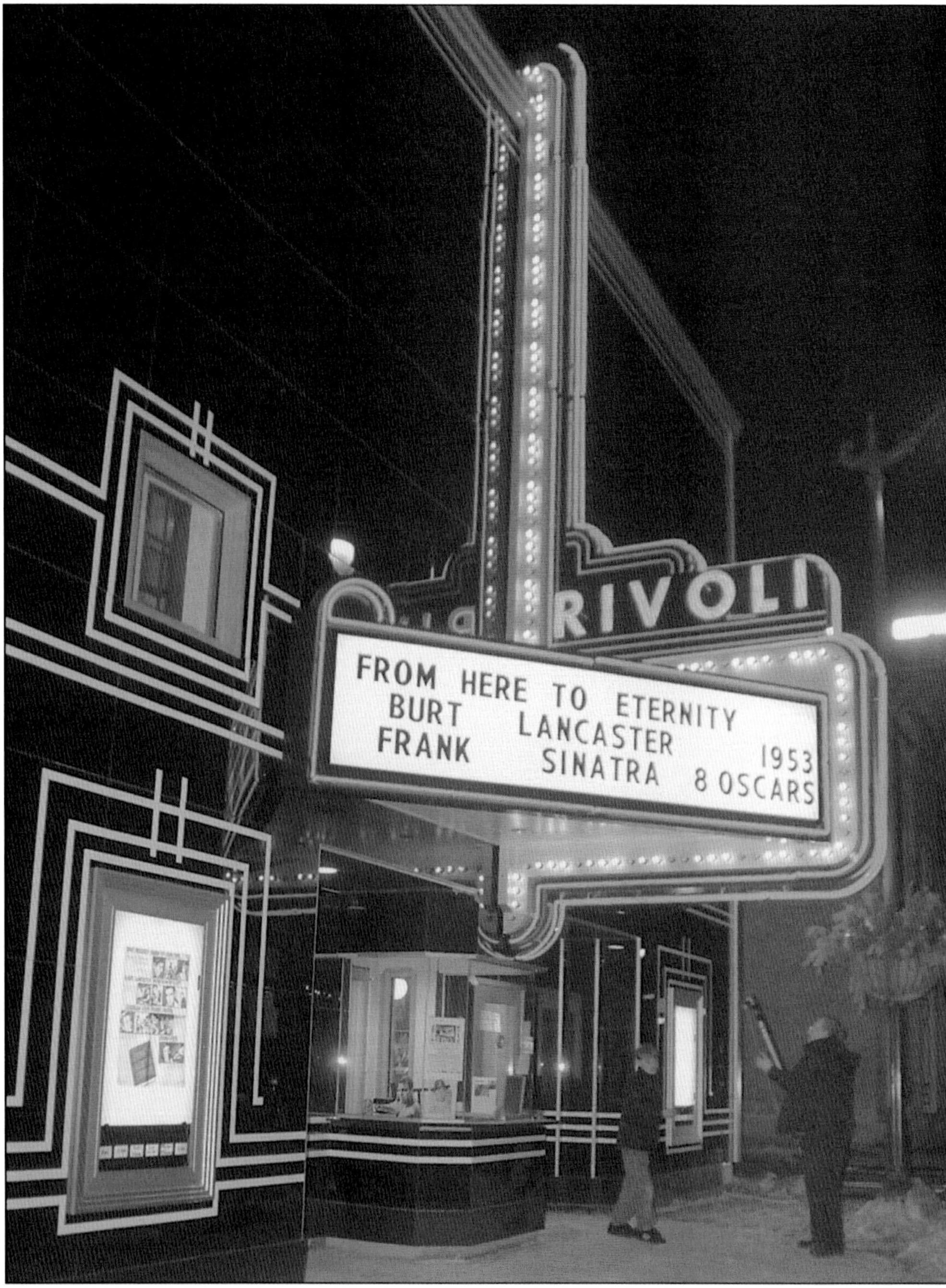

The restoration and operation of the Rivoli Theatre showed the very best of Cedarburg community spirit. Local organizations and residents contributed an estimated $1 million to restore the theater to its original 1930s decor, including an Art Deco facade of black Carrara glass, chrome trim, an Electrolite Silhouette marquee and sidewalk ticket booth, and interior changes. Perhaps most unique of all, the theater is operated almost exclusively by volunteers from throughout Cedarburg and surrounding communities, who sell tickets and run the concession counter. (Photograph by Mark Justesen, courtesy of the *News Graphic*.)

A group of Cedarburg residents recognized the importance of keeping the community's history and the stories of its older residents alive. In February 2000, they created the Cedarburg Fireside Chats, held at the Cedarburg Cultural Center, which invite a panel of residents to talk about their memories. Topics have included the Cedarburg fire department, the city's founders, churches, and family farms. Former mayor Jim Coutts (right) serves as the moderator. (Photograph by Mark Justesen, courtesy of the *News Graphic*.)

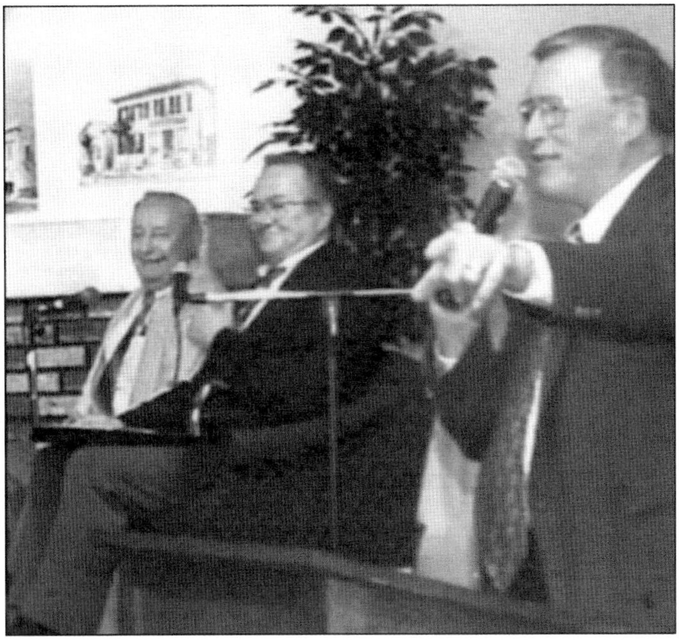

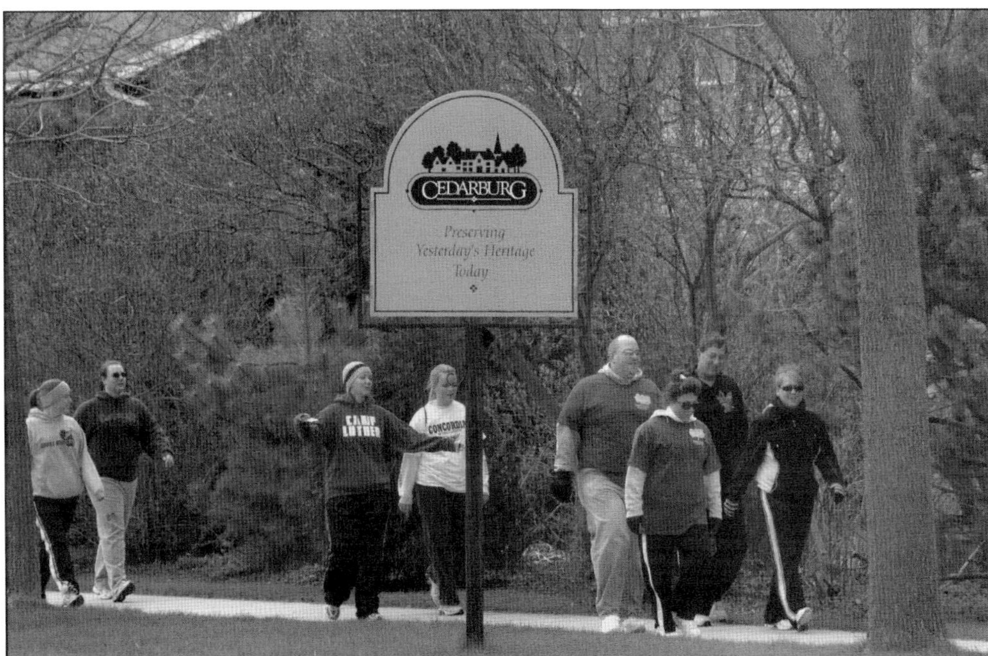

Cedarburg's embrace of its history was formally worked into the city's slogan, "Preserving Yesterday's Heritage Today." The logo was designed by Vic DiCristo, a graphic designer, musician, and Cedarburg resident. Here, walkers participate in a fundraising event along the Ozaukee Interurban Trail, a 30-mile paved pedestrian and bike trail that follows the old interurban railway line. (Photograph by Deb Kranitz.)

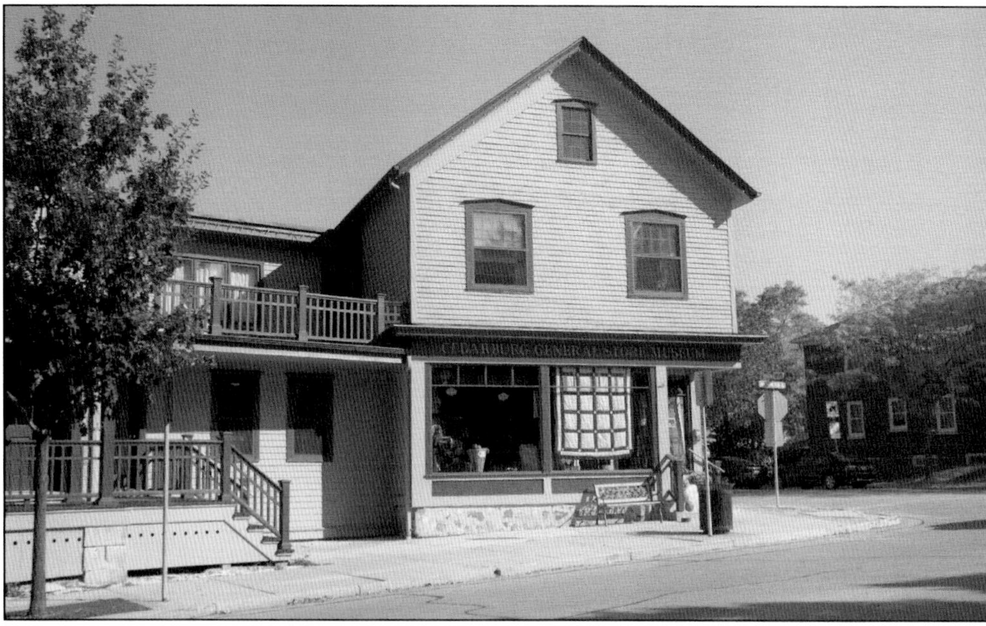

What was once the local A&P store on the corner of Washington Avenue and Spring Street was converted to the General Store Museum and the offices of the Cedarburg Chamber of Commerce in 1998. The 1860s-era frame building was restored by the Cedarburg Landmark Preservation Society. Staffed by volunteers, the General Store Museum is one of the first stops for tourists in Cedarburg. (Photograph by Mark Bertieri.)

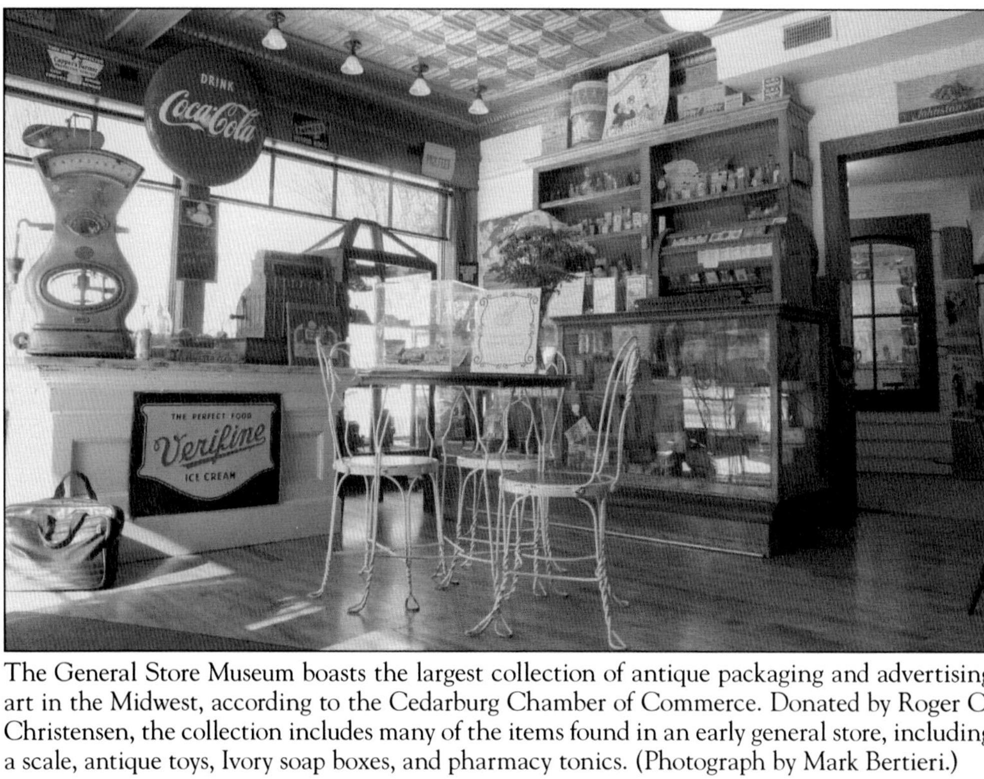

The General Store Museum boasts the largest collection of antique packaging and advertising art in the Midwest, according to the Cedarburg Chamber of Commerce. Donated by Roger C. Christensen, the collection includes many of the items found in an early general store, including a scale, antique toys, Ivory soap boxes, and pharmacy tonics. (Photograph by Mark Bertieri.)

Eight

TODAY

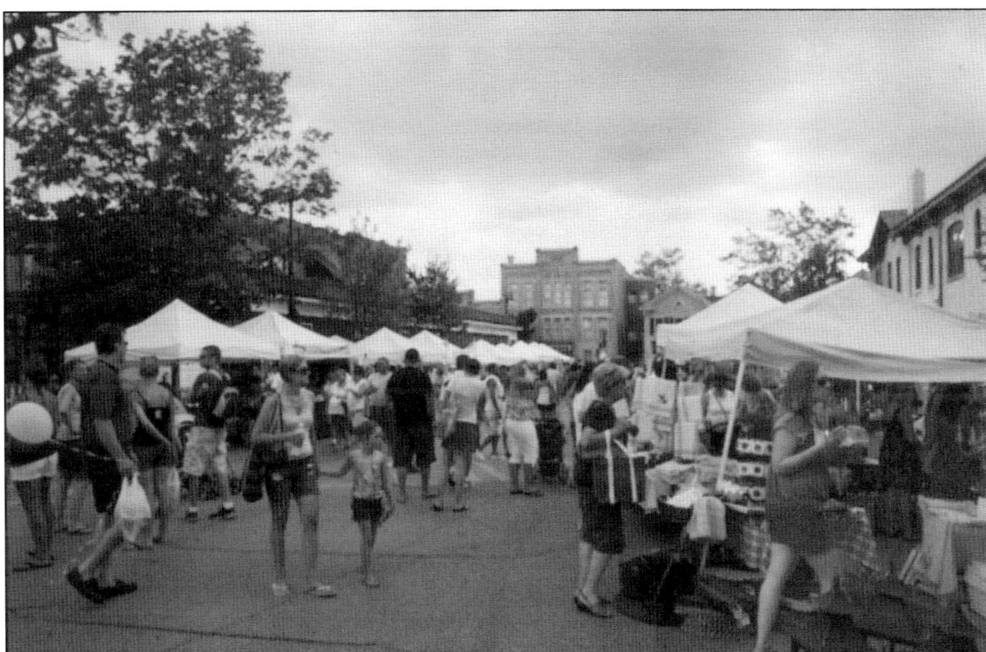

Started in 1985, the Cedarburg Strawberry Festival attracts thousands of visitors from around the Midwest for its fresh strawberries, homemade strawberry brats, and locally made strawberry wine. Just as important is the event's celebration of the arts. Closed to traffic for two days, Washington Avenue is an arts mecca, with artists of every medium displaying their wares. The Cedarburg Cultural Center also hosts an art show during the weekend. It is estimated that the Strawberry Festival attracts around 90,000 people in its two-day run. (Photograph by Mark Justesen, courtesy of the *News Graphic*.)

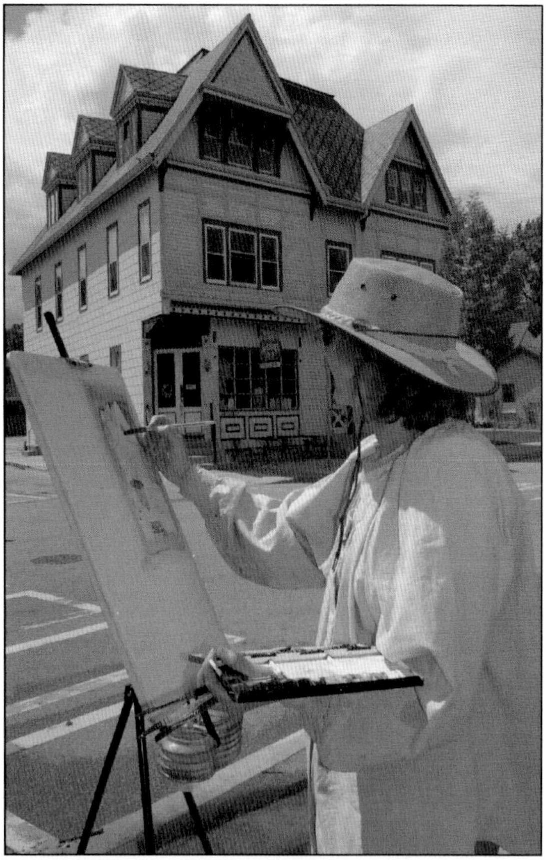

The plein air outdoor painting competition became a part of the Strawberry Festival in 2001 with the guiding hand of artist Sandy Pape. Today, painters can be seen throughout Cedarburg in the latter part of June, capturing the historic architecture and natural beauty. In this photograph, an artist paints the Settlers Inn at the corner of Washington Avenue and Cleveland Street. (Photograph by Deb Kranitz.)

The woolen mill that fell into disrepair in the 1960s is now one of the main attractions for visitors to the city. A plein air painter captures on canvas both the former blacksmith shop, which was converted to a restaurant in 2007, and the Cedar Creek Winery to the right. (Photograph by Deb Kranitz.)

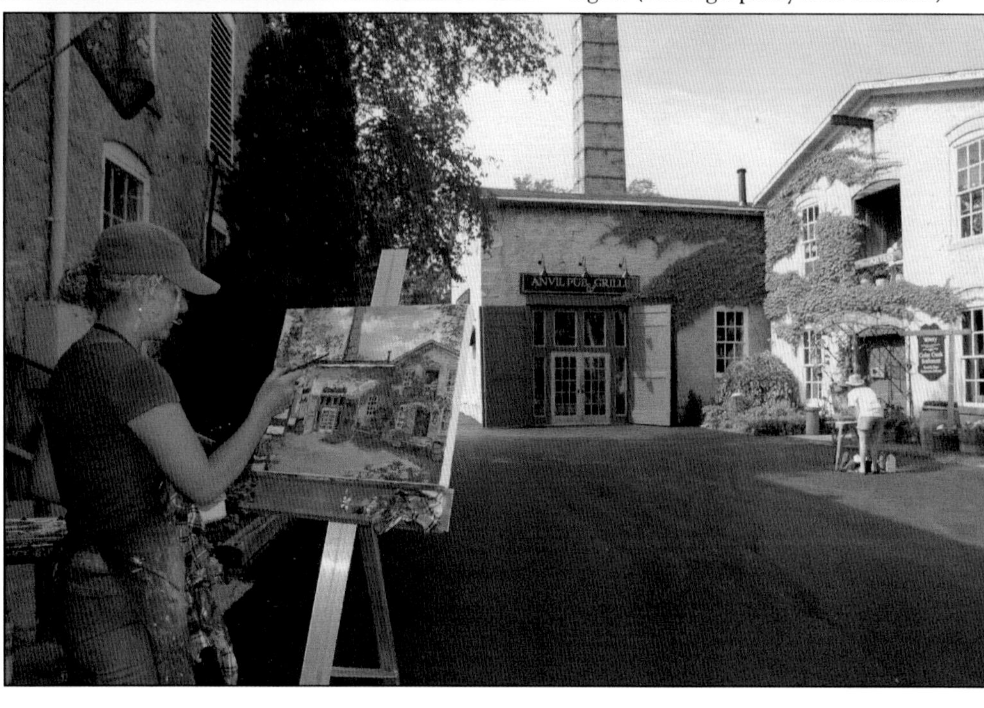

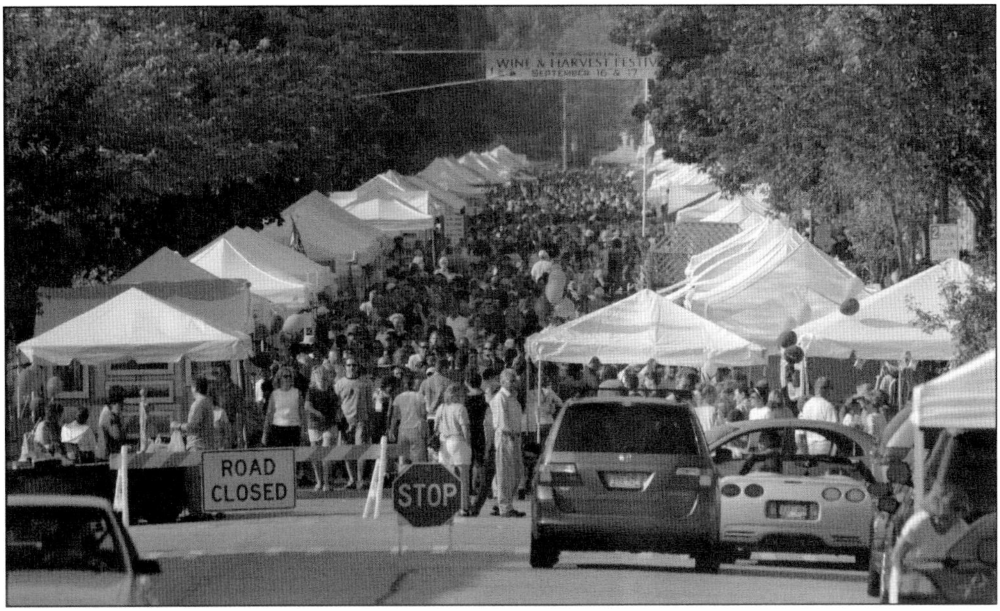

The Wine and Harvest Festival was started in 1972, and it not only launched the wines of the Cedar Creek Winery, but planted the seeds for three other annual festivals in the city. The Wine and Harvest Festival attracts an estimated 70,000 people during its two-day run each September. Events include a grape-stomping contest, pumpkin painting, and a pumpkin regatta on Cedar Creek. (Photograph by Deb Kranitz.)

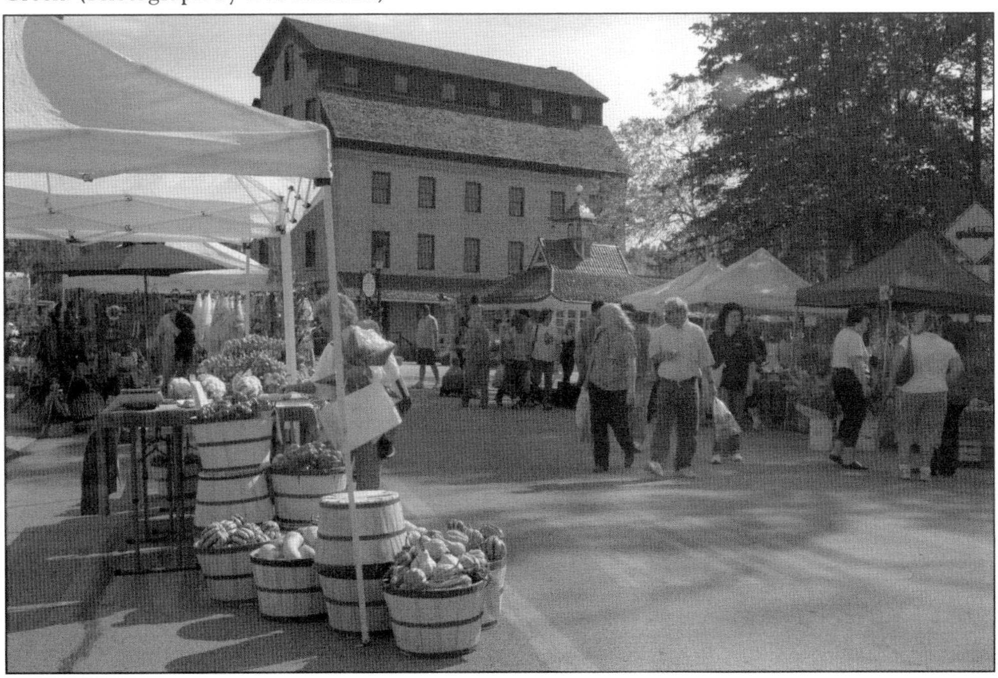

The 156-year-old gristmill serves as a backdrop every year to a farmers market held during the Wine and Harvest Festival. Farmers from around the region bring their fresh fruits, vegetables, and flowers to the farmers market area of the festival on Columbia Road. A hay wagon provides shuttle service to different areas of the festival. (Photograph by Deb Kranitz.)

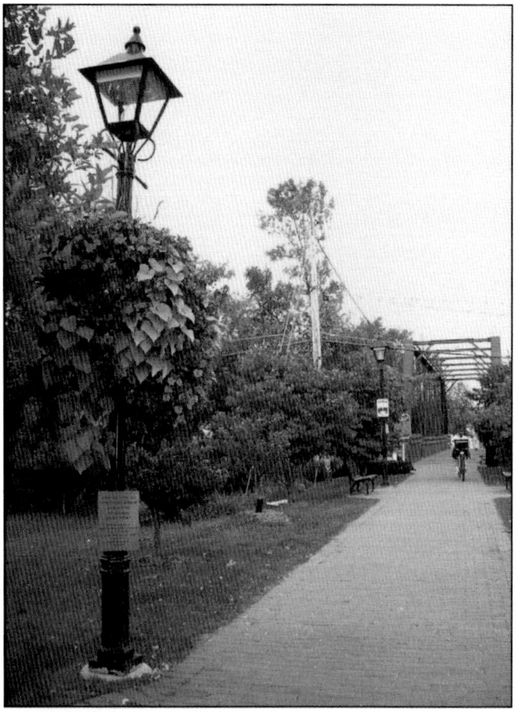

The interurban railway line that once connected Cedarburg with Milwaukee and Sheboygan is now a 30-mile paved path called the Ozaukee Interurban Trail, which spans Ozaukee County and cuts through the heart of Cedarburg. An estimated 5,000 bikers, walkers, runners, and others use the trail daily. Charity walks are often held along it, such as the Pig-to-Pig Walk from the Piggly Wiggly store in Cedarburg to the Piggly Wiggly store in Mequon. (Photograph by Deb Kranitz.)

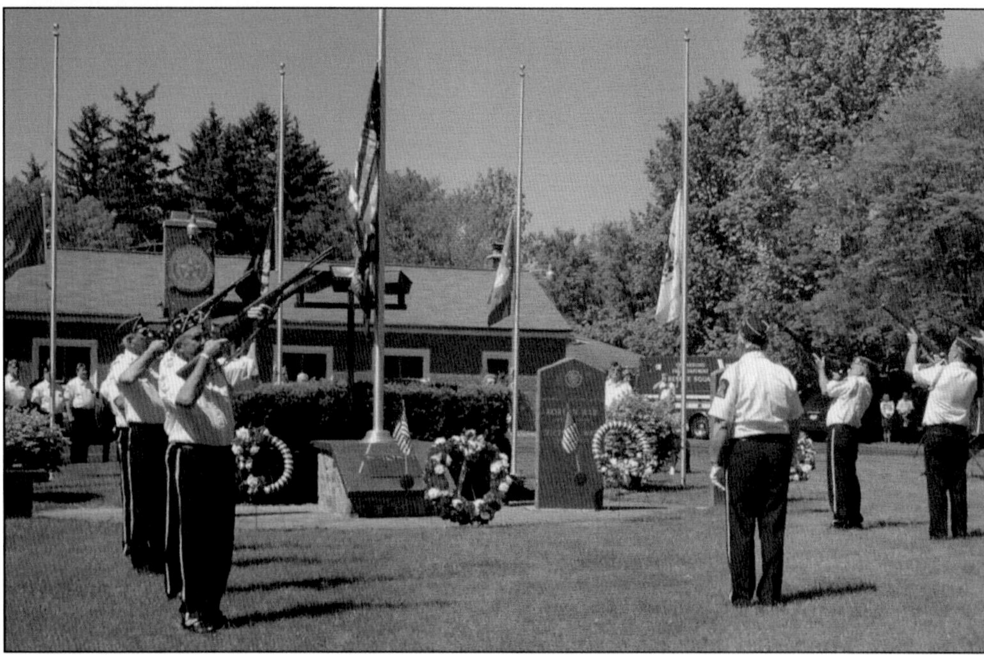

The Peter Wollner American Legion Post 288 has been an important member of the Cedarburg community since its charter was granted in 1920. The post not only provides support and camaraderie to its members, but its veterans visit schools and the elderly, hold a Memorial Day celebration, host a monthly fish fry, and volunteer throughout the community. The post sponsors local students to participate in Boys State and provides scholarships to local students. (Photograph by Mark Justesen, courtesy of the *News Graphic*.)

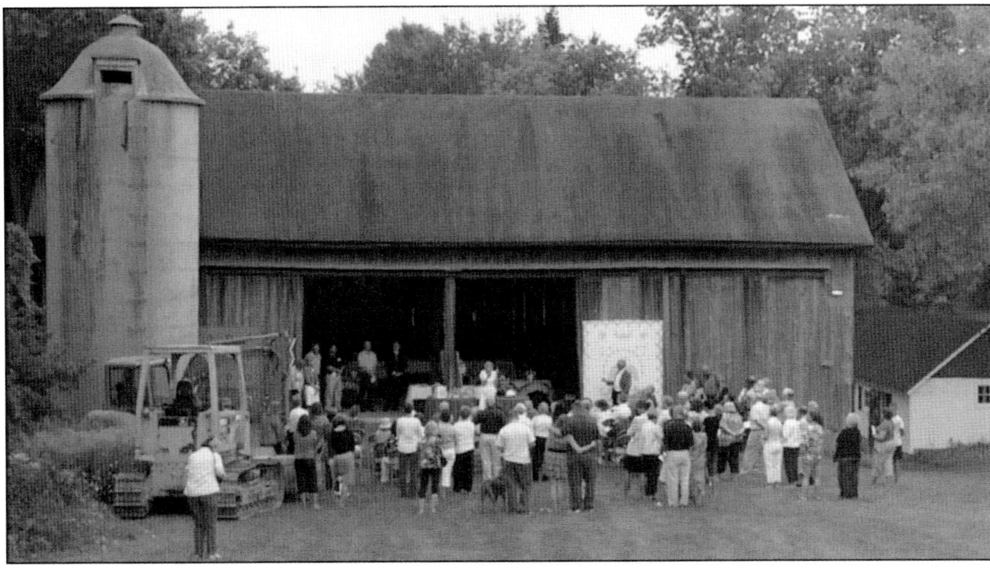

The former Hoffman-Boeker farmstead is now home to the Wisconsin Museum of Quilts and Textiles, which provides rotating exhibits, classes, and talks. Here, a crowd gathered in 2010 to kick off a major renovation project, which involves lifting the 155-year-old barn and laying a new foundation that will be made to look historical. A 2,689-square-foot, two-story building will be added to the north side of the barn and will include the main entryway and lobby, gift shop, catering kitchen, director's office, bathrooms, and an elevator. (Photograph by Deb Kranitz.)

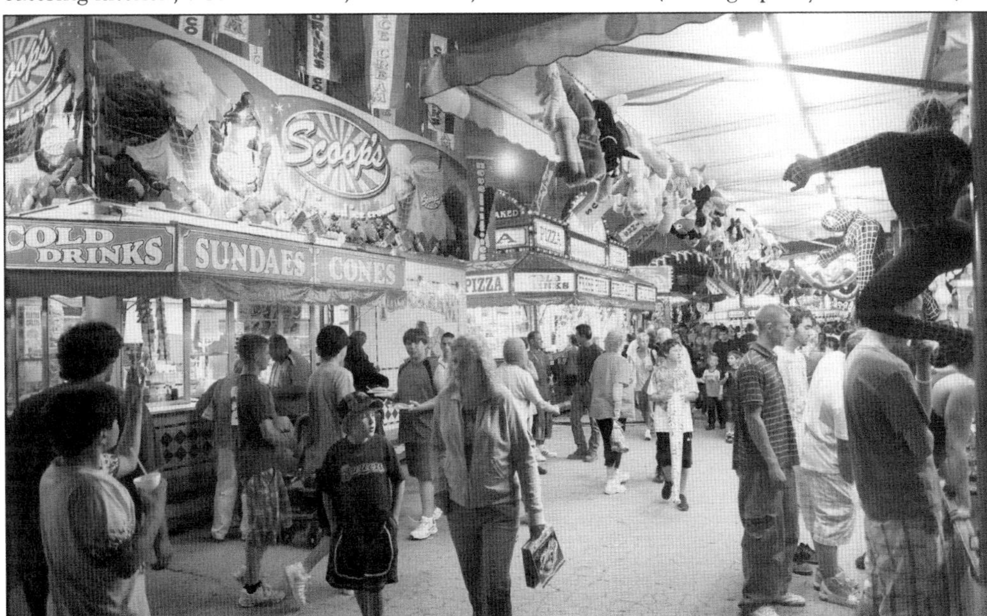

The Ozaukee County Fair celebrated its 150th anniversary in 2009 on the same grounds where the first fair was held in 1859. Much has changed, of course, like the bright lights and fast rides of the midway. Today's entertainment includes a teen battle of the bands, demolition derby, and an Ozaukee Idol singing contest. But much has remained the same, such as the 4-H exhibits, the animals, and the certainty that individuals and families will have a memorable time. It also remains one of the only free county fairs in the state. (Photograph by Mark Justesen, courtesy of the *News Graphic*.)

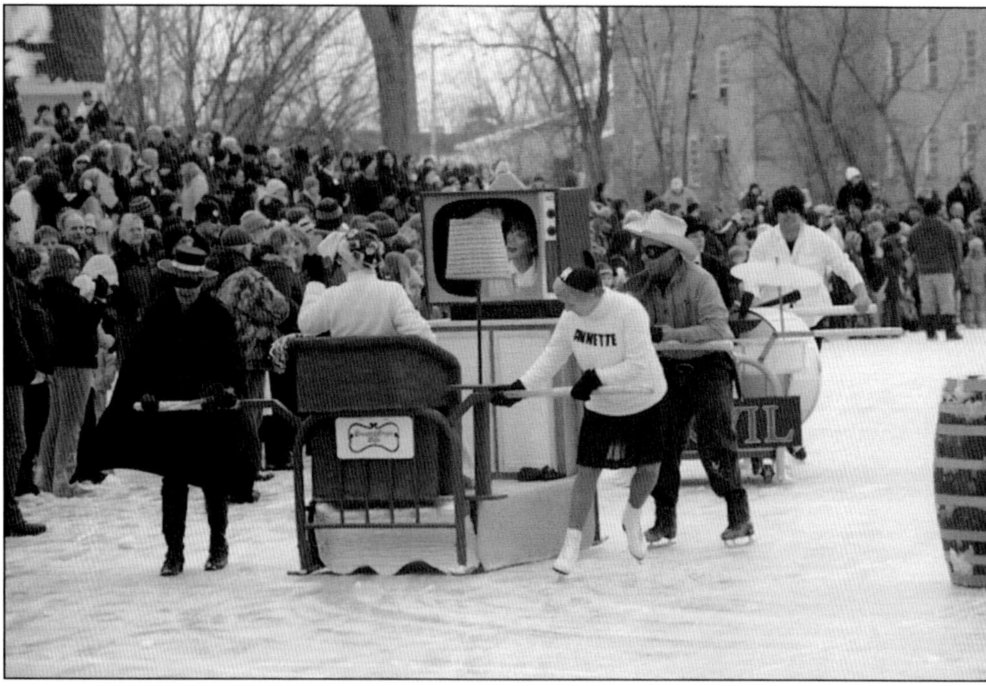

Cedarburg's Winter Festival has been held one weekend each February since 1974. The cold weather means it is not as well attended as the summer Strawberry Festival, but this uniquely local event attracts about 10,000 people to activities like the winter parade, snowshoe olympics, chili cook-off, Cedar-Ice-Burg golf open, and pancake breakfast. One of the most popular events is the bed races on the frozen Cedar Creek, pictured. Local businesses and schools form teams to decorate a bed and race it on the ice. (Photograph by Mark Justesen, courtesy of the *News Graphic*.)

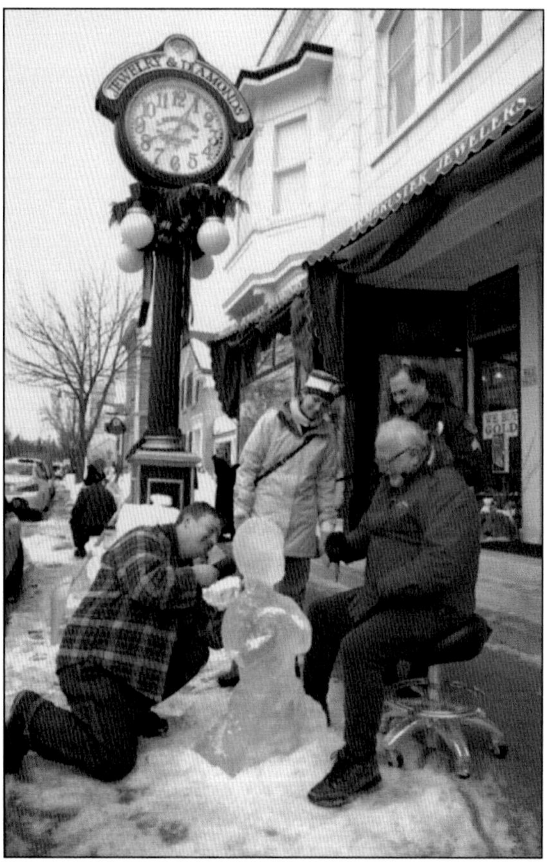

Another draw of the Cedarburg Winter Festival is the ice-sculpting, which pairs the fun of winter with Cedarburg's love of the arts. Sculptures must fit in with the theme of the festival each year. In 2011, there were two different Marilyn Monroe sculptures for the "Nifty Fifties" theme. Here, sculptors create a bust of Lucille Ball. (Photograph by Deb Kranitz.)

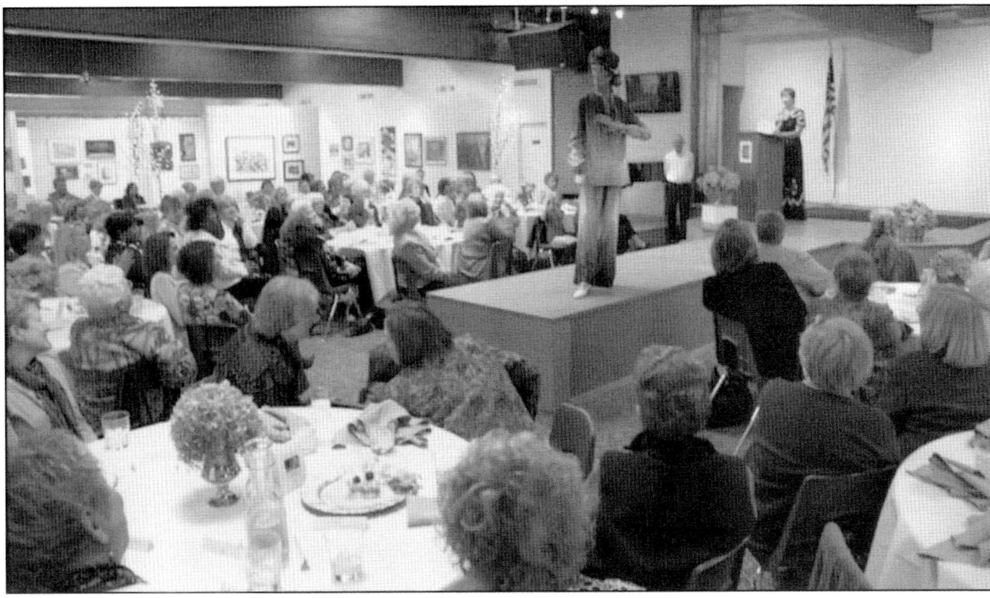

The Cedarburg Cultural Center was born in 1988, following a grassroots effort by those who wanted a place to preserve Cedarburg's many keepsakes as well as honor the city's love of the arts. The center now provides a museum, performing arts, visual arts, and classes. It operates the Kuhefuss House Museum and the General Store Museum. It is also the repository for thousands of historical photographs, including the Ed Rappold Collection. In this image, guests enjoy the Fashion through the Ages show. (Courtesy of the *News Graphic*.)

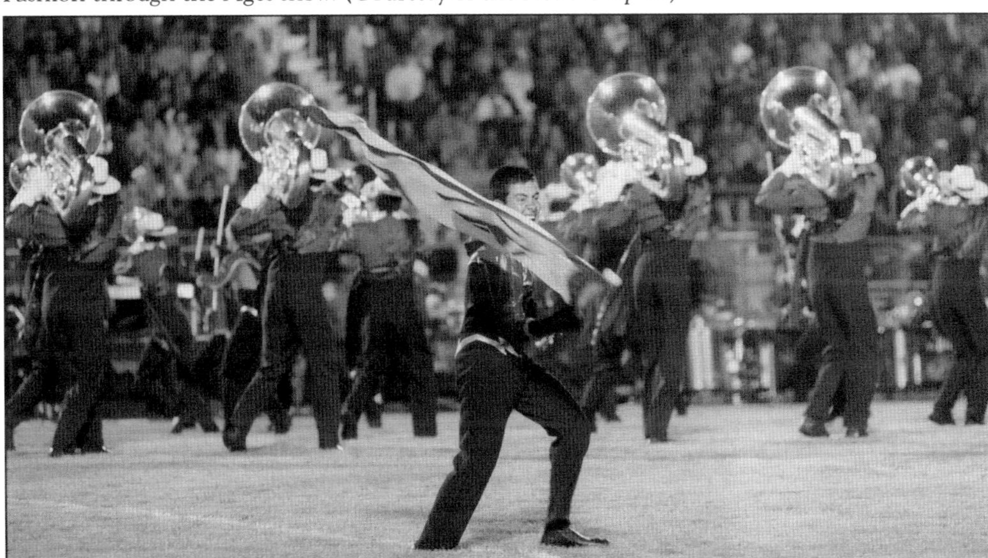

The Cedarburg Music Festival was an important tradition in Cedarburg in the 1970s and 1980s, but it disappeared in the late 1980s due to a lack of funding. The festival was resurrected in 2000 by the Cedarburg-Grafton Rotary Club and is held every year on July 3 at the Cedarburg High School Field House. The event features drum and bugle corps from as close as Wisconsin and as distant as Canada. It has raised more than $358,000 since 2000 for student scholarships and community projects. Pictured are the Madison Scouts, an all-male corps based in the state capital. (Photograph by Mark Justesen, courtesy of the *News Graphic*.)

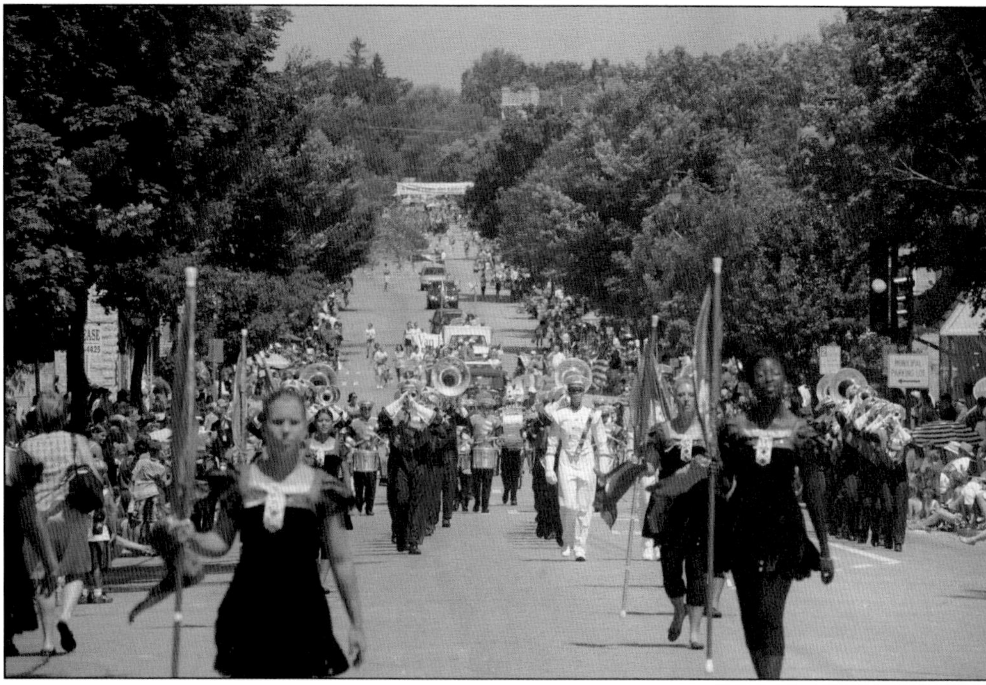

The Cedarburg Fourth of July parade is one of the largest in southeast Wisconsin. Next to Christmas and Thanksgiving, there is probably no holiday more popular among Cedarburg families than the Fourth of July. In 2010, the parade featured more than 100 units, including floats, antique fire trucks, dance troupes, drum and bugle corps, and an electric-powered shoe. One of the crowd favorites is the Goldens on Parade, a unit of up to 50 golden retrievers led by a Mustang convertible. (Photograph by Mark Justesen, courtesy of the *News Graphic*.)

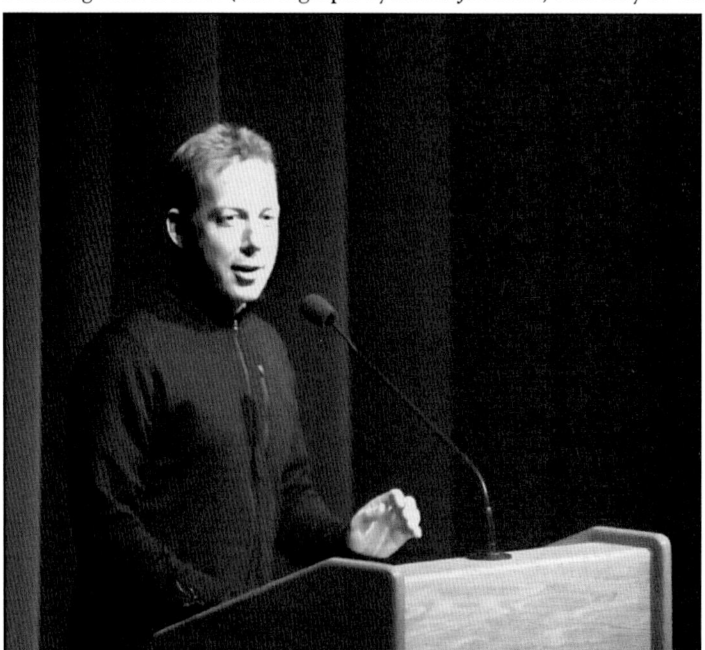

Cedarburg native Eric Larsen was celebrated by his hometown in 2010 with Eric Larsen Day after he became the first person to reach the North Pole, the South Pole, and the summit of Mount Everest within a year. Larsen is an explorer who is also raising awareness about the earth's changing climate. (Photograph by Mark Justesen, courtesy of the *News Graphic*.)

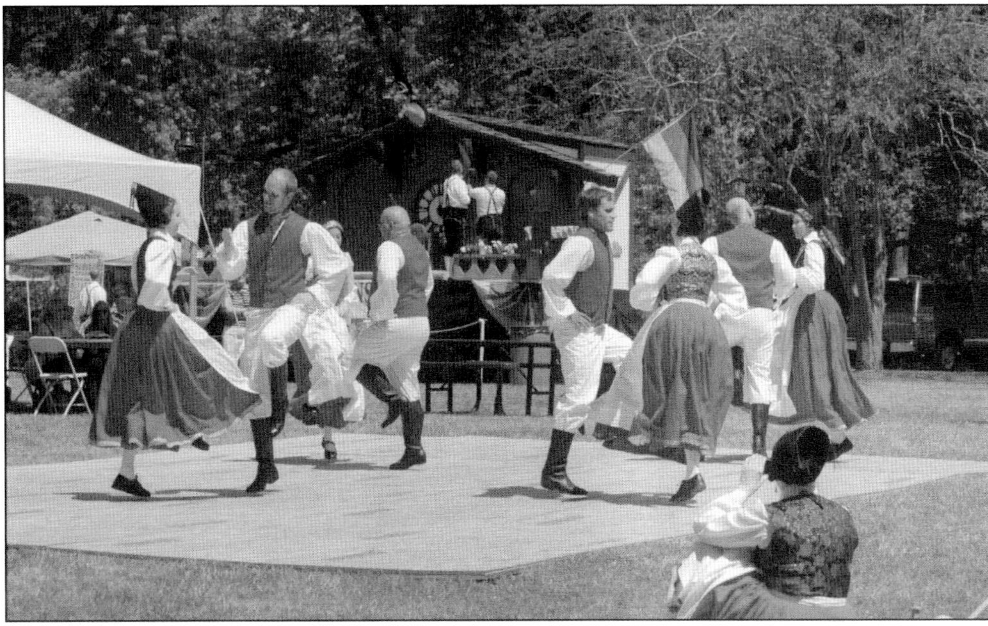

Cedarburg's youngest festival, the German Festival, was started in 2008 to honor the city's heritage. The event celebrates German culture with authentic music, food, games, and dancing. It also provides some unconventional entertainment, such as outhouse races, a German spelling bee, wife-carrying races, beer bucket races, and sauerkraut-eating contests. (Photograph by Deb Kranitz.)

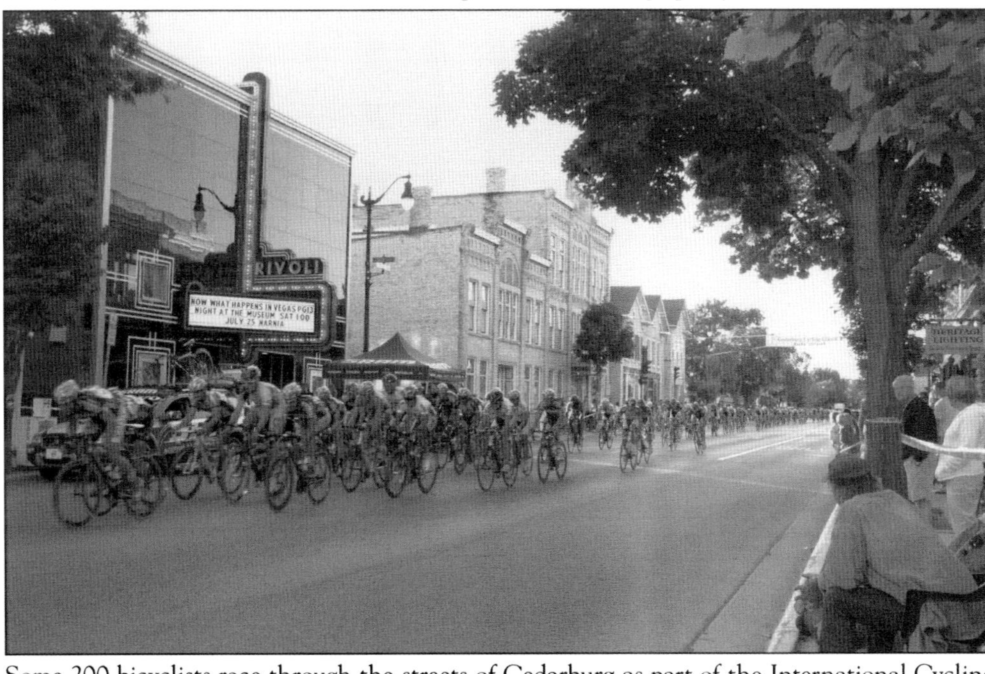

Some 200 bicyclists race through the streets of Cedarburg as part of the International Cycling Classic. The event was held in downtown Cedarburg during the summers of 2006 through 2009. It was part of a 17-city tour for the racers. The city also provided side races around one of the city's three elementary schools for the younger riders. Here, the bicyclists race past the restored Rivoli Theatre. (Photograph by Deb Kranitz.)

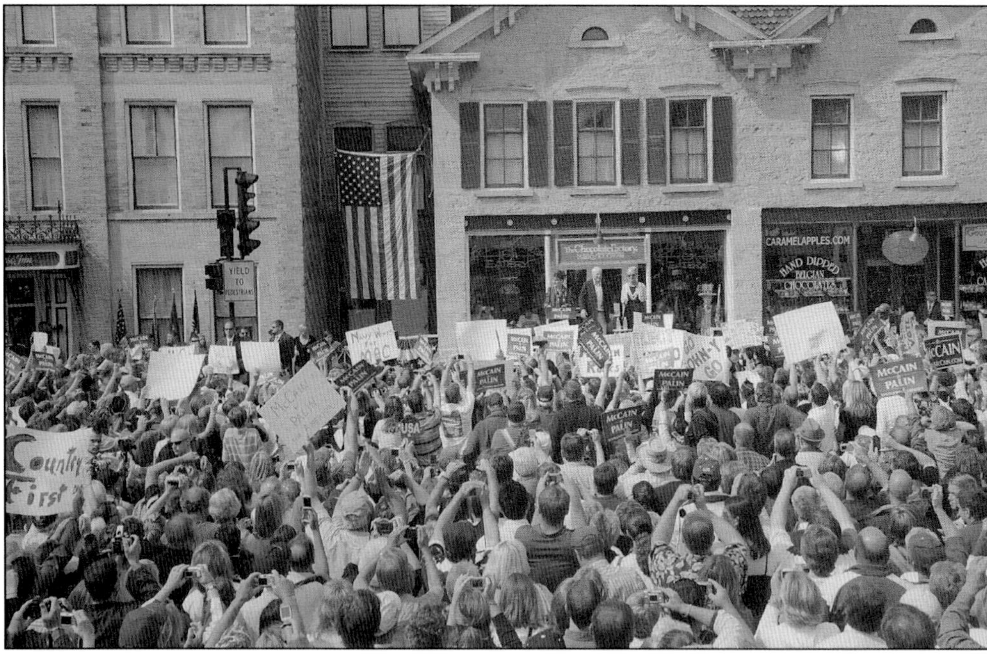

Presidential candidate John McCain and his running mate, Sarah Palin, kick-started their campaign in downtown Cedarburg following the 2008 Republican convention. Palin called Cedarburg "one of the most beautiful towns of all of America." It has been estimated that about 12,000 people attended the rally. (Photograph by Mark Justesen, courtesy of the *News Graphic*.)

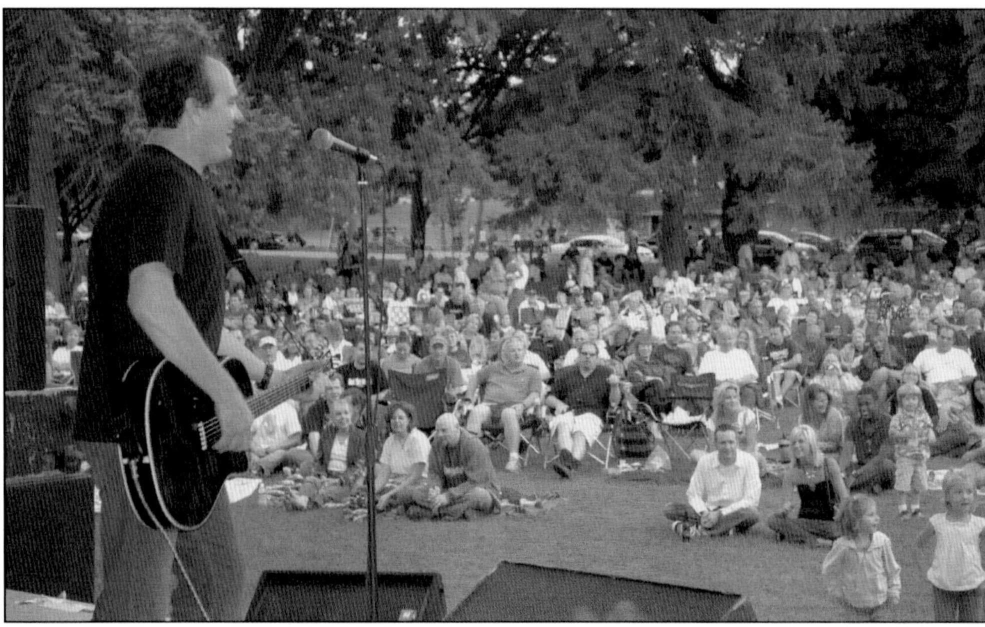

The Summer Sounds music concerts are a vital part of summer in Cedarburg. An estimated 1,500 attend the free concerts held every Friday evening at Cedar Creek Park, overlooking the creek. The events have been held since 2003 and feature some of the biggest musical acts from around the Midwest. Singer and songwriter Pat McCurdy (pictured) is a crowd favorite. (Photograph by Mark Justesen, courtesy of the *News Graphic*.)

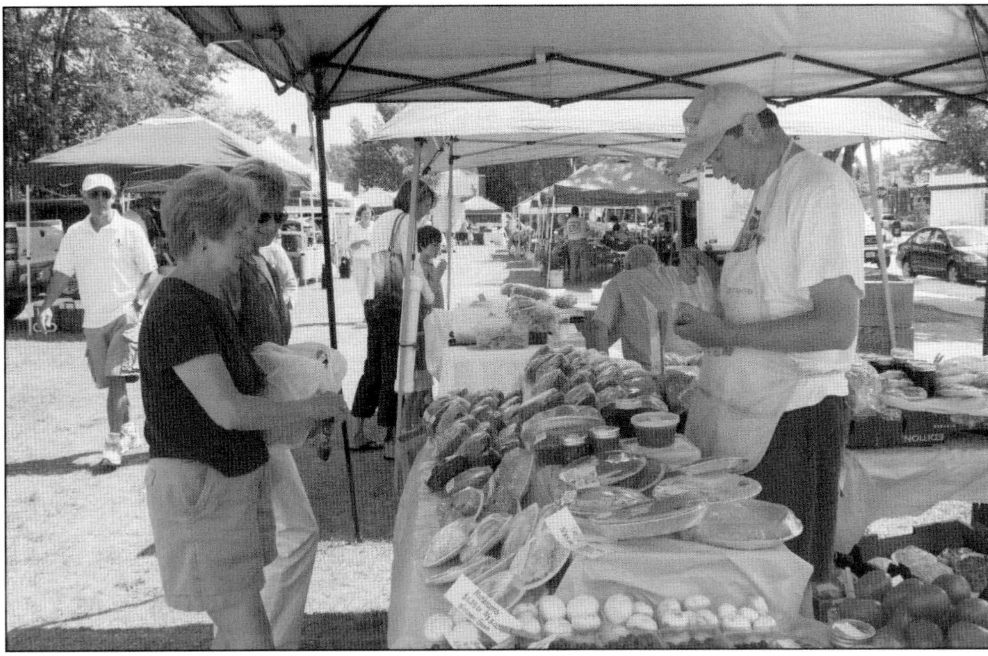

The Cedarburg farmers market is held on Fridays in downtown Cedarburg. The market features fresh produce, flowers, organic foods, herbs, and homemade soaps from vendors around Ozaukee and Washington Counties. Because Cedarburg is one of the major arts centers in the state, jewelry and other art can be purchased at the farmers market. (Photograph by Mark Bertieri.)

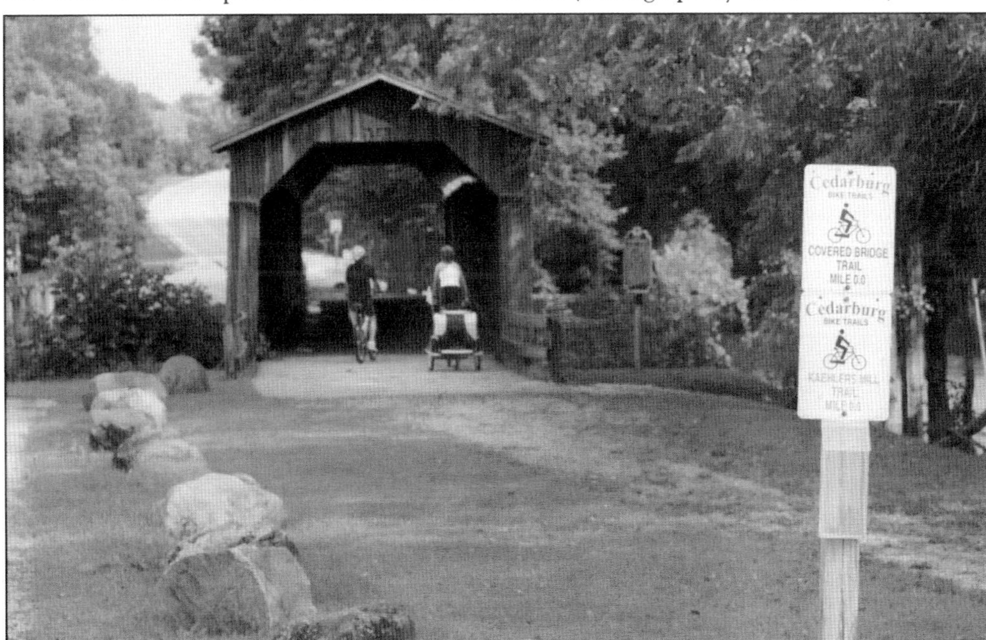

The covered bridge that once carried buggies and cars is now a popular spot for bikers and walkers. It is part of Covered Bridge Park and boasts nature trails, picnic sites, fishing, and access for snowmobiles, kayaks, and canoes. Several weddings are held in the park each year. (Photograph by Deb Kranitz.)

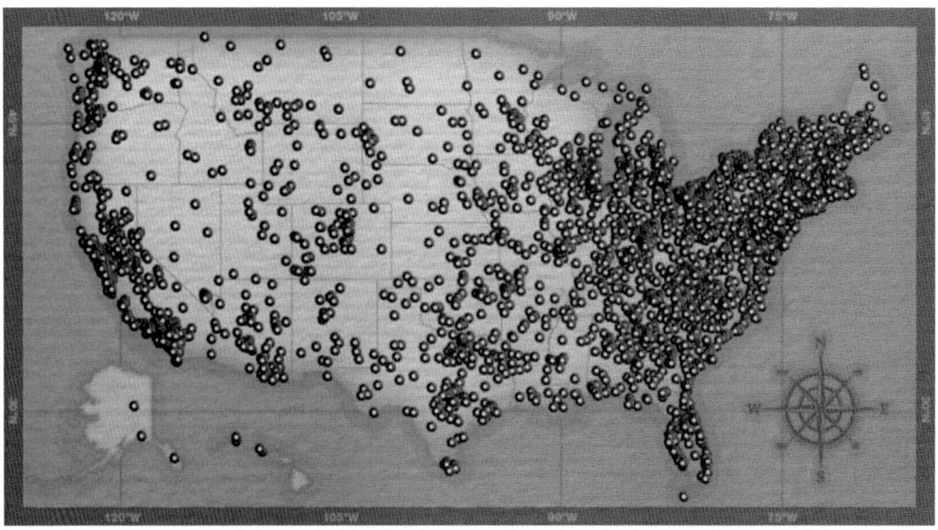